Value Functions

String Value Functions

SUBSTRING	Extracts a substring from a source string
UPPER	Converts a character string to all uppercase
LOWER	Converts a character string to all lowercase
TRIM	Trims off leading or trailing blanks
TRANSLATE	Transforms a source string from one character set to another
CONVERT	Transforms a source string from one character set to another

Numeric Value Functions

POSITION	Returns the starting position of a target string within a source string
CHARACTER_LENGTH	Returns the number of characters in a string
OCTET_LENGTH	Returns the number of octets (bytes) in a character string
BIT_LENGTH	Returns the length of a bit string
EXTRACT	Extracts a single field from a datetime or interval

Datetime Value Functions

CURRENT_DATE	Returns the current date
CURRENT_TIME(p)	Returns the current time; (p) is precision of seconds
CURRENT_TIME STAMP(p)	Returns the current date and the current time; (p) is precision of seconds

Set Functions

COUNT	Returns the number of rows in the specified table
MAX	Returns the maximum value that occurs in the specified table
MIN	Returns the minimum value that occurs in the specified table
SUM	Adds up the values in a specified column
AVG	Returns the average of all the values in the specified column

WHERE Clause Predicates

Comparison Predicates

=	Equal
<>	Not equal
<	Less than
<=	Less than or equal
>	Greater than
>=	Greater than or equal

Other Predicates

BETWEEN
IN
NOT IN
LIKE
NOT LIKE
NULL
ALL
SOME, ANY
EXISTS
UNIQUE
OVERLAPS
MATCH

SQL For Dummies, 2nd Edition

COMPUTER BOOK SERIES FROM IDG

Criteria for Normal Forms

First Normal Form (1NF)

Table must be two-dimensional, with rows and columns.

Each row contains data that pertains to one thing, or portion of a thing.

Each column contains data for a single attribute of the thing being described.

Each cell (intersection of row and column) of the table must be single-valued.

All entries in a column must be of the same kind.

Each column must have a unique name.

No two rows may be identical.

The order of the columns and of the rows does not matter.

Second Normal Form (2NF)

Table must be in first normal form (1NF).

All nonkey attributes (columns) must be dependent on all of the key.

Third Normal Form (3NF)

Table must be in second normal form (2NF).

Table has no transitive dependencies.

Domain Key Normal Form (DKNF)

Every constraint on the table is a logical consequence of the definition of keys and domains.

SQL Data Types

Exact Numerics

```
INTEGER
SMALLINT
NUMERIC
```

Approximate Numerics

```
REAL
DOUBLE PRECISION
FLOAT
```

Character Strings

```
CHARACTER
CHARACTER VARYING (VARCHAR)
NATIONAL CHARACTER
NATIONAL CHARACTER VARYING
```

Bit Strings

```
BIT
BIT VARYING
```

Datetimes

```
DATE
TIME
TIMESTAMP
TIME WITH TIMEZONE
TIMESTAMP WITH TIMEZONE
```

Intervals

```
INTERVAL DAY
INTERVAL YEAR
```

IDG BOOKS WORLDWIDE

...For Dummies: #1 Computer Book Series for Beginners

SQL

FOR

DUMMIES®

2ND EDITION

SQL FOR DUMMIES

2ND EDITION

by Allen G. Taylor

IDG BOOKS WORLDWIDE

IDG Books Worldwide, Inc.
An International Data Group Company

Foster City, CA ♦ Chicago, IL ♦ Indianapolis, IN ♦ Southlake, TX

SQL For Dummies® 2nd Edition

Published by
IDG Books Worldwide, Inc.
An International Data Group Company
919 E. Hillsdale Blvd.
Suite 400
Foster City, CA 94404
www.idgbooks.com (IDG Books Worldwide Web site)
www.dummies.com (Dummies Press Web site)

Library of Congress Catalog Card No.: 97-70737

ISBN: 0-7645-0105-4

Printed in the United States of America

10 9 8 7 6 5 4 3 2

2O/QR/QY/ZX/IN

Distributed in the United States by IDG Books Worldwide, Inc.

Distributed by Macmillan Canada for Canada; by Transworld Publishers Limited in the United Kingdom; by IDG Norge Books for Norway; by IDG Sweden Books for Sweden; by Woodslane Pty. Ltd. for Australia; by Woodslane Enterprises Ltd. for New Zealand; by Longman Singapore Publishers Ltd. for Singapore, Malaysia, Thailand, and Indonesia; by Simron Pty. Ltd. for South Africa; by Toppan Company Ltd. for Japan; by Distribuidora Cuspide for Argentina; by Livraria Cultura for Brazil; by Ediciencia S.A. for Ecuador; by Addison-Wesley Publishing Company for Korea; by Ediciones ZETA S.C.R. Ltda. for Peru; by WS Computer Publishing Corporation, Inc., for the Philippines; by Unalis Corporation for Taiwan; by Contemporanea de Ediciones for Venezuela; by Computer Book & Magazine Store for Puerto Rico; by Express Computer Distributors for the Caribbean and West Indies. Authorized Sales Agent: Anthony Rudkin Associates for the Middle East and North Africa.

For general information on IDG Books Worldwide's books in the U.S., please call our Consumer Customer Service department at 800-762-2974. For reseller information, including discounts and premium sales, please call our Reseller Customer Service department at 800-434-3422.

For information on where to purchase IDG Books Worldwide's books outside the U.S., please contact our International Sales department at 415-655-3200 or fax 415-655-3295.

For information on foreign language translations, please contact our Foreign & Subsidiary Rights department at 415-655-3021 or fax 415-655-3281.

For sales inquiries and special prices for bulk quantities, please contact our Sales department at 415-655-3200 or write to the address above.

For information on using IDG Books Worldwide's books in the classroom or for ordering examination copies, please contact our Educational Sales department at 800-434-2086 or fax 817-251-8174.

For press review copies, author interviews, or other publicity information, please contact our Public Relations department at 415-655-3000 or fax 415-655-3299.

For authorization to photocopy items for corporate, personal, or educational use, please contact Copyright Clearance Center, 222 Rosewood Drive, Danvers, MA 01923, or fax 508-750-4470.

is a trademark under exclusive license to IDG Books Worldwide, Inc., from International Data Group, Inc.

IDG BOOKS WORLDWIDE

About the Author

Allen G. Taylor is a 27-year veteran of the computer industry and the author of 15 computer-related books, including *dBASE for Windows Solutions, File Formats, Voodoo OS/2,* and *Unix Guide for DOS Users.* He is a professor of computer science at Lewis and Clark College, an industry consultant and seminar leader in database design and application development, and speaks nationally on improving quality and productivity through the appropriate application of technology. Allen lives with his family on a small farm outside of Oregon City, Oregon.

ABOUT IDG BOOKS WORLDWIDE

Welcome to the world of IDG Books Worldwide.

IDG Books Worldwide, Inc., is a subsidiary of International Data Group, the world's largest publisher of computer-related information and the leading global provider of information services on information technology. IDG was founded more than 25 years ago and now employs more than 8,500 people worldwide. IDG publishes more than 275 computer publications in over 75 countries (see listing below). More than 60 million people read one or more IDG publications each month.

Launched in 1990, IDG Books Worldwide is today the #1 publisher of best-selling computer books in the United States. We are proud to have received eight awards from the Computer Press Association in recognition of editorial excellence and three from *Computer Currents*' First Annual Readers' Choice Awards. Our best-selling *...For Dummies*® series has more than 30 million copies in print with translations in 30 languages. IDG Books Worldwide, through a joint venture with IDG's Hi-Tech Beijing, became the first U.S. publisher to publish a computer book in the People's Republic of China. In record time, IDG Books Worldwide has become the first choice for millions of readers around the world who want to learn how to better manage their businesses.

Our mission is simple: Every one of our books is designed to bring extra value and skill-building instructions to the reader. Our books are written by experts who understand and care about our readers. The knowledge base of our editorial staff comes from years of experience in publishing, education, and journalism — experience we use to produce books for the '90s. In short, we care about books, so we attract the best people. We devote special attention to details such as audience, interior design, use of icons, and illustrations. And because we use an efficient process of authoring, editing, and desktop publishing our books electronically, we can spend more time ensuring superior content and spend less time on the technicalities of making books.

You can count on our commitment to deliver high-quality books at competitive prices on topics you want to read about. At IDG Books Worldwide, we continue in the IDG tradition of delivering quality for more than 25 years. You'll find no better book on a subject than one from IDG Books Worldwide.

John Kilcullen
CEO
IDG Books Worldwide, Inc.

Steven Berkowitz
President and Publisher
IDG Books Worldwide, Inc.

Eighth Annual Computer Press Awards ➤1992

WINNER

Ninth Annual Computer Press Awards ➤1993

WINNER

Tenth Annual Computer Press Awards ➤1994

WINNER

Eleventh Annual Computer Press Awards ➤1995

Dedication

This book is dedicated to Georgina A. Taylor, who introduced me to the magic of reading and enriched my life immeasurably in the process.

Author's Acknowledgments

Many people have contributed to help improve the quality and content of this book. I would especially like to thank David Kalman and Chris Date for their helpful advice. I am deeply indebted to Phil Shaw for his careful scrutiny of the manuscript and many valuable suggestions. It has been a joy to work with my editor, Madhu Prasher, as well as with Amy Pedersen, Anne Marie Walker, and Chris Williams. I am especially indebted to the fine folks at Dummies Press who have helped make this book possible. Thank you Robert Wallace, William Barton, Patricia Pan, Jennifer Davies, Susan Christophersen, and Michael Sullivan.

I very much appreciate the support I have received from vendors, especially Nan Borreson and Karen Giles of Borland International, as well as Eric Rudie at Oracle Corporation. I want to thank all the members of my database program development course at Lewis and Clark College, who have "beta-tested" much of the material in this book.

Thanks to my agent Matt Wagner for his ongoing assistance in furthering my career, and to my brother David Taylor, who, as far as I know, is the only person in the world who has bought a copy of every one of my books, including foreign translations.

My biggest thanks go to my wife Joyce, for encouraging me to be myself.

Publisher's Acknowledgments

We're proud of this book; please send us your comments about it by using the IDG Books Worldwide Registration Card at the back of the book or by e-mailing us at feedback/dummies@idgbooks.com. Some of the people who helped bring this book to market include the following:

Acquisitions, Development, and Editorial

Project Editor: Robert Wallace

Acquisitions Editor: Michael Kelly, Quality Control Manager

Associate Permissions Editor: Heather H. Dismore

Copy Editors: William A. Barton, Susan Christophersen, Jennifer Davies, Gwenette Gaddis, Patricia Yuu Pan

Technical Editor: Eric Rudie

Editorial Managers: Leah P. Cameron and Mary C. Corder

Editorial Assistant: Michael D. Sullivan

Production

Project Coordinator: Valery Bourke

Layout and Graphics: Brett Black, Lou Boudreau, Valery Bourke, Dominique DeFelice, Maridee V. Ennis, Todd Klemme, Yvette Lillge, Tom Missler, Brent Savage, Kate Snell, Michael A. Sullivan

Proofreaders: Joel K. Draper, Renee Kelty, Nancy Price, Christine Sabooni, Robert Springer

Indexer: Ty Koontz

General and Administrative

IDG Books Worldwide, Inc.: John Kilcullen, CEO; Steven Berkowitz, President and Publisher

IDG Books Technology Publishing: Brenda McLaughlin, Senior Vice President and Group Publisher

Dummies Technology Press and Dummies Editorial: Diane Graves Steele, Vice President and Associate Publisher; Judith A. Taylor, Brand Manager; Kristin A. Cocks, Editorial Director

Dummies Trade Press: Kathleen A. Welton, Vice President and Publisher; Stacy S. Collins, Brand Manager

IDG Books Production for Dummies Press: Beth Jenkins, Production Director; Cindy L. Phipps, Supervisor of Project Coordination, Production Proofreading, and Indexing; Kathie S. Schutte, Supervisor of Page Layout; Shelley Lea, Supervisor of Graphics and Design; Debbie J. Gates, Production Systems Specialist; Tony Augsburger, Supervisor of Reprints and Bluelines; Leslie Popplewell, Media Archive Coordinator

Dummies Packaging and Book Design: Patti Sandez, Packaging Specialist; Lance Kayser, Packaging Assistant; Kavish+Kavish, Cover Design

♦

The publisher would like to give special thanks to Patrick J. McGovern, without whom this book would not have been possible.

♦

Contents at a Glance

Table of Contents

Part II: Using SQL to Build Databases *69*

Chapter 4: Building and Maintaining a
Simple Database Structure 71

Chapter 5: Building a Multitable Database 87

Part IV: Controlling Operations *237*

Introduction

*W*elcome to database development using the industry standard query language (SQL). Many different database management system (DBMS) tools are on the market that run on a large variety of hardware platforms. The differences among the tools can be great indeed, but all serious products have one thing in common: They all support SQL data access and manipulation. What DBMS you use or which operating system or what hardware the DBMS runs on doesn't matter. If you know SQL, you can build relational databases and get useful information out of them.

About This Book

Relational database management systems are vitally important to many organizations. People often think that creating and maintaining these systems are extremely complex activities — the domain of database gurus who possess a degree of enlightenment beyond that of ordinary mortals. This book sweeps away the database mystique. Database design and use are really straightforward activities that you can definitely do and do well. In this book, you:

- Get to the roots of databases
- Find out how a DBMS is structured
- Discover the major functional components of SQL
- Build a database
- Protect a database from harm
- Operate on database data
- Determine how to get the information you want out of a database

The purpose of this book is to help you build relational databases and get valuable information out of them by using SQL.

What Is SQL?

SQL is an industry standard data sublanguage, specifically designed for creating, manipulating, and controlling relational databases. Most organizations keep their critical information in relational databases. If you want to understand what's in an organization's database and to know how to get information from it, it's important for you to know SQL.

Who Should Read This Book?

If you need to store data or retrieve information from a DBMS, you can do a much better job if you have a working knowledge of SQL. You don't need to be a programmer to use SQL, and you don't need to be conversant in any programming languages, such as COBOL, FORTRAN, C, or Basic. SQL's syntax is very much like English.

If you are a programmer, you can incorporate SQL into your programs. SQL adds powerful data manipulation and retrieval capability to conventional languages. This book tells you what you need to know if you want to take advantage of SQL's rich assortment of tools and features from inside your programs.

How This Book Is Organized

This book contains eight major parts. Each part contains several chapters. You may want to read this book in order the first time through, although you don't need to. After that initial read, this book becomes a handy reference guide. You can turn directly to whatever section is appropriate to answer your current question.

Part I: Basic Concepts

Part I introduces the concept of a database and distinguishes relational databases from other types. It describes the most popular database architectures, as well as the major components of SQL.

Part II: Using SQL to Build Databases

You don't need SQL to build a database. This part gives an example of how to build a database by using an interactive Rapid Application Development (RAD) tool, and then you get to build the same database by using SQL. In addition to the essential step of defining database tables, this part covers a variety of other important database features: domains, character sets, collations, translations, keys, and indexes.

Throughout this part, I place major emphasis on protecting your database from corruption, which is a bad thing that can happen in a number of ways. SQL gives you the tools, but you must use them to prevent problems caused by bad database design, harmful interactions, operator error, and equipment failure.

Part III: Retrieving Data

After you have some data in your database, you want to do things with it. You may want to add to the data, change it, or delete it. Ultimately, you want to retrieve useful information from the database. SQL provides tools that enable you to accomplish all these objectives. These tools give you low-level, detailed control over your data. If you conceive of something you want to do with your data, you can probably do it with SQL.

Part IV: Controlling Operations

A big part of database management is protecting the data from harm, which comes in a variety of shapes and forms. People may accidentally or intentionally put erroneous data into database tables, for example. You can protect yourself against this kind of threat by controlling who can access your database and what they can do with it. Another threat to data comes from unintended interaction of concurrent users' operations. SQL provides powerful tools to prevent this kind of problem too. SQL provides much of the protection automatically, but you need to understand how the protection mechanisms work to ensure that you get all the protection you need.

Part V: SQL in the Real World

SQL is different from most other computer languages in that it operates on a whole set of data items at once, rather than dealing with them one at a time. This difference in operational modes makes combining SQL with other languages a challenge, but it's a challenge you can easily face by using the information in this book. I describe in depth the role SQL plays in transferring data across the Internet or an organizational intranet.

Part VI: Advanced Topics

In this part, you include set-oriented SQL statements in your programs and figure out how to get SQL to deal with data one item at a time.

Part VI also covers error handling. SQL provides you with a lot of information whenever something goes wrong in the execution of a SQL statement, and you find out how to retrieve and interpret that information.

Part VII: The Part of Tens

This section provides some important tips on what to do, and what not to do, in designing, building, and using a database.

Part VIII: Reference Material

You find two appendixes in this section. One lists every one of SQL-92's 134 reserved words, and the other lists which of the features described in this book are guaranteed to be present in Entry Level SQL, Intermediate Level SQL, and Full SQL. Part VIII also contains a glossary of important terms.

Icons Used in This Book

Tips save you a lot of time and keep you out of trouble.

Pay attention to the information marked by this icon — you may need it later.

This icon helps you keep track of the special terms you need to know to understand SQL and relational databases.

 Heeding the advice that this icon points to can save you from major grief. Ignore it at your peril.

 This icon alerts you to the presence of technical details that are interesting but not absolutely essential to understanding the topic being discussed.

Get Started

Now for the fun part! Databases are the best tools ever invented for keeping track of the things you care about. After you understand databases and can use SQL to make them do your bidding, you wield tremendous power. Co-workers come to you when they need critical information. Managers will seek your advice. Youngsters ask for your autograph. But most important, you know, at a very deep level, how your organization really works.

Part I
Basic Concepts

The 5th Wave   By Rich Tennant

" NO, THE SOLUTION TO OUR SYSTEM BEING DOWN
IS _NOT_ FOR US TO WORK ON OUR KNEES."

In this part . . .

1 n Part I, I present the big picture. Before talking about SQL itself, I explain what databases really are and how they're different from data that you store in unstructured files. I go over the most popular database models and discuss the physical systems on which these databases run. Then I move on to SQL itself. I give you a brief look at what SQL is and how the language came about, and then I identify and discuss its major components.

Chapter 1

Relational Database Fundamentals

*S*QL is an industry-standard language specifically designed to enable people to create databases, add new data to databases, maintain the data, and retrieve selected parts of the data. A number of different kinds of databases exist, each adhering to a different conceptual model. SQL was originally developed to operate on data in databases that follow the *relational model.* In this chapter, I discuss data storage, how the relational model compares with other major models, and the important features of relational databases.

Before I talk about SQL, however, I need to make sure that you understand what I mean by the term *database.* In fact, I'm going to start by going back one step farther to discuss how computers have changed the way people record and maintain information.

Keeping Track of Things

Today, people use computers to perform many tasks that they once carried out by using other tools. Computers have replaced typewriters, for example, as the primary means of creating and modifying documents. They've replaced electromechanical calculators as the best way to do math. They've also replaced millions of pieces of paper, file folders, and file cabinets as the principal storage medium for important information. Compared to these old tools, of course, computers do a lot more, a lot faster — and with greater accuracy. These increased benefits do come at a cost, however: Computer users no longer have direct physical access to their data.

If computers occasionally fail to work as people expect, office workers sometimes wonder whether computerization really improved anything at all. In the old days, a file folder rarely "crashed." If it did, you merely knelt down, picked up the papers, and put them back in the folder. A disk crash is another matter entirely. You can't "pick up" the lost bits and bytes. Barring earthquakes or other major disasters, file cabinets never "go down," and they never give you an error message. Computers, on the other hand, are sensitive to mechanical, electrical, and human failures that can make your data permanently unavailable.

Even so, computers really are an improvement over the old tools. By taking the necessary precautions, you can protect yourself from accidental data loss. After you protect yourself this way, you can then start cashing in on the greater speed and accuracy that computers provide.

If you're storing important data, you have the following four main concerns:

✔ Storing data needs to be quick and easy, because you're likely to do it often.

✔ The storage medium must be reliable. You don't want to come back later and find some of (or all) your data missing.

✔ Data retrieval needs to be quick and easy, regardless of the number of items you store.

✔ You need an easy way to sift the exact information that you want from the tons of data that you don't want.

Small is beautiful

Computers really shine in the area of data storage. Computers can store all kinds of information — text, numbers, sounds, graphic images, TV programs, or animations — as binary data. A computer can store data at very high densities, enabling you to keep large quantities of information in a very small space. As technology continues to advance, more and more data can occupy smaller and smaller spaces. This trend is spurring the use of computers in ways that once seemed quite improbable. Today, the gas pumps at your neighborhood filling station contain computers. Your car probably has several computers. Before long, you may even see computerized shoes that alter the resilience of their soles depending on whether you're walking, running, or taking a jump shot.

State-of-the-art computer databases satisfy these four criteria. If you store more than a dozen or so data items, you probably want to store those items in a database.

What Is a Database?

In recent years, people have used the term *database* rather loosely, and as a result, the term has lost some of its usefulness. To some people, a database is any collection of data items. Other people define the term more strictly.

In this book, I define a *database* as a self-describing collection of integrated records.

A *record* is a representation of some physical or conceptual object. Say, for example, that you want to keep track of a businesses' customers. You assign a record for each customer. Each record has multiple attributes, such as name, address, and telephone number.

A database is *self-describing* in that the database contains a description of its own structure. This description is called *metadata*. The database is *integrated* in that it includes the *relationships* among data items as well as including the data items themselves.

A database consists of both data and metadata. Metadata is data that describes the structure of the data within a database.

The database stores this metadata in an area called the *data dictionary,* which describes the tables, columns, indexes, constraints, and other items that make up the database.

Because a flat file system (described later in this chapter) has no metadata, applications written to work with flat files must contain the equivalent of the metadata as part of the application program.

Database Size and Complexity

Databases come in all sizes, from a simple collection of a few records to millions of records.

A *personal database* is designed for use by a single person on a single computer. Such a database is usually rather simple in structure and small in size. A *departmental* or *workgroup database* is for use by the members of a single department or workgroup within an organization. This type of database is generally larger than a personal database and is necessarily more complex, because such a database must handle multiple users trying to access the same data at the same time. An *organizational database* can be huge. Organizational databases may model the critical information flow of entire large organizations.

What Is a Database Management System?

A *database management system (DBMS)* is a set of programs that you use to define, administer, and process databases and their associated applications. A *database* is, in essence, a structure that you build to hold data that's valuable to you or your organization. A DBMS is the tool you use to build that structure and operate on the data contained within the database.

Many DBMSes are on the market today. Some run only on mainframe computers, some only on minicomputers, and some only on personal computers. A strong trend, however, is for such products to work on multiple platforms or on networks that contain all three classes of machines.

A DBMS that runs on platforms of multiple classes is said to be *scalable*.

Regardless of the size of the computer that hosts the database and regardless of whether the machine is connected to a network, the flow of information between the database and the user is the same. Figure 1-1 shows that the user communicates with the database through the DBMS. The DBMS masks the physical details of the database storage so that the application only needs to know about the logical characteristics of the data, not how the data is stored.

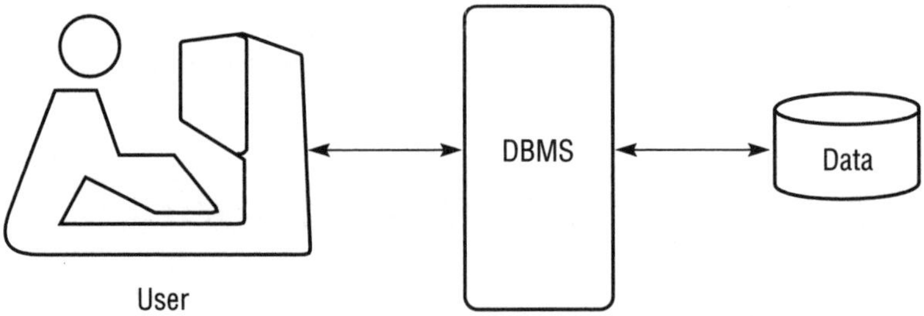

Figure 1-1:
The flow of information between the user and the database.

User

DBMS

Data

The value is not in the data, but in the structure

Years ago, some overly clever person calculated that, if you reduce a human being to his component carbon, hydrogen, oxygen, and nitrogen atoms (plus traces of others), the person would be worth only 97 cents. This clearly misleading assessment did grave damage to people's self images around the world. People aren't composed of collections of atoms. Our atoms combine into enzymes, proteins, hormones, and many other substances that cost millions of dollars per ounce on the pharmaceutical market. The structure of the combinations of atoms is what gives them this value. Database structure makes possible the interpretation of seemingly meaningless data. The structure brings to the surface patterns, trends, and tendencies in the data. Unstructured data, as is true of uncombined atoms, has little or no value.

Flat Files

Flat files got their name from the fact that these types of files are nothing more than a collection of data records. Flat files have minimal structure. They contain one data record after another in a format specified at the time the file was designed. Flat files contain the data, the whole data, and nothing but the data. Because the file doesn't store structural information (metadata), overhead (stuff in the file that is not data) is minimal.

Say that you want to keep track of the names and addresses of your company's customers in a flat file system. The system may have a structure something like that of the following example:

```
Harold Percival26262 S. Howards Mill Rd Westminster CA92683
Jerry Appel    32323 S. River Lane Rd   Santa Ana   CA92705
Adrian Hansen  232   Glenwood Court      Anaheim     CA92640
John Baker     2222  Lafayette St        Garden GroveCA92643
Michael Pens   77730 S. New Era Rd       Irvine      CA92715
Bob Michimoto  25252 S. Kelmsley Dr      Stanton     CA92610
Linda Smith    444   S.E. Seventh St     Costa Mesa  CA92635
Robert Funnell 2424  Sheri Court         Anaheim     CA92640
Bill Checkal   9595  Curry Dr            Stanton     CA92610
Jed Style      3535  Randall St          Santa Ana   CA92705
```

As you can see, the file contains nothing but data. Each field is of a fixed length (the Name field, for example, is always exactly 15 characters long), and no structure separates one field from another. The person who created the database assigned field positions and lengths. Any program using this file must "know" how each field was assigned.

On the plus side, operating on flat files can be very fast, because these files contain nothing but data. On the minus side, application programs must include logic that manipulates the data in the file at a very low level. The application must know exactly where and how the file stores its data. For small systems, flat files work fine. The larger a system is, however, the more cumbersome a flat file system becomes. Using a database instead of a flat file system eliminates duplication of effort and makes applications more portable across various hardware and operating system platforms. A database also makes writing application programs easier, because the programmer doesn't need to know the physical details of where and how the files store their data.

Databases eliminate duplication of effort, because the DBMS handles the details of data manipulation. Applications written to operate on flat files must include those details in the application code. If multiple applications all access the same flat file data, these applications must all (redundantly) include that data manipulation code. By using a DBMS, you don't need to include such code in the applications at all.

Clearly, if an application includes data-manipulation code specific to a particular hardware platform, migrating the application to a new platform is not an easy task. You first must change all the hardware-specific code. As a result, migrating a flat file-based application to another platform is much harder than migrating a similar DBMS-based application.

Database Models

Different as databases may be in size, they are generally always structured according to one of three database models: *hierarchical, network,* or *relational.* The first databases to see wide use were large organizational databases built according to either the hierarchical or the network model. Systems built according to the relational model followed several years later.

Hierarchical databases have a simple hierarchical structure that allows fast data access. They suffer from redundancy problems and a structural inflexibility that makes database modification difficult. Network databases have minimal redundancy but pay for that advantage with structural complexity.

Nowadays, new installations of database-management systems are almost exclusively of the relational type. Organizations that already have a major investment in hierarchical or network technology may add to the existing model, but those groups with no need to maintain compatibility with "legacy systems" nearly always choose the relational model for their databases.

Relational model

E. F. Codd of IBM first formulated the relational database model in 1970, and this model started appearing in products about a decade later. Ironically, IBM did not deliver the first relational DBMS. That distinction went to a small start-up company, which named its product Oracle.

Relational databases have replaced databases built according to other models because the relational type has valuable attributes that distinguish relational databases from those other database types. Probably the most important of these attributes is that, in a relational database, you can change the database structure without requiring changes to applications that were based on the earlier structures. Suppose, for example, that you add one or more new columns to a database table. You don't need to change any previously written applications that will continue to process that table, unless you alter one or more of the columns with which those applications deal. (Of course, if you remove a column to which an existing application refers, you experience problems no matter what database model you follow. One of the best ways to make a database application crash is to ask it to retrieve a kind of data that the database with which you're dealing doesn't contain.)

Why relational is better

In applications written with DBMSes that follow the hierarchical or the network model, database structure is "hard-coded" into the application. If you add a new attribute to the database, you must change your application to accommodate the change, whether the application uses the new attribute or not.

Because of the structural flexibility of relational databases, applications written for those databases are easier to maintain than are applications written to work with other kinds of databases. Furthermore, the same structural flexibility enables you to retrieve combinations of data that you hadn't anticipated needing at the time of the database's design.

Components of a relational database

Relational databases gain their flexibility from the fact that their data resides in tables that are largely independent of each other. You can add, delete, or change data in a table without affecting the data in the other tables, provided the affected table is not a *parent* of any of the other tables. (Parent-child table relationships are explained in Chapter 5.) In this section, I show what these tables consist of and how they relate to the other parts of a relational database.

Guess who's coming to dinner?

At holiday time, many of my relations come to my house and sit down at my table. Databases have relations, too, but each of their relations has its own table. A relational database is made up of one or more relations.

A *relation* is a two-dimensional array of rows and columns, containing single-valued entries and no duplicate rows. Each cell in the array can have only one value, and no two rows may be identical.

Most people are familiar with two-dimensional arrays of rows and columns, in the form of electronic spreadsheets such as Microsoft Excel or Lotus 1-2-3. The offensive statistics listed on the back of a major-league baseball player's baseball card is another example of such an array. On the baseball card are columns for year, team, games played, at-bats, hits, runs scored, runs batted in, doubles, triples, home runs, bases on balls, steals, and batting average. A row covers each year that the player has played in the major leagues. You could also store this data in a relation (a table), which has the same basic

Historical perspectives

In the early 1980s, personal databases appeared for the first time on personal computers. The earliest products were based on flat file systems, but some early products attempted to follow the relational model. As they've evolved, the most popular PC DBMSes have come progressively closer to being truly relational, as defined by Dr. Codd. Today, most people consider the leading DBMS products that claim to be relational as qualifying for that descriptor. Since the latter part of the 1980s, more and more PCs in organizations are hooked together into workgroups or departmental networks. To fill this new market niche, relational DBMSes that originated on large mainframe computers have migrated down to, and relational PC DBMSes have migrated up from, stand-alone personal computers.

structure. Figure 1-2 shows a relational database table holding the offensive statistics for a single major-league player. In practice, such a table would hold the statistics for an entire team, or perhaps the whole league.

Figure 1-2:
A table
showing a
baseball
player's
offensive
statistics.

Player	Year	Team	Game	At Bat	Hits	Runs	RBI	2B	3B	HR	Walk	Steals	Bat. Avg.
Roberts	1988	Padres	5	9	3	1	0	0	0	0	1	0	.333
Roberts	1989	Padres	117	329	99	81	25	15	8	3	49	21	.301
Roberts	1990	Padres	149	556	172	104	44	36	3	9	55	46	.309

Columns in the array are self-consistent in that a column has the same meaning in every row. If a column contains a player's last name in one row, the column must contain a player's last name in all rows. The order in which the rows and columns appear in the array has no significance. As far as the DBMS is concerned, therefore, which column is first, which is next, and which is last doesn't matter. The DBMS processes the table the same way regardless of the order of the columns. The same is true of rows. The order of the rows simply doesn't matter to the DBMS.

The development community commonly calls relations *tables.* Academics and theoreticians, on the other hand, prefer the term *relation,* but both terms mean the same thing. In this book, I call them tables.

Every column in a database table embodies a single attribute of the table. The meaning of a column is the same for every row of the table. A table may, for example, contain the names, addresses, and telephone numbers of all an organization's customers. Each row in the table (also called a *record,* or a *tuple*) holds the data for a single customer. Each column holds a single attribute, such as customer number, customer name, customer street, customer city, customer state, customer postal code, or customer telephone number. Figure 1-3 shows some of the rows and columns of such a table.

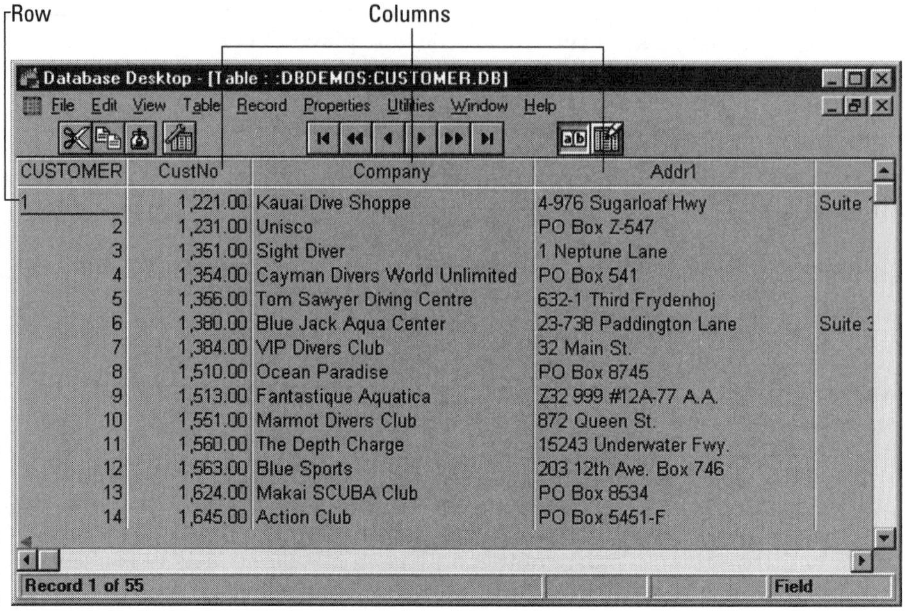

Row   Columns

Figure 1-3:
Each
database
row contains
a record;
each
database
column
holds a
single
attribute.

Enjoy the view

One of my favorite views is that of the Yosemite Valley as seen from the mouth of the Wawona tunnel, late on a spring afternoon. Golden light bathes the sheer face of El Capitan; Half Dome glistens in the distance; and Bridal Veil Falls forms a silver cascade of sparkling water, while a trace of wispy clouds weaves a tapestry across the sky. Databases have views as well. Database views may not be quite as beautiful as that of the Yosemite Valley, but such views can prove very useful in working with your data.

Tables can contain many columns and rows. Sometimes all that data interests you, and sometimes it doesn't. Only some of the columns of a table may interest you or only rows that satisfy a certain condition. Some columns of one table and some other columns of a related table may interest you. To eliminate data that is not relevant to your current needs, create a view. A *view* is a subset of a database that an application can process. It may contain parts of one or more tables.

Note: Views are sometimes called *virtual tables*. To the application or the user, views behave exactly the same as tables. Views, however, have no independent existence. Views are a way of looking at data but are not the data itself.

Say, for example, that you're working with a database that has a CUSTOMER table and an INVOICE table. The CUSTOMER table has columns CUSTOMER_ID, FIRST_NAME, LAST_NAME, STREET, CITY, STATE, ZIPCODE, and PHONE. The INVOICE table has columns INVOICE_NUMBER, CUSTOMER_ID, DATE, TOTAL_SALE, TOTAL_REMITTED, and FORM_OF_PAYMENT.

A national sales manager wants to look at a screen that contains only the customer's first name, last name, and telephone number. Creating from the CUSTOMER table a view that contains only those three columns makes available to the manager all needed information without the distraction of the unwanted data in the other columns. Figure 1-4 shows the derivation of the national sales manager's view.

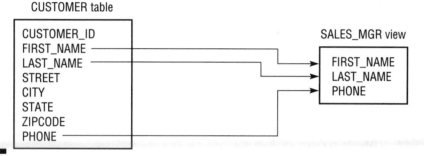

Figure 1-4:
The sales manager's view derives from the CUSTOMER table.

A branch manager may want to look at the names and phone numbers of all customers whose zip code falls between 90000 and 93999 (Southern and Central California). A view that places a restriction on the rows it retrieves as well as the columns it displays does the job. Figure 1-5 shows the sources for the branch manager's view's columns.

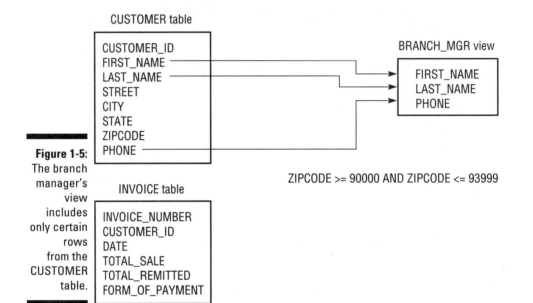

Figure 1-5: The branch manager's view includes only certain rows from the CUSTOMER table.

The accounts payable manager may want to look at customer names from the CUSTOMER table and DATE, TOTAL_SALE, TOTAL_REMITTED, and FORM_OF_PAYMENT from the INVOICE table, where TOTAL_REMITTED is less than TOTAL_SALE. The latter would be the case if full payment hasn't yet been made. This need requires a view that draws from both tables. Figure 1-6 shows data flowing into the accounts payable manager's view from both CUSTOMER and INVOICE tables.

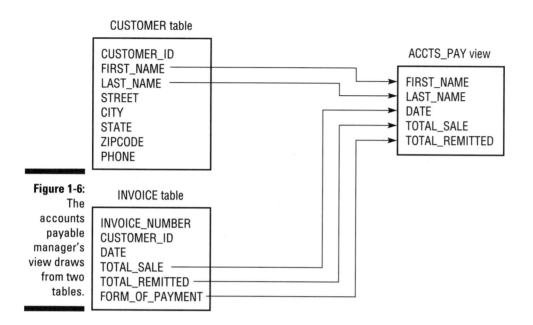

CUSTOMER table

ACCTS_PAY view

Figure 1-6:
The accounts payable manager's view draws from two tables.

INVOICE table

Views are useful because they enable you to extract and format database data without physically altering the stored data. In Chapter 6, I show you how to create a view using SQL.

Schemas, domains, and constraints

A database is more than a collection of tables. Additional structures, on several levels, help to maintain the integrity of the data. A database's *schema* provides an overall organization to the tables. The *domain* of a table column tells you what values you may store in the column. You can apply *constraints* to a database table to prevent anyone (including yourself) from storing invalid data in the table.

Schemas

The structure of an entire database is its *schema,* or *conceptual view.* This structure is sometimes also called the *complete logical view* of the database. The schema is metadata and, as such, is a part of the database. The metadata itself, which describes the structure of the database, is stored in tables that are just like the tables that store the regular data.

Domains

An attribute of a relation (that is, a column of a table) can assume some finite number of values. The set of all such values is the *domain* of the attribute.

Say, for example, that you're an automobile dealer who handles the newly introduced Curarri GT 4000 sports coupe. You keep track of the cars you have in stock in a database table that you name INVENTORY. One of the columns of that table you name COLOR, which holds the color of the exterior of each car. The GT 4000 comes in only four colors: blazing crimson, midnight black, snowflake white, and metallic gray. Those four colors are the domain of the COLOR attribute.

Constraints

Constraints are an important, although often overlooked, component of a database. Constraints are rules that determine what values the attributes of a table can assume.

By applying tight constraints to a column, you can prevent people from entering invalid data into that column. Of course, every value that is legitimately in the domain of the column must satisfy all the column's constraints. As I mention in the preceding section, the domain of a column is the set of all values that the column can contain. A constraint is a restriction on what a column may contain. The characteristics of a table column, plus the constraints that apply to that column, determine the column's domain. By applying constraints, you can prevent the entry into a column of data that falls outside the column's domain.

In the auto-dealership example, you could constrain the database to accept only those four values in the COLOR column. If a data-entry operator then tries to enter in the COLOR column a value of, for example, forest green, the system refuses to accept the entry. Data entry can't proceed until the operator enters a valid value into the COLOR field.

Database Design Considerations

A database is a representation of a physical or conceptual structure, such as an organization, an automobile assembly, or the performance statistics of all the major-league baseball clubs. The accuracy of the representation depends on the level of detail of the database design. The amount of effort that you put into database design should depend on the type of information you want to get out of the database. Too much detail is a waste of effort, time, and disk space. Too little detail may render the database worthless. Decide how much detail you need now and how much you may need in the future and then provide exactly that level of detail in your design — no more and no less.

Today's database management systems, complete with attractive graphical user interfaces and intuitive design tools, can give the would-be database designer a false sense of security. These systems can make designing a database seem comparable to building a spreadsheet or engaging in some other relatively straightforward task. No such luck. Database design is difficult. If you do it incorrectly, you get a database that becomes gradually more corrupt as time goes on. Often, the problem doesn't turn up until after you devote a great deal of effort to data entry. By the time you know that you have a problem, it's already serious. In many cases, the only solution is to completely redesign the database and reenter all the data.

Note: This book doesn't tell you how to design a database (although in Chapter 5 I give you some pointers). I assume that you or somebody else has already created a valid design. I then tell you how to implement that design by using SQL. If you suspect that you don't have a good database design, by all means, fix your design before you try to build the database. The earlier you detect and correct problems in a development project, the cheaper are the corrections you must make.

Chapter 2

SQL Fundamentals

SQL is the most widely used tool for communicating with a relational database. SQL is a flexible tool that you can use in a variety of ways. In this chapter, I explain what SQL is and what SQL isn't — specifically, what distinguishes SQL from other types of computer languages. Then I introduce the commands and data types that standard SQL supports and explain a couple of key concepts: *null values* and *constraints*. Finally, I give an overview of how SQL fits into the client/server environment, as well as the Internet and organizational intranets.

What SQL Is and Isn't

The first thing you need to understand about SQL is that SQL isn't a *procedural language,* as are FORTRAN, Basic, C, COBOL, Pascal, or Ada. To solve a problem in one of those languages, you write a procedure that performs one operation after another until you complete the task. The procedure may be a linear sequence or may loop back on itself, but in either case, the programmer specifies the order of execution. SQL, on the other hand, is *nonprocedural.* To solve a problem by using SQL, you simply tell SQL *what* you want instead of telling the system *how to get* you what you want. The DBMS decides the best way to get you what you request.

Note: The next version of the SQL specification, due out in 1999 and currently code-named SQL3, is to incorporate procedural language facilities such as BEGIN blocks, IF statements, functions, and procedures. The SQL developers are adding these facilities so that you can store programs at the server, where multiple clients can optimize and use these programs repeatedly. Other extensions to SQL3 support object-oriented data management.

To illustrate what I mean by "tell the system what you want," suppose that you have an EMPLOYEE table and you want to retrieve from that table the rows that correspond to all your "senior" people. You want to define a senior person as anyone older than age 40 or anyone earning more than $50,000 per year. You can make the desired retrieval by using the following query:

```
SELECT * FROM EMPLOYEE WHERE AGE>40 OR SALARY>50000 ;
```

This statement retrieves all rows from the EMPLOYEE table where either the value in the AGE column is greater than 40 or the value in the SALARY column is greater than 50,000. In SQL, you're not responsible for specifying how to retrieve the information. The database engine examines the database and decides for itself how to fulfill your request. You need only to specify what data you want to retrieve.

A *query* is a question you ask the database. If any of the data in the database satisfies the conditions of your query, SQL retrieves that data.

Current implementations of SQL lack many of the basic programming constructs that are fundamental to most other languages. Real-world applications usually require at least some of these programming constructs, which is why SQL is actually a data *sublanguage.* You need to use SQL in combination with one of the procedural languages, such as C, to create a complete application. SQL3 is to include some of the flow-control constructs, making SQL a more complete language. After those constructs become part of commonly available implementations of SQL, users are going to have less need to use another language along with SQL. Users will still need both languages but will switch back and forth less often.

You can extract information from a database in either of two ways. The first method is to make an *ad hoc query* from a computer console by just typing an SQL statement and reading the results from the screen. The second is to execute a program that collects information from the database and then reports on the information. You can use SQL either way.

Queries from a computer console are appropriate if you want a quick answer to a specific question. To meet an immediate need, you may require information that you never needed before from a database. You're likely never to need that information again either, but you need it now. Enter the appropriate SQL query statement from the console, and in due time, the result appears on your screen.

On the other hand, incorporating an SQL query directly into a program makes sense if the query is somewhat complex and you're likely to need to run the same query again in the future. That way, you need to formulate the query only once. Chapter 14 explains how to incorporate SQL code into programs that are written in another language.

A (Very) Little History

As did relational database theory, SQL itself originated in one of IBM's research laboratories. In the early 1970s, as IBM researchers performed early development on relational DBMS (or RDBMS) systems, they created a data sublanguage to operate on these systems. They originally named this sublanguage *SEQUEL* (*S*tructured *E*nglish *QUE*ry *L*anguage). Unfortunately, the IBM folks failed to conduct a thorough trademark search on the name SEQUEL and ran into a conflict. They couldn't call the product SEQUEL, so by the time they finally released it, they'd named their product SQL instead.

IBM's work with relational databases and SQL were well known in the industry even before IBM introduced its SQL/DS in 1981. By that time, Relational Software, Inc. (now Oracle Corporation), had already released its first RDBMS. These early products immediately set the standard for a new class of database management systems. They incorporated SQL, which became the de facto standard for data sublanguages. Vendors of other relational database management systems came out with their own versions of SQL. These other implementations typically contained all the core functionality of the IBM products but were extended in ways that took advantage of the particular strengths of the underlying RDBMS. As a result, although nearly all vendors used some form of SQL, compatibility across platforms was poor.

An *implementation* is a particular RDBMS running on a specific hardware platform.

Soon a movement began with the aim to create a universally recognized SQL standard to which everyone could adhere. In 1986, ANSI released a formal standard they named *SQL-86*. ANSI updated that standard in 1989 to *SQL-89*. As DBMS vendors proceed through new releases of their products, they try to bring their implementations ever closer to this standard. This effort has brought true SQL portability much closer to reality.

The most recent version of the SQL standard is *SQL-92* (ANSI Document No. X3.135-1992). SQL-92 is a major revision of SQL-89. In this book, I describe SQL as SQL-92 defines the language. Any specific implementation of SQL, of course, differs from the standard to a certain extent. Because the full SQL-92 standard is so very comprehensive, currently available implementations are unlikely to support it fully for a long time. In the meantime, however, DBMS vendors are working to support a low and an intermediate subset of the standard SQL language. Appendix B lists the features that these low and intermediate subsets provide. ANSI document No. X3.135-1992 is available from the American National Standards Institute, 1430 Broadway, New York, NY 10018; 212-642-4900.

SQL Commands

The SQL command language consists of a limited number of commands that specifically relate to data handling. Some of these commands perform data-definition functions; some perform data-manipulation functions; and others perform data-control functions. I cover the data-definition commands in Chapter 3, the data-manipulation commands in Chapter 6, and the data-control commands in Chapters 12 and 13. Table 2-1 (later in this chapter) provides a complete list of SQL-92 commands. You're unlikely to find an implementation that includes all these commands with the capabilities that the SQL-92 specification defines for them. Actual implementations are much more likely to comply with the low and intermediate subsets that I outline in Appendix B. An implementation's documentation should disclose its level of compliance.

Reserved Words

In addition to the commands, a number of other words have a special significance within SQL. These words, along with the commands, are reserved for specific uses and so you may not use them as variable names or in any other way that differs from their intended use. You can easily see why not to give tables, columns, and variables names that appear on the reserved word list. Confusion would abound if statements such as the following were possible:

```
SELECT SELECT FROM SELECT WHERE SELECT = WHERE ;
```

A complete list of SQL-92 reserved words appears in Appendix A.

Data Types

Depending on their histories, different SQL implementations support a variety of data types. The SQL-92 specification, however, recognizes only six general types: *exact numerics, approximate numerics, character strings, bit strings, datetimes,* and *intervals.* Within each of these general types may be several subtypes.

If you use an SQL implementation that supports one or more data types that the SQL-92 specification doesn't describe, you can keep your database more portable by avoiding these undescribed data types. By using a nonstandard data type, you make a conscious decision that you're never going to need to migrate your database to another RDBMS.

Table 2-1	SQL Statements
ADD	ALLOCATE DESCRIPTOR
ALTER	ALTER DOMAIN
ALTER TABLE	AUTHORIZATION
AVG	BEGIN
CHECK	CLOSE
COMMIT	CONNECT
CONTINUE	COUNT
COUNT(*)	CREATE ASSERTION
CREATE CHARACTER SET	CREATE COLLATION
CREATE DOMAIN	CREATE SCHEMA
CREATE TABLE	CREATE TRANSLATION
CREATE VIEW	DEALLOCATE DESCRIPTOR
DEALLOCATE PREPARE	DECLARE CURSOR
DECLARE CURSOR FOR	DEFAULT
DELETE	DELETE FROM
DESCRIBE	DESCRIBE INPUT
DROP	ESCAPE
EXECUTE	EXECUTE IMMEDIATE
FETCH	FOREIGN KEY
GET	GET DESCRIPTOR

(continued)

Table 2-1 *(continued)*	
GET DIAGNOSTICS	GO
GOTO	GRANT
HAVING	INSERT INTO
MAX	MIN
OPEN	ORDER BY
PREPARE	REFERENCES
REVOKE	ROLLBACK
SELECT	SET
SUM	UPDATE

Exact numerics

As you can probably deduce from the name, the *exact numeric* data types enable you to express the value of a number exactly. Four data types fall into this category: INTEGER, SMALLINT, NUMERIC, and DECIMAL.

INTEGER data type

Data of INTEGER type has no fractional part, and its precision depends on the specific SQL implementation. The database developer can't specify the precision.

The *precision* of a number is the maximum number of digits the number can have.

SMALLINT data type

The SMALLINT type is also for integers, but the precision of a SMALLINT in a specific implementation can't be any larger than the precision of an INTEGER on the same implementation. Implementations on IBM System/370 computers commonly represent SMALLINT and INTEGER with 16-bit and 32-bit binary numbers respectively. In many implementations, SMALLINT and INTEGER are the same.

If you're defining a database table column to hold integer data and you know that the range of values in the column is never going to exceed the precision of SMALLINT data on your implementation, assign the column the SMALLINT type rather than the INTEGER type. This assignment may enable your DBMS to conserve storage space.

NUMERIC data type

NUMERIC data can have a fractional component in addition to its integer component. You can specify both the precision and the scale of NUMERIC data. (Precision, remember, is the maximum number of digits possible.)

The *scale* of a number is the number of digits in its fractional part. The scale of a number can't be negative or larger than that number's precision.

If you specify the NUMERIC data type, your SQL implementation gives you exactly the precision and scale that you request. You may specify NUMERIC and get a default precision and scale or, NUMERIC (*p*) and get your specified precision and the default scale or, NUMERIC (*p,s*) and get both your specified precision and your specified scale. The parameters *p* and *s* are placeholders that would be replaced by actual values in a data declaration.

Say, for example, that the NUMERIC data type's default precision for your implementation of SQL is 12 and the default scale is 6. If you specify a database column as having a data type of NUMERIC, the column can hold numbers up to 999,999.999999. If, on the other hand, you specify a data type of NUMERIC (10) for a column, that column can hold only numbers with a maximum value of 9,999.999999. The parameter (10) specifies the maximum number of digits possible in the number. If you specify a data type of NUMERIC (10,2) for a column, that column can hold numbers with a maximum value of 99,999,999.99. In this case, you may still have ten total digits, but only two of the digits can fall to the right of the decimal point.

NUMERIC data is for values such as 595.72. That value has a precision of 5 (the total number of digits) and a scale of 2 (the number of digits to the right of the decimal point). A data type of NUMERIC (5,2) is appropriate for such numbers.

DECIMAL data type is similar to NUMERIC. This data type can have a fractional component, and you can specify its precision and scale. The difference is that the precision your implementation supplies may be greater than what you specify, and if so, the implementation uses the greater precision. If you do not specify precision or scale, the implementation uses default values, as it does with the NUMERIC type.

An item that you specify as NUMERIC (5,2) can never contain a number with an absolute value greater than 999.99. An item that you specify as DECIMAL (5,2) can always hold values up to 999.99, but if the implementation permits larger values, the DBMS doesn't reject values larger than 999.99.

Use the NUMERIC or DECIMAL type if your data has fractional positions and the INTEGER or SMALLINT type if your data always consists of whole numbers. Use the NUMERIC type if you want to maximize portability, because a value that you define as NUMERIC (5,2), for example, holds exactly the same range of values on all systems.

Approximate numerics

Some quantities have a range of possible values so large (many orders of magnitude) that a computer with a given register size can't represent all the values exactly. (Examples of *register sizes* are 32 bits, 64 bits, and 128 bits.) Usually in such cases, exactness isn't necessary, and a close approximation is acceptable. SQL-92 defines three approximate numeric data types to handle this kind of data.

REAL data type

The REAL data type gives you a single-precision floating-point number, the precision of which depends on the implementation. In general, the hardware you're using determines precision. A 64-bit machine, for example, gives you more precision than does a 32-bit machine.

DOUBLE PRECISION data type

The DOUBLE PRECISION data type gives you a double-precision floating-point number, the precision of which again depends on the implementation. Surprisingly, the meaning of the word DOUBLE also depends on the implementation. Double-precision arithmetic is primarily employed by scientific users. Different scientific disciplines have different needs in the area of precision. Some implementations of SQL cater to one category of user, and other implementations cater to other categories of user.

In some systems, the DOUBLE PRECISION type has exactly twice the capacity of the REAL data type for both mantissa and exponent. (In case you've forgotten what you learned in high school, you can represent any number as a *mantissa* if you multiply the number by ten raised to the power given by an exponent. You can also write 1,997, for example, as 1.997E3. The number 1.997 is the *mantissa,* which you multiply by ten raised to the third power; in that case, *3* is the *exponent.*) You gain no benefit by representing numbers that are fairly close to one (such as 1,997 or even 1,997,000) with an approximate numeric data type. Exact numeric types work just as well and take up less space in memory. For numbers that are either much smaller or much larger than one, however, such as 6.023E-23 (a very small number), you must use an approximate numeric type. The exact numeric types can't hold such numbers. On other systems, the DOUBLE PRECISION type gives you somewhat more than twice the mantissa capacity and somewhat less than twice the exponent capacity as the REAL type. On yet another type of system, the DOUBLE PRECISION type gives double the mantissa capacity but the same exponent capacity as the REAL type. In this case, accuracy doubles, but range does not.

The SQL-92 specification does not try to arbitrate or establish by fiat what DOUBLE PRECISION means. The specification requires only that the precision of a DOUBLE PRECISION number is greater than the precision of a REAL number. This constraint is a rather weak one but is perhaps the best possible in light of the great differences you encounter in hardware.

FLOAT *data type*

The FLOAT data type is most useful if you think that your database may someday migrate to a hardware platform with different register sizes than the one on which you originally design it. By using the FLOAT data type, you can specify a precision — for example, FLOAT (5). If your hardware supports the specified precision with its single-precision circuitry, single-precision arithmetic is what your system uses. If the specified precision requires double-precision arithmetic, the system uses double-precision arithmetic.

Using FLOAT rather than REAL or DOUBLE PRECISION makes porting your databases to other hardware easier, because the FLOAT data type enables you to specify precision. The precision of REAL and DOUBLE PRECISION numbers is hardware dependent.

If you aren't sure whether to use the exact numeric data types (NUMERIC/ DECIMAL) or the approximate numeric data types (FLOAT/REAL), use the exact numeric types. The exact data types are less demanding of system resources and, of course, give exact rather than approximate results. If the range of possible values of your data is large enough to require the use of the approximate data types, you can probably determine this fact in advance.

Character strings

These days, databases store many different types of data, including graphic images, sounds, and animations. I expect odors to come next. Can you imagine a three-dimensional 1024 × 768 24-bit color image of a large slice of pepperoni pizza on your screen, while an odor sample taken at DiFilippi's Pizza Grotto replays through your super-multimedia card? Such a setup may get frustrating — at least until you can afford to add taste-type data to your system as well. Alas, you can expect to wait a long time indeed before odor and taste become standard SQL data types. These days, the data types that you use most commonly — after the numeric types, of course — are the character-string types.

You have two main types of character data: fixed character data (CHARAC- TER or CHAR) and varying character data (CHARACTER VARYING or VARCHAR). You also have two variants of these types of character data: NATIONAL CHARACTER and NATIONAL CHARACTER VARYING.

CHARACTER *data type*

If you define the data type of a column as CHARACTER or CHAR, you can specify the number of characters the column holds by using the syntax CHARACTER (x), where x is the number of characters. If you specify a column's data type as CHARACTER (16), for example, the maximum length of any data you can enter in the column is 16 characters. If you don't specify an argument (that is, you don't provide a value in place of the *x*), SQL assumes a field length of one character. If you enter data into a CHARACTER field of a specified length and you enter fewer characters than the specified number, SQL fills the remaining character spaces with blanks.

CHARACTER VARYING data type

The CHARACTER VARYING data type is useful if entries in a column can vary in length, but you don't want SQL to pad the field with blanks. This data type enables you to store exactly the number of characters that the user enters. No default value exists for this data type. To specify this data type, use the form CHARACTER VARYING (*x*) or VARCHAR (*x*), where *x* is the maximum number of characters permitted.

NATIONAL CHARACTER and NATIONAL CHARACTER VARYING data types

The NATIONAL CHARACTER and NATIONAL CHARACTER VARYING data types function the same as the CHARACTER and CHARACTER VARYING data types, except that the character set you're specifying is different from the default character set. You can specify the character set as you define a table column. If you want, each column can use a different character set. The following example of a table-creation statement uses multiple character sets:

```
CREATE TABLE XLATE (
    LANGUAGE_1    CHARACTER (40),
    LANGUAGE_2    CHARACTER VARYING (40)  CHARACTER SET GREEK,
    LANGUAGE_3    NATIONAL CHARACTER (40),
    LANGUAGE_4    CHARACTER (40)           CHARACTER SET KANJI
    )
```

The LANGUAGE_1 column contains characters in the implementation's default character set. The LANGUAGE_3 column contains characters in the implementation's national character set. The LANGUAGE_2 column contains Greek characters. And the LANGUAGE_4 column contains Kanji characters.

Bit strings

SQL-92 also has a data type for strings of bits that don't represent alphanumeric characters or numbers. The BIT and BIT VARYING data types accept any arbitrary bit string. You specify fixed-length binary data by using the BIT (*x*) format, where *x* is the number of bits. BIT without an argument defaults to one bit. If you want to accommodate data that sometimes is one length and sometimes another, use BIT VARYING (*x*), where *x* denotes the maximum number of bits that the data field accepts. You may also use the BIT and BIT VARYING data types to hold binary or hexadecimal data or to hold flags that indicate whether individual logical switches are on or off.

Datetimes

The SQL-92 standard defines five different data types that deal with dates and times. These data types are called *datetime data types,* or simply *datetimes.* Considerable overlap exists among these data types, so some implementations you encounter may not support all five.

Implementations that do not fully support all five data types for dates and times may experience problems with databases that you try to migrate from another implementation. If you have trouble with a migration, check how both the source and the destination implementations represent dates and times.

DATE data type

The DATE type stores year, month, and day values of a date. The year value is four digits long, and the month and day values are both two digits long. A DATE value can represent any date from the year 0001 to the year 9999. The length of a DATE is ten positions, as in 1957-08-14.

TIME data type

The TIME data type stores hour, minute, and second values of time. The hours and minutes occupy exactly two digits. The seconds value is also two digits but may also include an optional fractional part. This data type, therefore, represents a time of 32 minutes and 58.436 seconds past 9 a.m., for example, as 09:32:58.436.

The precision of the fractional part is implementation-dependent but is at least six digits long. A TIME value takes up eight positions if the value has no fractional part or nine positions plus the number of fractional digits if the value does include a fractional part. The ninth position holds the decimal point. You specify TIME type data either as TIME or as TIME (p), where p is the number of positions. The default assumption is zero fractional digits. The example in the preceding paragraph represents a data type of TIME (12).

TIMESTAMP data type

TIMESTAMP data includes both date and time information. The lengths and the restrictions on the values of the components of TIMESTAMP data are the same as they are for DATE and TIME data, except for one difference: The default length of the fractional part of the time component of a TIMESTAMP is six digits rather than zero. If the value has no fractional digits, the length of a TIMESTAMP is 19 positions. If fractional digits are present, the length is

20 positions plus the number of fractional digits. The twentieth position is for the decimal point. You specify a field as TIMESTAMP type by using either TIMESTAMP or TIMESTAMP (p), where p is the number of digit positions. The value of p can't be negative, and the implementation determines its maximum value.

TIME WITH TIME ZONE data type

The TIME WITH TIME ZONE data type is exactly the same as the TIME data type except that this type adds information about the offset from *Universal Time* (formerly known as Greenwich Mean Time or GMT). The value of the offset may range anywhere from –12:59 to +13:00. This additional information takes up additional digit positions. A TIME WITH TIME ZONE value with no fractional part is 14 positions long. If you specify a fractional part, the field length is 15 positions plus the number of fractional digits.

TIMESTAMP WITH TIME ZONE data type

The TIMESTAMP WITH TIME ZONE data type functions exactly the same as the TIMESTAMP data type except that this data type also adds information about the offset from Universal Time. The additional information takes up six additional digit positions, giving 25 positions for a field with no fractional part and 26 positions plus the number of fractional digits for fields that do include a fractional part.

Intervals

The *interval* data types relate closely to the datetime data types. An interval is the difference between two datetime values. In many applications that deal with dates, times, or both, you sometimes need to determine the interval between two dates or two times. SQL-92 recognizes two distinct types of intervals: the *year-month* interval and the *day-time* interval. A year-month interval is the number of years and months between two dates. A day-time interval is the number of days, hours, minutes, and seconds between two instants within a month. You can't mix calculations involving a year-month interval with calculations involving a day-time interval, because months come in varying lengths (28, 29, 30, or 31 days long).

Data type summary

Table 2-2 enumerates the various data types and displays literals that conform to each type.

Table 2-2	Data Types
Data Type	*Example Value*
CHARACTER (20)	'Amateur Radio
VARCHAR (20)	'Amateur Radio'
SMALLINT or INTEGER	7500
NUMERIC or DECIMAL	3425.432
REAL, FLOAT, or DOUBLE PRECISION	6.023E-23
BIT (5)	B'11011'
BIT (16)	X'3FD0'
DATE	DATE '1997-08-14'
TIME (2)[1]	TIME '12:46:02.43'
TIME (3) WITH TIME ZONE	TIME '12:46:02.432-08:00'
TIMESTAMP (0)	TIMESTAMP '08-14-1997 12:46:02'
INTERVAL DAY	INTERVAL '4' DAY

[1]Argument specifies number of fractional digits.

Remember that your specific implementation of SQL may not support all the data types that I describe in this section. Furthermore, your implementation may support nonstandard data types that I don't describe here.

Null Values

If a database field contains a data item, that field has a specific value. A field that does not contain a data item is said to have a *null value*. In a numeric field, a null value is not the same as a value of zero. In a character field, a null value is not the same as a blank. Both a numeric zero and a blank character are definite values. A null value indicates that a field's value is undefined — its value is not known.

A number of situations exist in which a field may have a null value. The following list describes a few of these situations:

- ✔ *The value exists, but you don't know what the value is yet:* You set MASS to null in the Top row of the QUARK table because the mass of the top quark is not yet accurately determined.

- ✔ *The value doesn't exist yet:* You set TOTAL_SOLD to null in the *SQL For Dummies, 2nd Edition* row of the BOOKS table, because the first set of quarterly sales figures is not yet reported.

✔ *The field isn't applicable for this particular row:* You set SEX to null in the See-Threepio row of the EMPLOYEE table, because See-Threepio is a droid who has no gender.

✔ *The value is out of range:* You set SALARY to null in the Michael Jordan row of the EMPLOYEE table, because you designed the SALARY column as type NUMERIC (8,2) and Michael's contract calls for pay in excess of $999,999.99.

A field can have a null value for many different reasons. Don't jump to any hasty conclusions about what any particular null value means.

Constraints

Constraints are restrictions that you apply to the data that someone can enter into a database table. You may know, for example, that entries in a particular numeric column must fall within a certain range. If anyone makes an entry that falls outside that range, that entry must be an error. By applying a range constraint to the column, you prevent this type of error.

Traditionally, the application program that uses the database applies any constraints to a database. The most recent DBMS products, however, enable you to apply constraints directly to the database. This approach has several advantages. If multiple applications all use the same database, you need to apply the constraints only once rather than multiple times. Additionally, adding constraints at the database level is usually simpler than adding them to an application. In many cases, you need only to tack a clause onto your CREATE statement.

I discuss constraints and *assertions,* which are constraints that apply to more than one table, in detail in Chapter 5 in the section on integrity.

Using SQL in a Client/Server System

SQL is a data sublanguage that works on a stand-alone system or on a multiuser system. SQL works particularly well in a client/server system. On such a system, users on multiple client machines that connect to a server machine can access via a local area network (LAN) or other communications channel a database that resides on the server to which they're connected. The application program on a client machine contains SQL data-manipulation commands. The portion of the DBMS residing on the client sends these commands to the server across the communications channel that connects the server to the client. At the server, the server portion of the DBMS interprets and executes the SQL command and then sends the results back to the client across the communication channel. You can encode very complex operations into SQL at the client and then decode and perform those operations at the server. This type of setup results in the most effective use of the bandwidth of that communication channel.

If you retrieve data by using SQL on a client/server system, only the data you want travels across the communication channel from the server to the client. In contrast, a simple resource-sharing system, with minimal intelligence at the server, must send huge blocks of data across the channel to give you the small piece of data that you want. Needless to say, this sort of massive transmission can slow operations considerably. The client/server architecture complements the characteristics of SQL to provide good performance at a moderate cost on small, medium, and large networks.

The server

Unless it receives a request from a client, the server does nothing. It just stands around and waits. If multiple clients require service at the same time, however, servers need to respond quickly. Servers generally differ from client machines in that they have large amounts of very fast disk storage. Servers are optimized for fast data access and retrieval. And because they must handle traffic coming in simultaneously from multiple client machines, servers need a fast processor.

What the server is

The *server* (short for *database server*) is the part of a client/server system that holds the database. The server also holds the server portion of a database management system. This part of the DBMS interprets commands coming in from the clients and translates these commands into operations in the database. The server software also formats the results of retrieval requests and sends the results back to the requesting client.

What the server does

The job of the server is relatively simple and straightforward. All a server needs to do is read, interpret, and execute commands that come to it across the network from clients. Those commands are in one of several data sublanguages. A sublanguage doesn't qualify as a complete language — it implements only part of a language. A data sublanguage deals only with data handling. The sublanguage has operations for inserting, updating, deleting, and selecting data but doesn't have flow control structures such as DO loops, local variables, functions, procedures, or I/O to printers. SQL is the most common data sublanguage in use today and has become an industry standard. Proprietary data sublanguages are gradually being supplanted by SQL on machines in all performance classes.

The client

The *client* part of a client/server system consists of a hardware and a software component. The hardware is the client computer and its interface to the local area network. This hardware may be very similar or even identical to the server hardware. The software is the distinguishing component of the client.

What the client is

The primary job of the client is to provide a user interface. As far as the user is concerned, the client machine is the computer and the user interface is the application. The user may not even realize that the process involves a server. The server is usually out of sight — sometimes even in another room. Aside from the user interface, the client also contains the application program and the client part of the DBMS. The application program performs the specific task you require, such as accounts receivable or order entry. The client part of the DBMS executes the application program commands and exchanges data and SQL data-manipulation commands with the server part of the DBMS.

What the client does

The client part of a DBMS displays information on the screen and responds to user input transmitted via the keyboard, mouse, or other input device. The client may also process data coming in from a telecommunications link or from other stations on the network. The client part of the DBMS does all the application-specific "thinking." To a developer, the client part of a DBMS is the interesting part. The server part just handles the requests of the client part and does so in a repetitive, mechanical fashion.

Using SQL on the Internet/Intranet

Database operation on the Internet and on intranets differs fundamentally from operation in a traditional client/server system. The difference is primarily on the client end. In a traditional client/server system, much of the functionality of the DBMS resides on the client machine. On an Internet-based database system, most or all of the DBMS resides on the server. The client may host nothing more than a Web browser. At most, the client holds a browser and a browser extension, such as a Netscape plug-in or an ActiveX control. Thus the conceptual "center of mass" of the system shifts toward the server. This shift has several advantages, as noted in the following list:

✔ The client portion of the system (browser) is low cost.

✔ You have a standardized user interface.

✔ The client is easy to maintain.

✔ You have a standardized client/server relationship.

✔ You have a common means of displaying multimedia data.

The main disadvantages of performing database manipulations on the Internet involve security and data integrity, as the following list describes:

✔ To protect information from unwanted access or tampering, both the Web server and the client browser must support strong encryption.

✔ Browsers don't perform adequate data-entry validation checks.

✔ Database tables residing on different servers may become desynchronized.

Client and server extensions designed to address these concerns make the Internet a feasible location for production database applications. The architecture of intranets is similar to that of the Internet, but security is less of a concern. Because the organization maintaining the intranet has physical control over all the client machines as well as the servers and the network that connects these components together, an intranet suffers much less exposure to the efforts of malicious hackers. Data-entry errors and database desynchronization, however, do remain concerns. Chapter 16 covers database on the Internet in detail, and Chapter 17 discusses the organizational intranet.

Chapter 3

The Components of SQL

*S*QL is a special-purpose language, specifically designed for the creation and maintenance of data in relational databases. An ANSI standard, which was most recently revised in 1992, defines and controls SQL. Vendors of relational database management systems all have their own implementations of SQL. Those implementations differ from the standard to a greater or lesser degree. Close adherence to the standard is most important to people who may want to run their database and its associated applications on more than one platform.

Although SQL is not a general-purpose programming language, SQL does contain everything you need to create, maintain, and provide security for a relational database. The part of SQL that you use to create databases is called the *Data Definition Language (DDL)*. You perform database maintenance by using the *Data Manipulation Language (DML)*. The *Data Control Language (DCL)* provides security for your database. This chapter introduces the DDL, DML, and DCL.

SQL's Data Definition Language provides you with everything you need to completely define a database, modify its structure after you create the database, and destroy the database after you no longer need it. The Data Manipulation Language is a powerful tool for entering data into, changing, or extracting data from a database. The richness of DML enables you to specify exactly what you want to do with a database. The Data Control Language provides you with the armor you need to protect your database from harm. A database can become corrupted in many ways. If you correctly use the tools that the DCL provides, you can prevent many of those problems. The amount of protection that the DCL provides may vary from one implementation to another. If your implementation doesn't provide sufficient protection, you must add that protection to your application program.

Data Definition Language (DDL)

The Data Definition Language is the part of SQL you use to create, change, or destroy the basic elements of a relational database. Basic elements include tables, views, schemas, catalogs, and possibly other things as well. In this section, I discuss the containment hierarchy that relates these elements to each other and look at the commands that operate on these elements.

In Chapter 1, I mention tables and schemas, noting that a *schema* is an overall structure that includes tables within it. Tables and schemas, therefore, are two elements of a relational database's *containment hierarchy.* You can break down the containment hierarchy as follows: Tables contain columns and rows. Schemas contain tables and views. Catalogs contain schemas. And the database itself contains catalogs.

Creating tables

A database table is a two-dimensional array made up of rows and columns. You can create a table by using SQL's CREATE TABLE command. Within the command, you specify the name and data type of each column.

After you create a table, you can start loading the table with data. (Loading data is a DML, not a DDL, function.) If requirements change, you can change a table's structure after you create the table by using the ALTER TABLE command. Eventually, a table may outlive its usefulness or in some other way become obsolete. If that day arrives, you can eliminate the table by using the DROP command. The various forms of the CREATE and ALTER commands, together with the DROP command, make up SQL's DDL.

Say that you're a database designer and you don't want your database tables to gradually turn to guacamole as you make updates over time. You decide to structure your database tables according to the best normalized form to ensure maintenance of data integrity. *Normalization,* which is an extensive field of study in its own right, is a way of structuring database tables so that updates do not introduce anomalies. Each table you create contains columns that correspond to attributes that are tightly linked to each other.

You may, for example, create a CUSTOMER table with the attributes CUSTOMER.CUSTOMER_ID, CUSTOMER.FIRST_NAME, CUSTOMER.LAST_NAME, CUSTOMER.STREET, CUSTOMER.CITY, CUSTOMER.STATE, CUSTOMER.ZIPCODE, and CUSTOMER.PHONE. All these attributes are more closely related to the customer entity than to any other entity in a database that may contain many tables. These attributes contain all the relatively permanent information that your organization keeps on its customers.

Most database management systems provide a graphical tool for creating database tables. You can, however, also create such tables by using an SQL command. The following example demonstrates a command that creates your CUSTOMER table:

```
CREATE TABLE CUSTOMER (
    CUSTOMER_ID            INTEGER            NOT NULL,
    FIRST_NAME             CHARACTER (15),
    LAST_NAME              CHARACTER (20)     NOT NULL,
    STREET                 CHARACTER (25),
    CITY                   CHARACTER (20),
    STATE                  CHARACTER (2),
    ZIPCODE                INTEGER,
    PHONE                  CHARACTER (13) ) ;
```

For each column, you specify its name (for example, CUSTOMER_ID), its data type (for example, INTEGER), and possibly one or more constraints (for example, NOT NULL).

Figure 3-1 shows a portion of the CUSTOMER table with some sample data in the table.

Figure 3-1:
The CUSTOMER table that you can create by using the CREATE TABLE command.

CUSTOMER_ID	FIRST_NAME	LAST_NAME	STREET	CITY	STAT	ZIPCODE
1	Harold	Percival	26262 S. Howards Mill Rd.	Westminster	CA	92683
2	Jerry	Appel	32323 S. River Lane Rd.	Santa Ana	CA	92705
3	Adrian	Hansen	232 Glenwood Ct.	Hollis	NH	3049
4	John	Baker	2222 Lafayette St.	Garden Grove	CA	92643
5	Michael	Pens	730 S. New Era Rd.	Irvine	CA	92715
6	Bob	Michimoto	25252 S. Kelmsley Dr.	Stanton	CA	92610
7	Linda	Smith	444 S.E. Seventh St.	Hudson	NH	3051
8	Robert	Funnell	2424 Sheri Ct.	Anaheim	CA	92640
9	Bill	Checkal	9595 Curry Dr.	Stanton	CA	92610
10	Jed	Style	3535 Randall St.	Santa Ana	CA	92705

If the SQL implementation you're using complies with SQL-89 but does not fully implement SQL-92, the syntax you need to use may differ from the syntax that I give in this book.

Imagine that you have the task of creating a database for your organization. Excited by the prospect of building a useful, valuable, and totally righteous structure of great importance to the future of your company, you sit right down at your computer and start entering SQL CREATE commands. Right?

Well, no. Not quite. In fact, that's a prescription for disaster. Many database development projects go awry at the very start, as excitement and enthusiasm overtake careful planning. Even if you're sure you have a clear idea in your mind of how to structure your database, write everything out on paper before touching your keyboard. The following list identifies some procedures that you need to keep in mind as you plan your database:

- ✔ Identify all tables.
- ✔ Define the columns that each table must contain.
- ✔ Give each table a primary key that you can guarantee is unique.
- ✔ Make sure that every table in the database has at least one column in common with one other table in the database. These shared columns serve as logical links that enable you to relate information in one table to the corresponding information in another table.
- ✔ Put each table in third normal form (3NF) or better to ensure the prevention of insertion, deletion, and update anomalies. (I discuss database normalization in Chapter 5.)

After you complete the design on paper and verify that it is sound, you're ready to transfer the design to the computer by using SQL CREATE commands.

A room with a view

At times, you want to retrieve some specific information from the CUSTOMER table. You don't want to look at everything — only some specific columns and rows. What you need is a view.

A *view* is a virtual table. In most implementations, a view has no independent physical existence. The view's definition exists only in the database's metadata, but the actual data comes from the table or tables from which you derive the view. The view's data is not physically duplicated somewhere else in online disk storage. Some views zero in on specific columns and rows of a single table. Others, known as *multitable views,* draw from two or more tables.

Single-table view

Sometimes, if you have a question, the data that gives you the answer resides in a single table in your database. If all the information you want to see exists on a single table, you can create a single-table view of the data. Say, for example, that you want to look at the names and telephone numbers of all customers who live in the state of New Hampshire. You can create a view from the CUSTOMER table that contains only the data you want. The following SQL command creates this view:

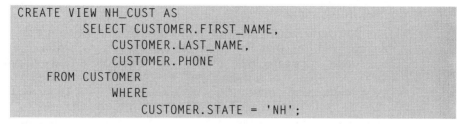

```
CREATE VIEW NH_CUST AS
        SELECT CUSTOMER.FIRST_NAME,
            CUSTOMER.LAST_NAME,
            CUSTOMER.PHONE
    FROM CUSTOMER
            WHERE
                CUSTOMER.STATE = 'NH';
```

Figure 3-2 diagrams how you derive the view from the CUSTOMER table.

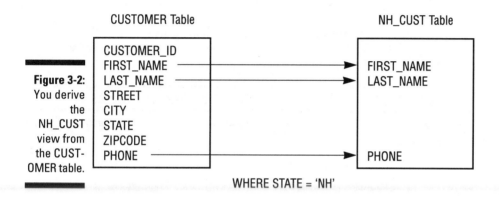

Figure 3-2: You derive the NH_CUST view from the CUST-OMER table.

This code is rigorously correct, but a little on the wordy side. You can accomplish the same thing with less typing if the SQL implementation you're using assumes that all table references are the same as the ones in the FROM clause. If your system makes that reasonable default assumption, you can reduce the command to the following lines:

```
CREATE VIEW NH_CUST AS
        SELECT FIRST_NAME,
            LAST_NAME,
            PHONE
        FROM CUSTOMER
            WHERE
                STATE = 'NH';
```

Although the second version is easier to write and read, this version is also more vulnerable to disruption from later ALTER TABLE commands. Such disruption isn't a problem for this simple case, which has no JOIN, but views with JOINs are much more "robust" if they use fully qualified names. I cover JOINs in Chapter 10.

Multitable view

More often than not, you need to pull data from two or more tables to answer your question. Say, for example, that you work for a sporting goods store, and you want a list of all customers who bought ski equipment in the last year so that you can send them a promotional mailing. You probably need information from the CUSTOMER table, the PRODUCT table, the INVOICE table, and the INVOICE_LINE table. You can create a multitable view that shows the data you need to answer your question. After you create the view, you can use that same view again and again. Each time you use the view, it reflects the changes that occurred in the underlying tables since the last time you used this view.

The sporting goods store database contains four tables: CUSTOMER, PRODUCT, INVOICE, and INVOICE_LINE. The tables are structured as shown in Table 3-1.

Table 3-1	Sporting Goods Store Database Tables		
Table	**Column**	**Data Type**	**Constraint**
CUSTOMER			
	CUSTOMER_ID	INTEGER	NOT NULL
	FIRST_NAME	CHARACTER (15)	
	LAST_NAME	CHARACTER (20)	NOT NULL
	STREET	CHARACTER (25)	
	CITY	CHARACTER (20)	
	STATE	CHARACTER (2)	
	ZIPCODE	INTEGER	
	PHONE	CHARACTER (13)	
PRODUCT			
	PRODUCT_ID	INTEGER	NOT NULL
	NAME	CHARACTER (25)	
	DESCRIPTION	CHARACTER (30)	
	CATEGORY	CHARACTER (15)	
	VENDOR_ID	INTEGER	
	VENDOR_NAME	CHARACTER (30)	
INVOICE			
	INVOICE_NUMBER	INTEGER	NOT NULL

Table	Column	Data Type	Constraint
	CUSTOMER_ID	INTEGER	
	INVOICE_DATE	DATE	
	TOTAL_SALE	NUMERIC (9,2)	
	TOTAL_REMITTED	NUMERIC (9,2)	
	FORM_OF_PAYMENT	CHARACTER (10)	
INVOICE_LINE			
	LINE_NUMBER	INTEGER	NOT NULL
	INVOICE_NUMBER	INTEGER	
	PRODUCT_ID	INTEGER	
	QUANTITY	INTEGER	
	SALE_PRICE	NUMERIC (9,2)	

Notice that some of the columns in Table 3-1 contain the constraint NOT NULL. These columns are either the primary keys of their respective tables or are columns that you, for some other reason, decide must contain a value. A table's primary key must uniquely identify each row. The primary key must contain a nonnull value in every row. I discuss keys in detail in Chapter 5.

The tables relate to each other through the columns that they have in common. Figure 3-3 shows these relationships.

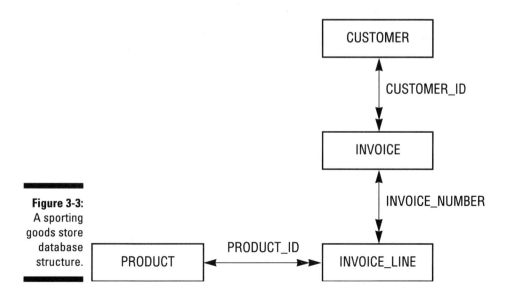

Figure 3-3:
A sporting
goods store
database
structure.

The CUSTOMER table bears a one-to-many relationship to the INVOICE table. One customer can make multiple purchases, generating multiple invoices. Each invoice, however, deals with one and only one customer. The INVOICE table bears a one-to-many relationship to the INVOICE_LINE table. An invoice may have multiple lines, but each line appears on one and only one invoice. The PRODUCT table also bears a one-to-many relationship to the INVOICE_LINE table. A product may appear on more than one line on one or more invoices. Each line, however, deals with one and only one product.

The CUSTOMER table links to the INVOICE table by the common CUSTOMER_ID column. The INVOICE table links to the INVOICE_LINE table by the common INVOICE_NUMBER column. The PRODUCT table links to the INVOICE_LINE table by the common PRODUCT_ID column. These links are the essence of what makes this database a relational database.

To give you the information you want about customers who've bought ski equipment, you need FIRST_NAME, LAST_NAME, STREET, CITY, STATE, and ZIPCODE from the CUSTOMER table; CATEGORY from the PRODUCT table; INVOICE_NUMBER from the INVOICE table; and LINE_NUMBER from the INVOICE_LINE table. You could create the view you want in stages by using the following commands:

```
CREATE VIEW SKI_CUST1 AS
    SELECT FIRST_NAME,
        LAST_NAME,
        STREET,
        CITY,
        STATE,
        ZIPCODE,
        INVOICE_NUMBER
    FROM CUSTOMER JOIN INVOICE
    USING (CUSTOMER_ID) ;
CREATE VIEW SKI_CUST2 AS
    SELECT FIRST_NAME,
        LAST_NAME,
        STREET,
        CITY,
        STATE,
        ZIPCODE,
        PRODUCT_ID
    FROM SKI_CUST1 JOIN INVOICE_LINE
    USING (INVOICE_NUMBER) ;
```

```
CREATE VIEW SKI_CUST3 AS
    SELECT FIRST_NAME,
        LAST_NAME,
        STREET,
        CITY,
        STATE,
        ZIPCODE,
        CATEGORY
    FROM SKI_CUST2 JOIN PRODUCT
    USING (PRODUCT_ID) ;
CREATE VIEW SKI_CUST AS
    SELECT DISTINCT FIRST_NAME,
        LAST_NAME,
        STREET,
        CITY,
        STATE,
        ZIPCODE
    FROM SKI_CUST3
    WHERE CATEGORY = 'Ski' ;
```

These CREATE VIEW statements combine data from multiple tables by using the JOIN operator. Figure 3-4 diagrams the process.

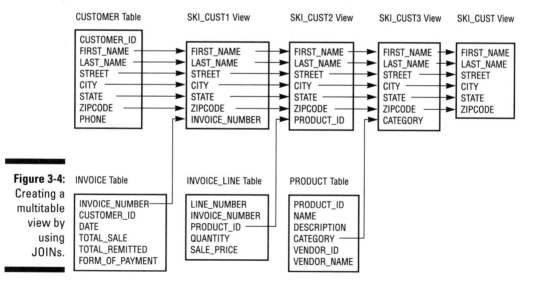

Figure 3-4: Creating a multitable view by using JOINs.

The first CREATE VIEW statement combines columns from the CUSTOMER table with a column of the INVOICE table to create the SKI_CUST1 view. The second CREATE VIEW statement combines SKI_CUST1 with a column from the INVOICE_LINE table to create the SKI_CUST2 view. The third CREATE VIEW statement combines SKI_CUST2 with a column from the PRODUCT table to create the SKI_CUST3 view. The fourth CREATE VIEW statement filters out all rows that don't have a CATEGORY of 'Ski.' The end result is a view (SKI_CUST) that contains the names and addresses of all customers who've bought at least one product in the 'Ski' category. The DISTINCT keyword in the fourth CREATE VIEW's SELECT clause ensures that you have only one entry for each customer, even if some customers made multiple purchases of ski items. (I cover JOINs in detail in Chapter 10.)

Collecting tables into schemas

A table consists of rows and columns and normally deals with a specific type of entity, such as customers, products, or invoices. Useful work generally requires information about several (or many) related entities. Organizationally, you collect the tables that you associate with these entities together into a schema.

A *schema* is a collection of related tables.

On a system where several unrelated projects may co-reside, you can assign all tables that are related to one another to one schema. Other groups of tables you can collect into schemas of their own.

By naming schemas, you can ensure that no one accidentally mixes in tables from one project with tables of another. Each project has its own associated schema, which you can distinguish from other schemas by name. Seeing certain table names (such as CUSTOMER, PRODUCT, and so on) appear in multiple projects, however, isn't uncommon. If any chance exists of a naming ambiguity, you want to qualify your table name by using its schema name as well (as in SCHEMA_NAME.TABLE_NAME). If you don't qualify a table name, SQL assigns that table to the default schema.

Ordering by catalog

For really large database systems, even multiple schemas may not prove sufficient. In a large distributed database environment with many users, you may even find duplication of a schema name. To prevent this situation from occurring, SQL-92 adds one more level to the containment hierarchy: the catalog.

A *catalog* is a named collection of schemas.

You can qualify a table name by using a catalog name as well as a schema name to ensure that no one confuses that table with a table of the same name in a schema with the same schema name. The catalog-qualified name appears in the following format:
`CATALOG_NAME.SCHEMA_NAME.TABLE_NAME.`

A database's containment hierarchy has catalogs at the highest level. A catalog contains schemas, and a schema contains tables and views. Tables and views contain columns and rows.

A catalog contains the schemas that contain user tables, but the catalog also contains the *information schema.* The information schema contains the system tables. The system tables hold the metadata associated with the other schemas. In Chapter 1, I define a database as a self-describing collection of integrated records. The metadata contained in the system tables is what makes the database self-describing.

Because you distinguish catalogs by their names, you can have multiple catalogs in a database. Each catalog can have multiple schemas, and each schema can have multiple tables. Of course, each table can have multiple columns and rows. The hierarchical relationships are shown in Figure 3-5.

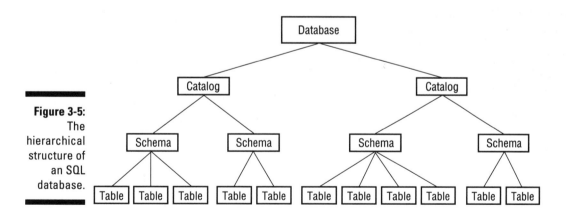

Figure 3-5: The hierarchical structure of an SQL database.

The DDL commands

SQL's Data Definition Language consists of the CREATE, ALTER, and DROP commands. The DDL deals with the structure of a database, while the Data Manipulation Language deals with the data contained within that structure. You use the various forms of the CREATE command to build the essential structures of the database. You use the ALTER command to change structures that you create. If you apply the DROP command to a table, that command destroys not only the table's data, but its structure as well. In the following sections, I give you brief descriptions of the DDL commands. In Chapters 4 and 5, I use these commands in examples.

CREATE

You can apply the SQL CREATE command to several SQL objects, including schemas, domains, tables, and views. By using the CREATE SCHEMA statement, you can create a schema, identify its owner, and specify a default character set. An example of such a statement appears as follows:

```
CREATE SCHEMA SALES
    AUTHORIZATION SALES_MGR
    DEFAULT CHARACTER SET ASCII ;
```

Use the CREATE DOMAIN statement to apply constraints to column values or to specify a collation order. The constraints you apply to a domain determine what objects the domain can contain and what objects it can't contain. You can create domains after you establish a schema. The following example shows how to use this command:

```
CREATE DOMAIN AGES AS INTEGER
   CHECK (AGE > 20) ;
```

You create tables by using the CREATE TABLE statement, and you create views by using the CREATE VIEW statement. Earlier in this chapter I show examples of the CREATE TABLE and the CREATE VIEW statements. If you use CREATE TABLE to create a new table, you can specify constraints on its columns at the same time. Sometimes, however, you may want to specify constraints that don't specifically attach to a table, but that apply to an entire schema. You can use the CREATE ASSERTION statement to specify such constraints. You also have CREATE CHARACTER SET, CREATE COLLATION, and CREATE TRANSLATION statements, which give you the flexibility of creating new character sets, collation sequences, or translation tables.

Collation sequences define the order in which you carry out sorts. *Translation tables* control the conversion of character strings from one character set to another.

ALTER

After you create a table, you're not necessarily stuck with that exact table forever. As you start to use the table, you may discover that it's not everything you need it to be. You can use the ALTER TABLE command to change the table by adding, changing, or deleting a column in the table. In addition to tables, you can also ALTER columns and domains.

DROP

Removing a table from a database schema is easy. Just use a DROP TABLE <tablename> command. You erase all the table's data, as well as the metadata that defines the table in the data dictionary — almost as if the table never existed.

Data Manipulation Language (DML)

As I state earlier in this chapter, the DDL is that part of SQL that creates, modifies, or destroys database structures. The DDL doesn't deal with data itself. The Data Manipulation Language (DML) is the part of SQL that operates on the data. Some DML statements read like ordinary English-language sentences and are easy to understand. Because SQL gives you very fine control of data, however, other DML statements can be very complex. If a DML statement includes multiple expressions, clauses, predicates, or subqueries, understanding just what that statement is trying to do can be a real challenge. After dealing with some of these statements, you may even consider switching to an easier line of work, such as brain surgery or quantum electrodynamics. Such drastic action is probably not necessary, however, because you can come to understand such SQL statements by mentally breaking them down into their basic components and analyzing them one chunk at a time.

The DML statements you can use are INSERT, UPDATE, DELETE, and SELECT. These statements can consist of a variety of parts, including multiple clauses. Each clause may incorporate value expressions, logical connectives, predicates, aggregate functions, and subqueries. You can make fine discriminations among database records and extract more information from your data by including these clauses in your statements. In Chapter 6, I discuss the operation of the DML commands, and in Chapters 7 through 11, I delve into the details of these commands.

Value expressions

Use *value expressions* to combine two or more values. Five different kinds of value expressions exist: *numeric, string, datetime, interval, and conditional.*

Numeric value expressions

To combine numeric values, use the addition (+), subtraction (−), multiplication (*), and division (/) operators. The following lines show a few examples of numeric value expressions:

```
12-7
15/3-4
6*(8+2)
```

The values in these examples are *numeric literals.* These values could also be column names, parameters, host variables, or subqueries — provided that those column names, parameters, host variables, or subqueries evaluate to a numeric value. Following are some examples:

```
SUBTOTAL+TAX+SHIPPING
6*MILES/HOURS
:month00s/12
```

The colon in the last example is a signal that the following term (months) is either a parameter or a host variable.

String value expressions

String value expressions may include the *concatenation operator* (||). Use concatenation to join two text strings together, as shown in Table 3-2.

Table 3-2	Examples of String Concatenation
Expression	*Result*
`'military ' || 'intelligence'`	`'military intelligence'`
`'oxy' || 'moron'`	`'oxymoron'`
`CITY|| ' ' ||STATE|| ' '||ZIP`	A single string with city, state, and zip code, each separated by a single space.

Some implementations of SQL use + as the concatenation operator rather than ||.

Some implementations may include string operators other than concatenation, but SQL-92 doesn't support such operators.

Datetime and interval value expressions

Datetime value expressions (surprise!) deal with dates and times. Data of `DATE`, `TIME`, `TIMESTAMP`, and `INTERVAL` types may appear in datetime value expressions. The result of a datetime value expression is always another datetime. You can add or subtract an interval from a datetime and also specify time zone information.

One example of a datetime value expression appears as follows:

```
DUE_DATE + INTERVAL '7' DAY
```

A library may use such an expression to determine when to send a late notice. Another example, specifying a time rather than a date, appears as follows:

```
TIME '18:55:48' AT LOCAL
```

The AT LOCAL keywords indicate that the time refers to the local time zone.

Interval value expressions deal with the difference (how much time passes) between one datetime and another. You have two kinds of intervals: *year-month* and *day-time*. You can't mix the two in an expression.

As an example of an interval, say that someone returns a library book after the due date. By using an interval value expression such as that of the following example, you can calculate how many days late the book is and assess a fine accordingly:

```
(DATE_RETURNED-DATE_DUE) DAY
```

Because an interval may be of either the year-month or the day-time variety, you need to specify which kind to use. In the preceding example, I specify DAY.

Conditional value expressions

CASE, NULLIF, and COALESCE are conditional value expressions, which I discuss extensively in Chapter 8. (Actually, NULLIF and COALESCE are macro expansions that provide a shorthand way of writing certain commonly needed CASE expressions.) The conditional value expressions give SQL the capability to take different actions, depending on which of several conditions is true. The conditional value expressions in SQL-92 make that version a much more powerful language than is SQL-89, which lacks these expressions.

Predicates

Predicates are the SQL equivalents of logical propositions. The following statement is an example of a proposition:

"The student is a senior."

In a table containing information about students, the domain of the CLASS column may be SENIOR, JUNIOR, SOPHOMORE, FRESHMAN, or NULL. You can use the predicate CLASS = SENIOR to filter out rows for which the predicate is false, retaining only those for which the predicate is true. Sometimes the value of a predicate in a row is unknown (NULL). In those cases, you may choose either to discard the row or to retain it. (After all, the student *could* be a senior.) The correct course depends on the specific situation.

CLASS = SENIOR is an example of a *comparison predicate*. SQL has six comparison operators. A simple comparison predicate uses one of these operators. Table 3-3 shows the comparison predicates and examples of their use.

Table 3-3	Comparison Operators and Comparison Predicates
Operator	*Comparison Expression*
= equal to	CLASS = SENIOR
<> not equal to	CLASS <> SENIOR
< less than	CLASS < SENIOR
> greater than	CLASS > SENIOR
<= less than or equal to	CLASS <= SENIOR
>= greater than or equal to	CLASS >= SENIOR

In the preceding example, only the first two entries (CLASS=SENIOR and CLASS< >SENIOR) make sense, because SOPHOMORE is considered greater than SENIOR, as SO comes after SE in the default collation sequence, which sorts in ascending alphabetical order. This interpretation, however, is probably not the one you want.

Logical connectives

Logical connectives enable you to build complex predicates out of simple ones. Say, for example, that you want to identify all the child prodigies in a database of high school students. Two propositions that could identify these students may read as follows:

"The student is a senior."

"The student's age is less than 14 years."

You can use the logical connective AND to create a compound predicate that isolates the student records that you want, as in the following example:

```
CLASS = SENIOR AND AGE < 14
```

If you use the AND connective, both of the component predicates must be true for the compound predicate to be true. Use the OR connective if you want the compound predicate to evaluate to true if either of the component predicates is true. NOT is the third logical connective. Strictly speaking, NOT doesn't connect two predicates but instead reverses the truth value of the single predicate to which you apply it. Take, for example, the following expression:

```
NOT (CLASS = SENIOR)
```

This expression is true only if CLASS is, in fact, not equal to SENIOR.

Set functions

Sometimes the information that you want to extract from a table doesn't relate to what the individual rows contain but concerns the data in the entire table taken as a set. SQL-92 provides five *set* (or *aggregate*) *functions* to deal with such situations. These functions are COUNT, MAX, MIN, SUM, and AVG. Each of these functions performs an action that draws data from a set of rows rather than from only a single row.

COUNT

The COUNT function returns the number of rows in the specified table. To count the number of precocious students in our high school database, use the following statement:

```
SELECT COUNT (*)
     FROM STUDENT
     WHERE GRADE = 12 and AGE < 14 ;
```

MAX

Use the MAX function to return the maximum value that occurs in the specified column. Say that you want to find the oldest student enrolled in your school. A statement such as the following returns the appropriate row:

```
SELECT FIRST_NAME, LAST_NAME, AGE
     FROM STUDENT
     WHERE AGE = (SELECT MAX(AGE) FROM STUDENT);
```

This statement returns all students whose age is equal to the maximum age. That is, if the age of the oldest student is 23, this statement returns the first and last names and the age of all students who are 23 years old.

This query makes use of a subquery. The subquery `SELECT MAX(AGE) FROM STUDENT` is embedded within the main query.

MIN

The `MIN` function works just like `MAX`, except that `MIN` looks for the minimum value in the specified column rather than the maximum. To find the youngest student enrolled, you can use the following query:

```
SELECT FIRST_NAME, LAST_NAME, AGE
    FROM STUDENT
    WHERE AGE = (SELECT MIN(AGE) FROM STUDENT);
```

This query returns all students whose age is equal to the age of the youngest student.

SUM

The `SUM` function adds up the values in a specified column. The column must be one of the numeric data types, and the value of the sum must be within the range of that type. Thus if the column is of type `SMALLINT`, the resulting sum must be no larger than the upper limit of the `SMALLINT` data type. In the retail database from earlier in this chapter, the `INVOICE` table contains a record of all sales. To find the total dollar value of all sales recorded in the database, use the `SUM` function as follows:

```
SELECT SUM(TOTAL_SALE) FROM INVOICE;
```

AVG

The `AVG` function returns the average of all the values in the specified column. As does the `SUM` function, `AVG` applies only to columns with a numeric data type. To find the value of the average sale, considering all transactions in the database, use the `AVG` function in the following way:

```
SELECT AVG(TOTAL_SALE) FROM INVOICE
```

Nulls, remember, have no value, so if any of the rows in the `TOTAL_SALE` column contain null values, those rows are ignored in the computation of the value of the average sale.

Subqueries

Subqueries, as you can see in the section on set functions earlier in this chapter, are queries within a query. Any place in an SQL statement where you can use an expression, you can also use a subquery. Subqueries provide a powerful tool for relating information in one table to information in another table, because you can embed a query into one table, within a query into another table. By nesting one subquery within another, you enable the access of information from two or more tables to generate a final result. If you understand how to use subqueries correctly, you can retrieve just about any information you want from a database.

SQL-89 has limited support of subqueries in that only one side of a comparison can function as a subquery. Implementations that adhere to SQL-89, but not fully to SQL-92, may restrict the places where you can use subqueries.

Data Control Language (DCL)

The Data Control Language has four commands: `COMMIT`, `ROLLBACK`, `GRANT`, and `REVOKE`. These commands all involve protecting the database from harm, either accidental or intentional.

Transactions

Your database is most vulnerable to damage while you or someone else is changing it. Even in a single-user system, making a change can prove dangerous to a database. A software or hardware failure while the change is in progress can leave a database in an indeterminate state between where it was before the change starts and where it would be after the change finishes.

SQL protects your database by restricting operations that can change the database so that these operations occur only within transactions. During a transaction, SQL acts on temporary copies of the data. Only at the conclusion of the transaction, after you issue the `COMMIT` statement, do the changes affect the database. If anything interrupts the transaction before the `COMMIT`, you can restore the system to its original state by issuing a `ROLLBACK` statement. After you roll back the database to its state before the transaction began, you can clear up whatever caused the problem and then attempt the transaction again.

As long as a hardware or software problem can possibly occur, your database remains susceptible to damage. To minimize the chance of damage, close the window of vulnerability as much as possible by performing all operations that affect the database within a transaction and then committing all these operations at one time. After you issue the `COMMIT` statement, all the actions in the transaction execute as quickly as possible. To damage data, a failure must occur during that brief period while the transaction is actually being committed.

In a multiuser system, database corruption or incorrect results are possible even if no hardware or software failures occur. Interactions between two or more users who access the same table at the same time can cause serious problems. By restricting changes so that they occur only within transactions, SQL addresses these problems as well.

By putting all operations that affect the database into transactions, you can isolate the actions of one user from those of another user. Such isolation is critical if you want to make sure that the results you obtain from the database are accurate.

You may wonder how the interaction of two users can produce inaccurate results. Say that user one reads a record in a database table. An instant later (more or less), user two changes the value of a numeric field in that record. Now user one writes a value back into that field, based on the value that she read initially. Because user one is unaware of user two's change, the value after user one's write operation is incorrect.

Another problem can result if user one writes to a record and then user two reads that record. If user one rolls back her transaction, user two is unaware of the rollback and bases his actions on the value that he read, which does not reflect the value that's actually in the database after the rollback.

Users and privileges

Aside from data corruption resulting from hardware and software problems or the unintentional interaction of two users, another major threat to data integrity is the users themselves. Some people should have no access to the data at all. Others should have only restricted access to some of the data but no access to the rest. Some should have unlimited access to everything. You need, therefore, a system for classifying users and for assigning access privileges to the users in different categories.

The creator of a schema is considered its owner. As the owner of a schema, you can grant access privileges to the users you specify. Any privileges that you don't explicitly grant are withheld. You can also revoke privileges that you've already granted. A user must pass an authentication procedure to prove his identity before he can access the files you've authorized him to use. That procedure is implementation dependent.

SQL gives you the capability to protect the following database objects:

- ✓ Tables
- ✓ Columns
- ✓ Views

✔ Domains

✔ Character sets

✔ Collations

✔ Translations

I discuss character sets, collations, and translations in Chapter 5.

SQL-92 supports six kinds of protection: *seeing, adding, modifying, deleting, referencing, and using.*

You permit access by using the GRANT statement and remove access by using the REVOKE statement. By controlling the use of the SELECT command, the DCL controls who can see a database object such as a table, column, or view. Controlling the INSERT command determines who can add new rows in a table. Restricting the use of the UPDATE command to authorized users controls who can modify table rows, and restricting the DELETE command controls who can delete table rows.

If one table in a database contains as a foreign key a column that is a primary key in another table in the database, you can add a constraint to the first table so that it references the second table. If one table references another, the owner of the first table may be able to deduce information about the contents of the second. As the owner of the second table, you may want to prevent such snooping. SQL-92's GRANT REFERENCES statement gives you that power. The following section discusses the problem of a renegade reference and how the GRANT REFERENCES statement prevents it. By using the GRANT USAGE statement, you can control who can use or even see the contents of a domain, character set, collation, or translation. (I cover this issue in Chapter 12.)

Table 3-4 summarizes the SQL statements that you use to grant and revoke privileges.

You can give different levels of access to different people, depending on their needs. The following commands offer a few examples of this capability:

```
GRANT SELECT
    ON customer
    TO SALES_MANAGER;
```

The preceding example enables one person, the sales manager, to see the customer table.

```
GRANT SELECT
    ON RETAIL_PRICE_LIST
    TO PUBLIC;
```

This second example enables anyone with access to the system to see the retail price list.

```
GRANT UPDATE
    ON RETAIL_PRICE_LIST
    TO SALES_MANAGER;
```

The preceding example here enables the sales manager to modify the price list. She can change the contents of existing rows, but she can't add or delete rows.

```
GRANT INSERT
    ON RETAIL_PRICE_LIST
    TO SALES_MANAGER;
```

This preceding example enables the sales manager to now add new rows to the retail price list.

```
GRANT DELETE
    ON RETAIL_PRICE_LIST
    TO SALES MANAGER;
```

Now, thanks to this last example, she can delete unwanted rows from the table, too.

Table 3-4	Types of Protection
Protection Operation	**Statement**
Enable to see a table	GRANT SELECT
Prevent from seeing a table	REVOKE SELECT
Enable to add rows to a table	GRANT INSERT
Prevent from adding rows to a table	REVOKE INSERT
Enable to change data in table rows	GRANT UPDATE
Prevent from changing data in table rows	REVOKE UPDATE
Enable to delete table rows	GRANT DELETE
Prevent from deleting table rows	REVOKE DELETE
Enable to reference a table	GRANT REFERENCES
Prevent from referencing a table	REVOKE REFERENCES
Enable to use a domain, character set, collation, or translation	GRANT USAGE ON DOMAIN, GRANT USAGE ON CHARACTER SET, GRANT USAGE ON COLLATION, GRANT USAGE ON TRANSLATION

Protection Operation	Statement
Prevent the use of a domain, character set, collation, or translation	REVOKE USAGE ON DOMAIN, REVOKE USAGE ON CHARACTER SET, REVOKE USAGE ON COLLATION, REVOKE USAGE ON TRANSLATION

Referential integrity constraints can jeopardize your data

You may think that, if you can control the seeing, creating, modifying, and deleting functions on a table, you're well-protected. Against most threats, you are. A knowledgeable hacker, however, can still ransack the house by using an indirect method.

A correctly designed relational database has *referential integrity,* which means that the data in one table in the database is consistent with the data in all the other tables. To ensure referential integrity, database designers apply constraints to tables that restrict what someone can enter into the tables. If you have a database with referential integrity constraints, a user can possibly create a new table that uses a column in a confidential table as a foreign key. That column then serves as a link through which someone can possibly steal confidential information.

Say, for example, that you're a famous Wall Street stock analyst. Many people believe in the accuracy of your stock picks, so whenever you recommend a stock to your subscribers, a lot of people buy that stock and its value goes up. You keep your analysis in a database, which contains a table named FOUR_STAR. Your top recommendations for your next newsletter are in that table. Naturally, you restrict access to FOUR_STAR so that word doesn't leak out to the investing public before your paying subscribers receive the newsletter.

You're still vulnerable, however, if anyone besides yourself can create a new table that uses the stock name field of FOUR_STAR as a foreign key, as shown in the following command example:

```
CREATE TABLE HOT_STOCKS (
    stock CHARACTER (30) REFERENCES FOUR_STAR
    );
```

The hacker can now try to insert the name of every stock on the New York Stock Exchange into the table. Those inserts that succeed tell the hacker which stocks match the stocks that you name in your confidential table. At computer speeds, the hacker doesn't need long to extract your entire list of stocks.

You can protect yourself from hacks such as the one in the preceding example by being very careful about entering statements similar to the following:

```
GRANT REFERENCES (stock)
     ON FOUR_STAR
     TO HACKER;
```

Avoid granting privileges to people who may abuse them.

This example offers one good reason for maintaining careful control of the REFERENCES privilege.

The following list describes two other reasons for careful control of REFERENCES:

- ✔ If the other person specifies the constraint in HOT STOCKS by using a RESTRICT option and you try to delete a row from your table, you're told by the DBMS that you can't, because doing so would violate a referential constraint.

- ✔ If you decide that you want to DROP your table, you find that you must either get the other person to first drop his constraint (or his table) or you must simply specify CASCADE and destroy his table along with yours.

The bottom line is that enabling another person to specify integrity constraints on your table not only introduces a potential security breach, but also means that the other user sometimes gets in your way.

Delegating responsibility for security

If you want to keep your system secure, you must severely restrict the access privileges you grant and the people to whom you grant these privileges. People who can't do their work because of lack of access, however, are likely to constantly hassle you. To preserve your sanity, you're probably going to need to delegate some of the responsibility for maintaining the security of your database. SQL provides for such delegation through the WITH GRANT OPTION clause. Consider the following example:

```
GRANT UPDATE
     ON RETAIL_PRICE_LIST
     TO SALES_MANAGER WITH GRANT OPTION
```

This statement is similar to the previous GRANT UPDATE example in that the statement enables the sales manager to update the retail price list. The statement also, however, gives her the right to grant the update privilege to anyone she wants. If you use this form of the GRANT statement, you must not only trust the grantee to use the privilege wisely, but you must also trust her to choose wisely in granting the privilege to others.

The ultimate in trust, and therefore the ultimate in vulnerability, is to execute a statement such as the following:

```
GRANT ALL PRIVILEGES
    ON FOUR_STAR
    TO BENEDICT_ARNOLD WITH GRANT OPTION;
```

Be *extremely* careful in using statements such as this one.

Part II
Using SQL to Build Databases

In this part . . .

The life of a database encompasses the following four important stages:

- ✔ Creating the database

- ✔ Filling the database with data

- ✔ Manipulating and retrieving selected data

- ✔ Deleting the data

I cover all these stages in this book, but in Part II, I focus on database creation. SQL includes all the facilities you need to create relational databases of any size or complexity. I explain what these facilities are and how to use them. I also describe some common problems that relational databases suffer from and tell you about provisions in SQL that can prevent such problems — or at least minimize their effects.

Chapter 4

Building and Maintaining a Simple Database Structure

• •

In This Chapter

▶ Building a database table by using graphical design tools

▶ Changing the structure of a database table by using graphical design tools

▶ Removing a database table by using graphical design tools

▶ Building, changing, and removing a database table by using SQL

▶ Migrating your database to another DBMS

• •

*T*he world's first electronic computer was activated right after the end of World War II; it operated on what's known as *binary logic*. The device was essentially a large collection of interconnected switches, and each switch was either on or off at any given time. The on and off states corresponded to the 1 and 0 of the binary number system. To use early electronic computers, computer scientists had to feed them a sequence of ones and zeros and then have them perform a computation. The result was another sequence of ones and zeros. This arrangement was very easy for the computer but very hard on the humans, who don't normally think in terms of ones and zeros. In those early days, no more than a handful of computers even existed on the planet. That was fortunate, because no more than a handful of people could program the things.

As technology moved from vacuum tubes to transistors to integrated circuits, computers gained speed and power. The devices were capable of taking over more of the work, making things easier for the people who used them. The first step in this process was to move from programming in *binary machine language* (the first-generation language) to programming in *assembly language* (the second-generation language). The next step involved higher-level (third-generation) languages such as FORTRAN, COBOL, Basic, Pascal, and C. Later, languages specifically designed for use with databases, such as dBASE, Paradox, and R:BASE (third-and-a-half-generation languages?) came into use. The latest step in this progression is the emergence of development environments such as Delphi, IntraBuilder, and C++ Builder (fourth-generation languages or 4GLs), which build applications with little or no procedural programming. You can use these graphical object-oriented tools (also known as *rapid application development,* or *RAD,* tools) to assemble application components into production applications.

SQL, as I state in Chapters 1 through 3, is not a complete language. It doesn't fit tidily into one of the generational categories I just mentioned. It makes use of commands in the manner of a third-generation language but is essentially nonprocedural, like a fourth-generation language. The bottom line is that how you classify SQL doesn't really matter. You can use it in conjunction with all the major third- and fourth-generation development tools. You can write the SQL code yourself, or you can move objects around on-screen and have the development environment generate equivalent code for you. The commands that go out to the remote database are pure SQL in either case.

In this chapter, I step you through the process of building, altering, and dropping a simple table by using a RAD tool, and then you find out how to build, alter, and drop the same table by using SQL.

Building a Simple Database by Using a RAD Tool

People use databases because they want to keep track of things important to them. Sometimes the things that they want to track are simple . . . and sometimes not. A good database management system provides what you need in either case. Some DBMSes give you SQL. Others, called *rapid application development (RAD) tools,* give you an object-oriented graphical environment. Some DBMSes support both approaches. In the following sections, I build a simple single-table database by using an object-oriented graphical database design tool so that you can see what the process involves. I use Borland's C++ Builder, but the procedure is similar for other Windows-based development environments.

A likely scenario

The first step is to decide what facts you want to track. Consider a likely example: Imagine that you just won $101 million in the Arizona Powerball lottery. People you haven't heard from in years and friends you'd forgotten you had are coming out of the woodwork. Some have sure-fire, can't-miss business opportunities in which they want you to invest. Others represent worthy causes that could benefit from your support. You're a responsible person, and you want to be a good steward of your new wealth. You realize that some of the business opportunities probably aren't as good as others. Some of the causes aren't as worthy as others. You'd better put all the options into a database so as not to lose any and to help you make fair and equitable judgments.

You decide to track the following items:

✔ First Name

✔ Last Name

✔ Address 1

✔ City

✔ State

✔ Country

✔ Postal Code

✔ Phone

✔ How Known

✔ Proposal

✔ Business or Charity?

Because you don't want to get too elaborate, you decide to put all the listed items into a single database table. You fire up your C++ Builder development environment and stare at the screen shown in Figure 4-1.

Too much is never enough

The screen contains a lot more information than previous-generation DBMS products displayed. In the old days (the 1980s), the typical DBMS presented you with a blank screen punctuated by a single-character prompt. Database management has come a long way since then, but determining what you should do first isn't necessarily any easier now. Sometimes too much information is just as confusing as too little. Actually, however, after you become familiar with the RAD tools, you can operate quite confidently and comfortably with them.

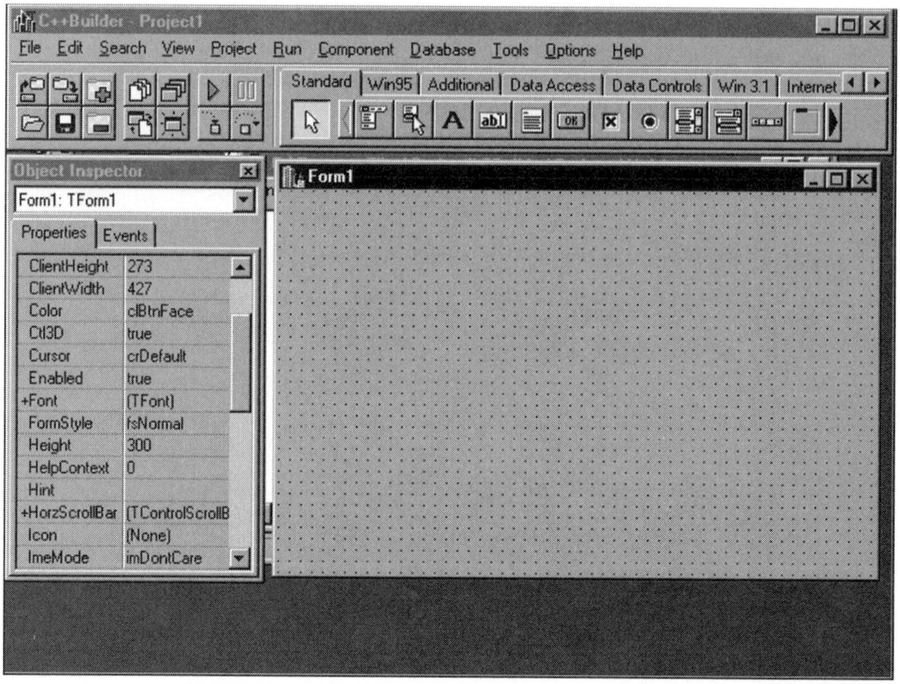

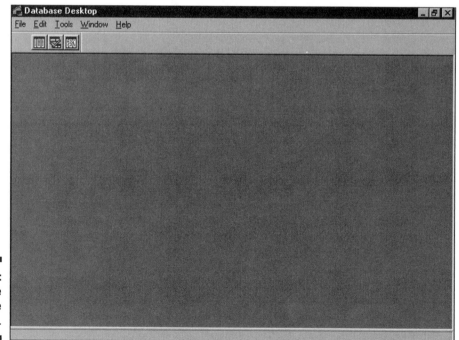

Figure 4-1:
The
opening
screen of
the C++
Builder
development
environment.

Figure 4-2:
The
Database
Desktop.

Borland's C++ Builder is a RAD tool. Its primary function is to develop applications of all types, including those that don't involve databases. In that sense, C++ Builder is similar to other RAD tools, such as Microsoft's Visual Basic/Access combination, PowerBuilder, and Borland's own dBASE for Windows and Paradox for Windows. C++ Builder has an advantage over those other tools in that its underlying language is C++, which is rapidly becoming the language of choice for serious software development.

C++ Builder includes a *Database Desktop* component, which serves the same purpose as the SQL Data Definition Language. The Database Desktop provides graphical tools for creating, maintaining, and destroying tables. Other RAD environments offer similar tools, which operate in similar ways.

From the main C++ Builder screen, choose Tools⇨Database Desktop from the menu bar. The window, shown in Figure 4-2, appears.

As you can see, the Database Desktop screen is marvelously free of clutter. In fact, the screen is marvelously free of just about everything. The Database Desktop does, however, offer a menu bar with a few choices. That's really all you need. Choose File⇨New⇨Table from this menu bar so that you can define a new database table. This action causes C++ Builder to display the Table Type dialog box.

A number of database file formats are in use on a variety of platforms. To be competitive, a development tool must have the capability to create and operate on at least most of the popular formats. C++ Builder gives you a choice of the most common formats on mainframes, UNIX machines, and personal computers. As an example, select the dBASE for Windows file type from the Table type list box in the center of the Create Table dialog box. Borland's dBASE for Windows is a popular personal-computer relational database management system. You can access dBASE files, as well as files in the other popular formats, by using SQL.

A really RAD way to create a table

After you select the dBASE for Windows file type in the Create Table dialog box, a table definition window similar to the one shown in Figure 4-3 appears.

In the Field Roster, you can enter the Field Name (which is the same as the table column name), the field Type, its Size, and the number of decimal places (Dec), if applicable. Make entries for all the fields you can identify. dBASE for Windows' use of the *field* nomenclature rather than *column* stems from its history. The original dBASE product, dBASE II, was not relational and used the terminology common for flat file systems.

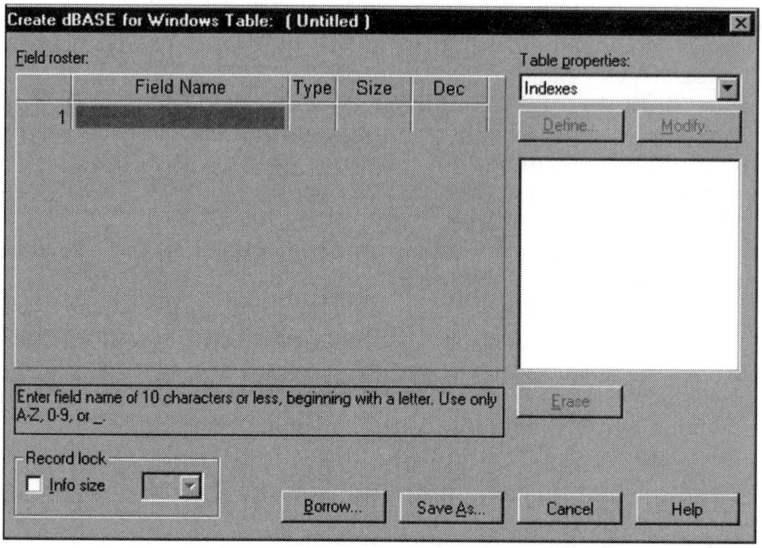

Figure 4-3:
A table
definition
window for
the Visual
dBASE file
type.

As a new multimillionaire, you want to add one more field that I haven't
mentioned yet. So many people have offered you enticing business deals
that a few of these folks have the same first and last names as other people
in the group. To keep them straight, you decide to add a unique proposal
number to each record in the database table. This way, you can tell one
David Lee from another.

Enter all the field information into the Field Roster, including appropriate
values for field type and size. After you finish, the Field Roster looks something like Figure 4-4.

Creating an index

Because the number of investment and charitable proposals you receive
could easily grow into the thousands, you need a quick way to pull out
records of interest. You may want to accomplish this task in a variety of
different ways. Say, for example, that you want to look at all the proposals
made by your brothers. You can isolate these effectively by basing your
retrieval on the contents of the LAST_NAME field, as shown in the following
example:

```
SELECT * FROM POWER
    WHERE LAST_NAME = 'Marx' ;
```

Create dBASE for Windows Table: (Untitled) ⊠

Field roster:

	Field Name	Type	Size	Dec
1	PROPOSALNO	F	5	0
2	FIRST_NAME	C	15	
3	LAST_NAME	C	20	
4	ADDRESS1	C	30	
5	CITY	C	25	
6	STATE	C	2	
7	POSTALCODE	C	10	
8	PHONE	C	14	
9	HOW_KNOWN	C	30	
10	PROPOSAL	C	50	
11	BUS_OR_CHA	C	1	

Table properties:

Indexes ▼

Define... Modify...

Specify a field size from 1 to 254.

Erase

Record lock

☐ Info size ▼

Borrow... Save As... Cancel Help

Figure 4-4:
A completed
Field
Roster.

That strategy, however, doesn't work for the proposals made by your brothers-in-law, but you can get those proposals by looking at another field, as shown in the following example:

```
SELECT * FROM POWER
   WHERE HOW_KNOWN = 'brother-in-law' ;
```

These queries work, but if POWER is large (tens of thousands of records), they may not work very quickly. SQL scans the entire table a row at a time, looking for entries that satisfy the WHERE clause. You can speed things up tremendously by applying *indexes* to the POWER table.

An *index* is a table of pointers. Each row in the index points to a corresponding row in the data table.

You can define an index for each different way that you may want to access your data. If you add, change, or delete rows in the data table, you don't need to re-sort the table. You need only to update the indexes. You can update an index much faster than you can sort an entire table. After you establish an index with the desired ordering, you can use that index to access rows in the data table almost instantaneously.

Because PROPOSALNO, the proposal number, is unique, as well as short, using that field is always the quickest way to reach an individual record. To use this field, however, you must know the proposal number of the record you want. You may want to create additional indexes, based on other fields, such as LAST_NAME, POSTALCODE, or HOW_KNOWN. For a table that you index on LAST_NAME, after a search finds the first row containing a

LAST_NAME of 'Marx', the search has found them all. The indexes for all the 'Marx' rows are stored one right after another. Chico, Groucho, Harpo, Zeppo, and Karl can all be retrieved almost as fast as Chico alone.

After you create an index, that creation adds additional overhead to your system, which tends to slow operations down a bit. You must balance this slowdown against the speed you gain by accessing records through an index. Indexing fields that you use frequently to access records in a large table generally pays off in the long run. Creating indexes for fields that you never use as retrieval keys, however, loses you far more than you gain. Creating indexes for fields that don't differentiate one record from another also makes no sense. The BUS_OR_CHA field, for example, merely divides the table records into two categories. This field doesn't make a good index.

The effectiveness of a specific index varies from one implementation to another. If you migrate a database from one platform to another, the indexes that gave the best performance on the first system may not perform the best on the new platform. In fact, they may cause a worse performance than if you hadn't indexed the database at all. You must optimize your indexes for each specific DBMS and hardware configuration. Try various indexing schemes to see which one gives you the best overall performance, considering both retrieval and update speed.

To create indexes for our example table, click the Define button in the Restructure dBASE IV Table: power.dbf dialog box. This action opens the Define Index dialog box, as shown in Figure 4-5.

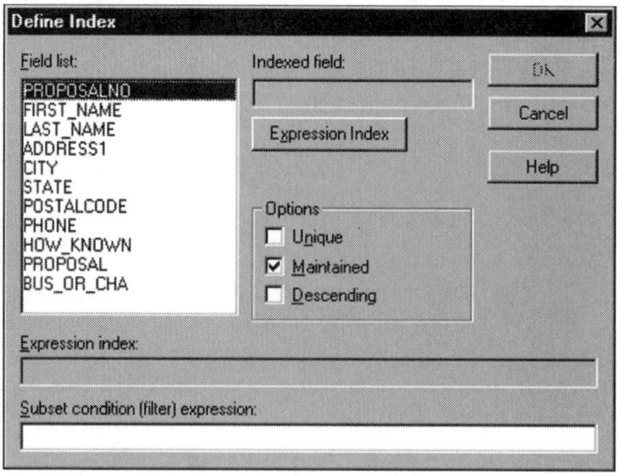

Figure 4-5:
The Define
Index
dialog box.

Define Index

Field list:
PROPOSALNO
FIRST_NAME
LAST_NAME
ADDRESS1
CITY
STATE
POSTALCODE
PHONE
HOW_KNOWN
PROPOSAL
BUS_OR_CHA

Indexed field:

Expression Index

OK
Cancel
Help

Options
☐ Unique
☑ Maintained
☐ Descending

Expression index:

Subset condition (filter) expression:

From the fields in the Field List at the left of the dialog box, select one or more that you want to serve as indexes. The indexes appear in the Indexed Field panel on the right. Select the PROPOSALNO field and then click the OK button. The Save Index As dialog box appears and suggests an Index tag name of PROPOSALNO. Click OK to accept the default index tag name and return to the Restructure dBASE IV Table: power.dbf dialog box. An SQL table can have multiple indexes. You may now create additional indexes by using other fields. You can index LAST_NAME, POSTALCODE, and HOW_KNOWN in the same way that you index PROPOSALNO.

After you create all your indexes, you can save the new table structure. Click the Save As button in the Restructure dBASE IV Table: power.dbf dialog box.

Of course, if you're using a RAD tool other than Borland C++ Builder or a file type other than dBASE, the specifics that I describe in this section don't apply to you. You go through a roughly equivalent procedure, however, to create a database table and its indexes with a different RAD tool.

Altering table structure

More often than not, the database tables you create aren't right the first time you build them. If you're working for someone else, you can be virtually certain that your client is going to come to you after you create your database and tell you that management wants to keep track of another data item — perhaps even several more. If you're building a database for your own use, deficiencies in your structure, which were totally invisible before you actually built the database, inevitably become apparent *after* you create the structure. Perhaps you start getting proposals from outside the USA and need to add a Country column. Or you decide that including an e-mail address may prove helpful. In any case, you must go back in and restructure what you created. All RAD tools have a restructure capability. To demonstrate a typical one, I use C++ Builder to modify the POWER proposal table.

Say that you need to add another address field, because for some people, one line of address isn't enough. From the Database Desktop, choose File⇨Open⇨Table to display the Open Table dialog box. Specify the correct drive (or the *alias* for that drive) and directory and then specify the table name. This action puts the table's structural skeleton on-screen, as shown in Figure 4-6.

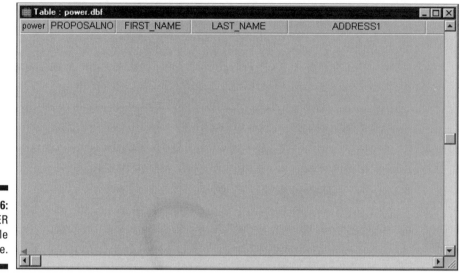

Table : power.dbf
power PROPOSALNO   FIRST_NAME   LAST_NAME   ADDRESS1

Figure 4-6:
The POWER
table
structure.

To add a column to the table, choose Table⇨Restructure from the menu bar.
In the Restructure dBASE IV Table: power.dbf dialog box that appears, you
can now place the Field Roster cursor on line 5 (the line below ADDRESS_1)
and press the Insert key. This action opens up a blank line on line 5, pushing
down the former contents of that line and everything below the line. Enter
Address_2 as the Field Name on this line, **C** as the Type, and **30** as the Size.
The result is shown in Figure 4-7.

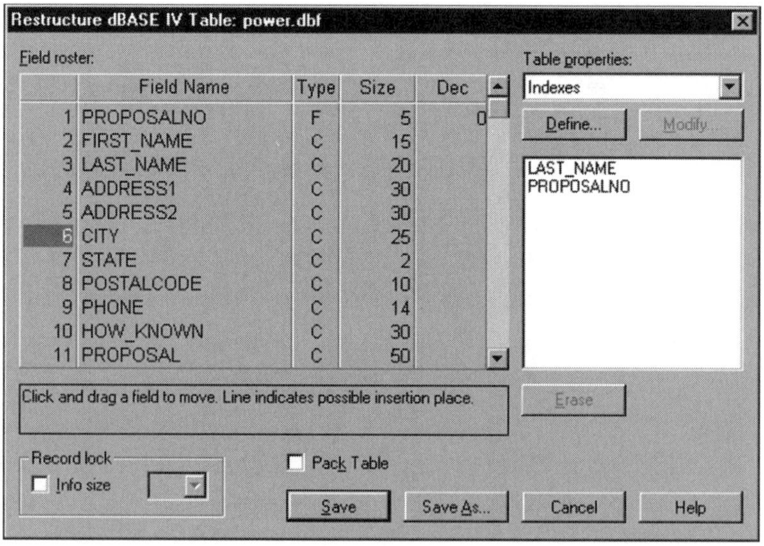

Figure 4-7:
The
restructured
POWER
table.

Dropping a table

In the course of creating a POWER table with exactly the structure you want, you may create a few intermediate forms that aren't quite right. The presence of these bogus tables on your system may prove confusing to people later, so your best course is to get rid of these tables while you can still remember which is which. To do so, choose Tools⇨Utilities⇨Delete from the Database Desktop main menu bar. The Delete dialog box appears, as shown in Figure 4-8. Highlight the name of the table you want to delete and press the Delete key.

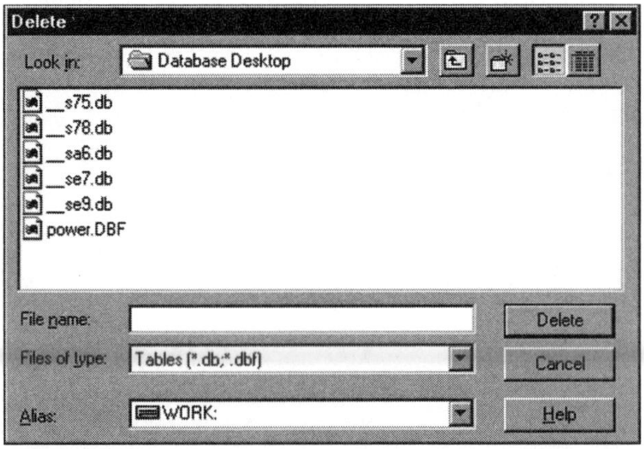

Figure 4-8:
The Delete
dialog box.

If the Database Desktop deletes a table, it deletes all related tables as well, including any indexes the table may have.

Build POWER with SQL's DDL Instead

All the database definition functions you can perform by using a RAD tool such as Borland's C++ Builder you can also accomplish by using SQL. Instead of clicking menu choices with the mouse, you enter commands from the keyboard. Some people, who prefer to manipulate visual objects, find the RAD tools easy and natural to understand and use. Other people, more oriented toward stringing words together into logical statements, find SQL commands easier and more natural. Because some things are more easily represented by using the object paradigm and others are more easily handled by using SQL, becoming proficient at using both methods is usually worthwhile.

In the following sections, I use SQL to perform the same table creation, alteration, and deletion operations that I used the RAD tool to perform in the preceding section.

Creating a table

To create a database table with SQL, you must enter the same information that you'd enter if you were creating the table with a RAD tool. The difference is that the RAD tool helps you by providing a field roster (or some similar data entry skeleton) and by preventing you from entering invalid field names, types, or sizes. SQL doesn't give you nearly as much help. You must know what you're doing before you start instead of figuring things out along the way. You must enter the entire CREATE TABLE statement before SQL even looks at it, let alone gives you any indication as to whether you made any errors in the statement.

The statement that creates a proposal tracking table identical to the one created earlier uses the following syntax:

```
CREATE TABLE POWER_SQL (
    PROPOSAL_NUMBER       SMALLINT,
    FIRST_NAME            CHAR (15),
    LAST_NAME             CHAR (20),
    ADDRESS1              CHAR (30),
    CITY                  CHAR (25),
    STATE                 CHAR (2),
    POSTAL_CODE           CHAR (10),
    PHONE                 CHAR (14),
    HOW_KNOWN             CHAR (30),
    PROPOSAL              CHAR (50),
    BUSIN_OR_CHARITY      CHAR (1) );
```

As you can see, the information in the SQL statement is essentially the same as what you entered into the RAD tool earlier in this chapter.

So which is the easier way to create a table — by using SQL or a RAD tool? Probably the method you're used to is the easier one for you. Which method you use is largely a matter of personal preference. The nice thing about SQL, however, is that the language is universal. The same standard syntax works regardless of the database management system you use.

SQL is a standard database language in the same way that COBOL is a standard programming language. If you learned COBOL in the mid-1960s, that knowledge is still very valuable today. On the other hand, if you'd become an expert in Borland's ObjectVision RAD Tool in 1992, the time that tool first appeared, you'd have no market for that expertise now, because ObjectVision is no longer on the market.

Any effort you put into learning SQL has long-term payoffs, because SQL is going to be around for a long time, just as COBOL has been. Effort you put into becoming an expert in a particular development tool is likely to yield a lesser return on investment. No matter how wonderful the latest RAD tool may be, you can be sure that it is going to be superseded by newer technology within one to three years. If you can recover your investment in the tool in that time, great! Use it. If not, you may be wise to stick with the tried and true. Train your people in SQL and your training investment is sure to pay dividends over a much longer period.

Creating an index

Indexes are a very important part of any relational database. Indexes serve as pointers into the tables that contain the data of interest. By using an index, you can go directly to a particular record, without needing to scan the table sequentially, one record at a time, to find that record. For large tables, indexes are a necessity. Without indexes, you may need to wait *years* rather than seconds for a result from a really large table.

Well, I suppose you wouldn't actually wait years. Some retrievals, however, may actually take that long if you let them keep running. Unless you have nothing better to do with your computer's time, you'd probably just abort the retrieval and do without the result. Life goes on.

Amazingly, the SQL-92 specification doesn't provide a means to create an index! The DBMS vendors must provide their own implementations of the function. Because these implementations aren't standardized, they may differ from one another. Most vendors provide the index creation function by adding a `CREATE INDEX` command to SQL. Even though two vendors may use the same words (`CREATE INDEX`), the way the command operates may not be the same. You're likely to find a lot of implementation-dependent clauses. You must carefully study your DBMS documentation to determine how to use that particular DBMS to create indexes.

Altering table structure

To change the structure of an existing table, you can use SQL's `ALTER TABLE` command. Interactive SQL at your client station is not as convenient as a RAD tool. The RAD tool displays your table's structure, which you can then modify. Using SQL, you must know in advance both the table's structure and how you want to modify it. At the screen prompt, you must enter the appropriate command to perform the alteration. If, however, you want to embed the table alteration instructions in an application program, using SQL is usually the easiest way to do so.

To add a second address field to the POWER_SQL table, use the following DDL command:

```
ALTER TABLE POWER_SQL
    ADD COLUMN ADDRESS2 CHAR (30);
```

You don't need to be an SQL guru to decipher this code. In fact, even professed computer illiterates can probably figure this one out. The command alters a table by the name of *POWER_SQL* by adding a column to the table. The column is named ADDRESS2, is of the CHAR data type, and is 30 characters long. This example demonstrates how easily you can change the structure of database tables by using SQL DDL commands.

Note: Although SQL provides this statement for adding a column to a table, SQL doesn't have facilities for dropping a column or for changing the name or data type of a column. If you want to perform any of those actions, you must create a new table and transfer the appropriate data from the old table to it.

Dropping a table

Getting rid of database tables you no longer want and that are cluttering up your hard disk is easy. Just use the DROP TABLE command, as follows:

```
DROP TABLE POWER_SQL ;
```

What could be simpler? If you drop a table, you erase all its data as well as its metadata. No vestige of the table remains.

Dropping an index

If you get rid of a table by issuing a DROP TABLE command, you delete any indexes associated with that table at the same time. Sometimes, however, you may want to keep a table but remove an index from it. SQL-92 doesn't define a DROP INDEX command, but some implementations include that command anyway. Such a command comes in handy if your system slows to a crawl and you discover that your tables aren't optimally indexed. Correcting an index problem can bring about a dramatic performance improvement that may surprise and delight users who've become accustomed to response times reminiscent of pouring molasses on a cold day in Vermont.

Portability Considerations

Any SQL implementation that you're likely to use has extensions that give it capabilities that the SQL-92 specification doesn't cover. Some of these features are likely to appear in the next release of the SQL specification, commonly referred to as SQL3. Others are unique to a particular implementation and probably destined to stay that way.

Often these extensions make creating an application that meets your needs easier, and you find yourself tempted to use them. Using the extensions may be your best course, but if you do, be aware of the tradeoffs. If you ever want to migrate your application to another SQL implementation, you may need to rewrite those sections in which you used extensions that your new environment doesn't support. Think about the probability of such a migration at some time in the future and also about whether the extension you're considering is unique to your implementation or fairly widespread. Forgoing use of an extension may be better in the long run, even if its use saves you some time. On the other hand, you may find no reason not to use the extension. Consider each case carefully. The more you know about existing implementations and the trends in their development, the better are the decisions you can make.

Chapter 5
Building a Multitable Database

A *database* is a representation or model of a physical or conceptual reality. The fidelity or resolution of that representation can be high (very detailed), low (only to a broad approximation), or somewhere in between.

Creating a high-fidelity model of a system takes more time, money, and expertise than does creating a low-fidelity model — a lot more. Consequently, you want to design your database structure so that the database contains exactly the level of detail that you need to serve your purpose — but no more.

Suppose that you work for an automobile dealership. You want to create an inventory of all the vehicles you have in stock. You probably want to track such facts as the year, model, color, engine, and options on each vehicle so that you can know what you have available for sale. You probably don't want to maintain detailed records of every part in the engine, the transmission, the differential, or any other part of the car. Such data is necessary in the manufacturer's database but not in the dealer's. On the other hand, you don't want to leave out any fact that may be important to sales, such as a car's color.

Some items in the system you model need to be major components of the database. Other items need to be present but in a subsidiary capacity. Some aspects of the system you don't need to include in the model at all, however, because those aspects don't affect the results that you want from the database. In the auto dealer database model, clearly VEHICLE is a major component. COLOR, on the other hand, is subsidiary to VEHICLE. ALTERNATOR_TYPE you probably don't need to include at all.

In this chapter, I take you through an example of how to design a multitable database. The first step is to identify what to include and what not to include. The next step is to decide how the included items relate to each other and set up tables accordingly. I discuss how to use keys, which provide a means of accessing individual records, and indexes, which enable you to access those records quickly.

That a database merely holds your data isn't enough. The database must also protect the data from becoming corrupted. In the latter part of this chapter, I discuss how to protect the integrity of your data. *Normalization* is one of the key methods you can use for protecting the integrity of a database, so I discuss the various "normal" forms and point out the kinds of problems that normalization solves.

Designing the Database

The best approach to database design is to follow this sequence of steps:

1. **Decide what objects are relevant to the problem.**
2. **Determine which of these objects should be tables and which should be columns in those tables.**
3. **Define tables according to your determination of how you need to organize the objects.**
4. **Optionally, you may want to designate a table column or a combination of columns as a key.**

   Keys provide a fast way of locating a particular row of interest in a table.

The following sections discuss these steps in detail, as well as some other technical issues that arise during database design.

Defining objects

The first step in designing a database is to decide which aspects of the system are important enough to include in the model. Treat each of these aspects as an object and create a list containing the names of all the objects you can think of. At this stage, don't try to decide how these objects relate to each other. Just try to list them all.

You may find it helpful to have a team of several people who are familiar with the system you're modeling. These people can brainstorm and respond to each other's ideas. Working together, you will probably develop a more complete and more accurate set of objects.

After you believe you have a reasonably complete set of objects, you can move on to the next step: deciding how these objects relate to each other. Some of the objects are major entities, crucial to giving you the results that you want. Others are subsidiary to or components of those major entities. Some objects, you ultimately may decide, don't belong in the model at all.

Identifying tables and columns

Major entities translate into database tables. Each major entity has a set of associated attributes, which translate into the columns of the table. Many business databases, for example, have a CUSTOMER table that keeps track of customers' names, addresses, and other permanent information. Each attribute of a customer, such as name, street, city, state, zip code, phone number, and Internet address, becomes a column in the CUSTOMER table.

No hard and fast rules exist about what to identify as tables and which of the attributes in the system belong to which table. You may have some reasons for assigning a particular attribute to one table and other reasons for assigning the attribute to another table. You must make a judgment based on what information you want to get from the database and how you want to use that information.

In deciding how to structure database tables, a critical consideration is to involve the future users of the database as well as the people who are to make decisions based on database information. If the "reasonable" structure you arrive at isn't consistent with the way that people will use the information, your system turns out frustrating to use at best — and could even produce wrong information, which is much worse than being hard to use. Don't let this happen! Put careful effort into deciding how to structure your tables.

Take a look at an example to demonstrate the thought process that goes into creating a multitable database. Say that you just established VetLab, a clinical microbiology laboratory that tests biological specimens sent in by veterinarians. Clearly, you want to track several kinds of things, such as the items in the following list:

- Clients
- Tests that you perform
- Employees
- Orders
- Results

Each of these entities has associated attributes. Each client has a name, address, and other contact information. Each test has a name and a standard charge. Employees have contact information as well as a job classification and rate of pay. For each order, you need to know who ordered the test, when the test was ordered, and exactly what test was ordered. For each test result, you need to know the outcome of the test, whether the results were preliminary or final, and the test order number.

Defining tables

Now you want to define a table for each entity and a column for each attribute. Table 5-1 shows how you may define the VetLab tables.

Table 5-1	VetLab Tables
Table	**Columns**
CLIENT	Client Name
	Address 1
	Address 2
	City
	State
	Postal Code
	Phone
	Fax
	Contact Person
TESTS	Test Name
	Standard Charge
EMPLOYEE	Employee Name
	Address 1
	Address 2
	City
	State
	Postal Code
	Home Phone
	Office Extension
	Hire Date
	Job Classification
	Hourly/Salary/Commission
ORDERS	Order Number
	Client Name
	Test Ordered
	Responsible Salesperson
	Order Date
RESULTS	Result Number
	Order Number
	Result
	Date Reported
	Preliminary/Final

You may create the tables defined in Table 5-1 by using either a rapid application development (RAD) tool or by using SQL's Data Definition Language (DDL) as shown below:

```
CREATE TABLE CLIENT (
     CLIENT_NAME          CHARACTER (30)     NOT NULL,
     ADDRESS_1            CHARACTER (30),
     ADDRESS_2            CHARACTER (30),
     CITY                 CHARACTER (25),
     STATE                CHARACTER (2),
     POSTAL_CODE          CHARACTER (10),
     PHONE                CHARACTER (13),
     FAX                  CHARACTER (13),
     CONTACT_PERSON       CHARACTER (30) ) ;

CREATE TABLE TESTS (
     TEST_NAME            CHARACTER (30)     NOT NULL,
     STANDARD_CHARGE      CHARACTER (30) ) ;

CREATE TABLE EMPLOYEE (
     EMPLOYEE_NAME        CHARACTER (30)     NOT NULL,
     ADDRESS_1            CHARACTER (30),
     ADDRESS_2            CHARACTER (30),
     CITY                 CHARACTER (25),
     STATE                CHARACTER (2),
     POSTAL_CODE          CHARACTER (10),
     HOME_PHONE           CHARACTER (13),
     OFFICE_EXTENSION     CHARACTER (4),
     HIRE_DATE            DATE,
     JOB_CLASSIFICATION   CHARACTER (10),
     HOUR_SAL_COMM        CHARACTER (1) ) ;

CREATE TABLE ORDERS (
     ORDER_NUMBER         INTEGER            NOT NULL,
     CLIENT_NAME          CHARACTER (30),
     TEST_ORDERED         CHARACTER (30),
     SALESPERSON          CHARACTER (30),
     ORDER_DATE           DATE ) ;

CREATE TABLE RESULTS (
     RESULT_NUMBER        INTEGER            NOT NULL,
     ORDER_NUMBER         INTEGER,
     RESULT               CHARACTER(50),
     DATE_REPORTED        DATE,
     PRELIM_FINAL         CHARACTER (1) ) ;
```

These tables relate to each other by the attributes (columns) that they share, as the following list describes:

✔ The CLIENT table links to the ORDERS table by the CLIENT_NAME column.

✔ The TESTS table links to the ORDERS table by the TEST_NAME (TEST_ORDERED) column.

✔ The EMPLOYEE table links to the ORDERS table by the EMPLOYEE_NAME (SALESPERSON) column.

✔ The RESULTS table links to the ORDERS table by the ORDER_NUMBER column.

For a table to serve as an integral part of a relational database, a good practice is to link that table to at least one other table in the database by using a common column. Figure 5-1 illustrates the relationships between the tables.

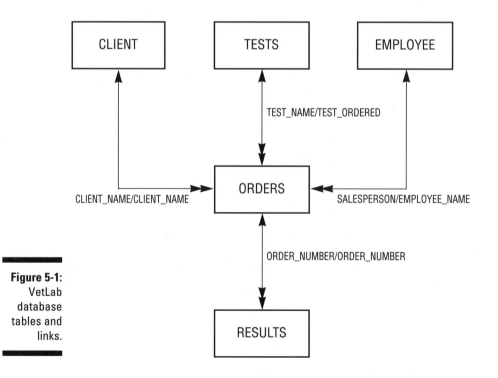

Figure 5-1:
VetLab
database
tables and
links.

The links in Figure 5-1 illustrate four different one-to-many relationships. The single arrowhead points to the "one" side of the relationship and the double arrowhead points to the "many" side. One client can make many orders, but each order is made by one and only one client. Each test can appear on many orders, but each order calls for one and only one test. Each order is taken by one and only one employee (or salesperson), but each salesperson can (and, you hope, does) take multiple orders. Each order can produce several preliminary test results and a final result, but each result is associated with one and only one order. As you can see in the figure, the attribute that links one table to another can have a different name in each table. Both attributes must, however, have matching data types.

Domains, character sets, collations, and translations

Although tables are the main components of a database, additional elements play a part, too. In Chapter 1, I define the *domain* of a column in a table as the set of all values that the column may assume. Establishing clear-cut domains for the columns in a table, through the use of constraints, is an important part of designing a database.

People who communicate in standard American English, however, aren't the only ones who use relational databases. Other languages — even some that use other character sets — work equally well. Even if your data isn't in a foreign language, some applications may still require a specialized character set. SQL-92 enables you to specify the character set you want to use. In fact, you can use a different character set for each column in a table. This kind of flexibility is generally unavailable in languages other than SQL.

A *collation* is a set of rules that determine how strings in a character set compare with one another. Every character set has a default collation. In the default collation of the ASCII character set, *A* comes before *B* and *B* comes before *C*. A comparison, therefore, considers *A* as less than *B* and considers *C* as greater than *B*. SQL-92, on the other hand, enables you to apply different collations to a character set. Again, this degree of flexibility isn't generally available in other languages.

Sometimes you encode data in a database in one character set, but you want to deal with the data in another character set. Perhaps you have data in the German character set, for example, but your printer doesn't support German characters that the ASCII character set doesn't include. A *translation* is a facility of SQL-92 that enables you to translate character strings from one character set to another. The translation may, for example, translate one character into two, such as a German *ü* to an ASCII *ue*, or the translation may translate lowercase characters to uppercase. You could even translate one alphabet into another, such as Hebrew into ASCII.

Get into your database fast with keys

A good rule for database design is to make sure that every row in a database table is distinguishable from every other row — that is, that each row in the table is unique. Sometimes you may want to extract data from your database for a specific purpose, such as a statistical analysis, and in so doing, you create tables where rows aren't necessarily unique. For your limited purpose, this sort of duplication doesn't matter. Tables that you may use in more than one way, however, should not contain duplicate rows.

A *key* is an attribute or a combination of attributes that uniquely identifies a row in a table. To access a row in a database, you must have some way of distinguishing that particular row from all the other rows. Because they must be unique, keys provide such an access mechanism. Because a key *must* be unique, you never want to place null values in keys. If you use null keys, two rows that each contain a null key field may not be distinguishable from each other.

In our veterinary lab example, you can designate appropriate columns as keys. In the CLIENT table, CLIENT_NAME makes a good key. This key can distinguish each client from all others. Entering a value in this column, therefore, becomes mandatory for every row in the table. TEST_NAME and EMPLOYEE_NAME make good keys for the TESTS and EMPLOYEE tables. ORDER_NUMBER and RESULT_NUMBER make good keys for the ORDERS and RESULTS tables. In each case, make sure that you enter a unique value for every row.

You can have two kinds of keys: *primary keys* and *foreign keys.* The keys that I discuss in the preceding paragraph are actually primary keys. Primary keys guarantee uniqueness. I discuss foreign keys later in this section.

To incorporate the idea of keys into the VetLab database, you can specify the primary key of a table as you create the table. In the following example, a single column is sufficient (assuming all VetLab's clients have unique names):

```
CREATE TABLE CLIENT (
    CLIENT_NAME        CHARACTER (30)     PRIMARY KEY,
    ADDRESS_1          CHARACTER (30),
    ADDRESS_2          CHARACTER (30),
    CITY               CHARACTER (25),
    STATE              CHARACTER (2),
    POSTAL_CODE        CHARACTER (10),
    PHONE              CHARACTER (13),
    FAX                CHARACTER (13),
    CONTACT_PERSON     CHARACTER (30)
    ) ;
```

Here, the constraint PRIMARY KEY replaces the constraint NOT NULL, given in the earlier definition of the CLIENT table. The PRIMARY KEY constraint implies the NOT NULL constraint, because a primary key can't have a null value.

Sometimes no single column in a table can guarantee uniqueness. In such cases, you can use a *composite key*. A composite key is a combination of columns that, together, guarantee uniqueness. Imagine that some of VetLab's clients are chains that have offices in several cities. In that case, CLIENT_NAME isn't sufficient to distinguish two different branch offices of the same client. To handle this situation, you can define a composite key, as follows:

```
CREATE TABLE CLIENT (
    CLIENT_NAME         CHARACTER (30)      NOT NULL,
    ADDRESS_1           CHARACTER (30),
    ADDRESS_2           CHARACTER (30),
    CITY                CHARACTER (25)      NOT NULL,
    STATE               CHARACTER (2),
    POSTAL_CODE         CHARACTER (10),
    PHONE               CHARACTER (13),
    FAX                 CHARACTER (13),
    CONTACT_PERSON      CHARACTER (30),
    CONSTRAINT BRANCH PRIMARY KEY
        (CLIENT_NAME, CITY)
    ) ;
```

A *foreign key* is a column or group of columns in a table that corresponds to or references a primary key in another table in the database. A foreign key need not itself be unique but must uniquely identify the column (or columns) in the table that the key references. If the CLIENT_NAME column is the primary key in the CLIENT table, every row in the CLIENT table must have a unique value in the CLIENT_NAME column. CLIENT_NAME is a foreign key in the ORDERS table. This foreign key corresponds to the primary key of the CLIENT table, but the key need not be unique in the ORDERS table. In fact, you hope the foreign key *isn't* unique. If each of your clients gave you only one order and then never ordered again, you'd go out of business rather quickly. You hope, in fact, that many rows in the ORDERS table correspond with each row in the CLIENT table, indicating that all your clients are repeat customers.

The following definition of the ORDERS table shows how you can add the concept of foreign keys to a CREATE statement:

```
CREATE TABLE ORDERS (
    ORDER_NUMBER        INTEGER             PRIMARY KEY,
    CLIENT_NAME         CHARACTER (30),
    TEST_ORDERED        CHARACTER (30),
    SALESPERSON         CHARACTER (30),
    ORDER_DATE          DATE,
    CONSTRAINT NAME_FK FOREIGN KEY (CLIENT_NAME)
        REFERENCES CLIENT (CLIENT_NAME),
    CONSTRAINT TEST_FK FOREIGN KEY (TEST_ORDERED)
        REFERENCES TESTS (TEST_NAME),
    CONSTRAINT SALES_FK FOREIGN KEY (SALESPERSON)
        REFERENCES EMPLOYEE (EMPLOYEE_NAME)
    ) ;
```

Foreign keys in the ORDERS table link that table to the primary keys of the CLIENT, TESTS, and EMPLOYEE tables.

Indexes

The SQL-92 specification doesn't address the topic of indexes, but that omission doesn't mean that indexes are rare or even optional parts of a database system. Every implementation of SQL supports indexes, but no universal agreement exists on how to support them. In Chapter 4, I show you how to create an index by using Borland's C++ Builder, a rapid application development (RAD) tool. You must refer to the documentation for your particular DBMS to see how the system implements indexes.

What's an index, anyway?

Data generally appears in a table in the order in which you originally entered the information. That order, however, may have nothing to do with the order in which you later want to process the data. Say, for example, that you want to process your CLIENT table in CLIENT_NAME order. The computer must first search the entire table to find the name that's closest to the front of the alphabet. After processing that row, the computer must search the entire table again to find the name that's the second closest to the front of the alphabet — and so on through the entire table. These searches take time. The larger the table, the longer the searches take. What if you have a table with 100,000 rows? What if you have a table with a million rows? In some applications, such table sizes are not rare. To scan through the entire table a million times to sort a million rows becomes unreasonable. Even with a very fast computer, you may not live long enough to see the result.

Indexes can be a great time saver. An *index* is a subsidiary or support table that goes along with a data table. For every row in the data table, you have a corresponding row in the index table. In the index table, however, the order of the rows is different.

Table 5-2 shows a small example data table.

Table 5-2	CLIENT Table			
CLIENT_NAME	*ADDRESS_1*	*ADDRESS_2*	*CITY*	*STATE*
Butternut Animal Clinic	5 Butternut Lane		Hudson	NH
Amber Veterinary, Inc.	470 Kolvir Circle		Amber	MI
Vets R Us	2300 Geoffrey Road	Suite 230	Anaheim	CA
Doggie Doctor	32 Terry Terrace		Nutley	NJ
The Equestrian Center	Veterinary Department	7890 Paddock Parkway	Gallup	NM
Dolphin Institute	1002 Marine Drive		Key West	FL
J. C. Campbell, Credit Vet	2500 Main Street		Los Angeles	CA
Wenger's Worm Farm	15 Bait Boulevard		Sedona	AZ

The rows are not in alphabetical order by CLIENT_NAME. In fact, they aren't in any useful order at all. The rows are simply in the order in which some-body entered the data.

An index for this CLIENT table may look like Table 5-3.

Table 5-3	Client Name Index for the CLIENT Table
CLIENT_NAME	*Pointer to Data Table*
Amber Veterinary, Inc.	2
Butternut Animal Clinic	1
Doggie Doctor	4
Dolphin Institute	6
J. C. Campbell, Credit Vet	7
The Equestrian Center	5
Vets R Us	3
Wenger's Worm Farm	8

The index contains the field that forms the basis of the index (in this case CLIENT_NAME) and a pointer into the data table. The pointer in each index row gives the row number of the corresponding row in the data table.

Why would I want one?

If I want to process a table in CLIENT_NAME order, and I have an index arranged in CLIENT_NAME order, I can perform my operation almost as fast as I could if the data table itself was in CLIENT_NAME order. I can work through the index sequentially, moving immediately to each index row's corresponding data record by using the pointer in the index.

If you use an index, the processing time of a table is proportional to N, where N is the number of records in the table. Without an index, the processing time for the same operation is proportional to N^2. For small tables, the difference is insignificant, but for large tables, the difference is very great indeed. On large tables, some operations aren't at all practical to perform without the help of indexes.

As an example, say that you have a table containing 100,000 records ($N = 100,000$) and processing each record takes one millisecond (one-thousandth of a second). If you have an index, processing the entire table takes only 100 seconds — less than two minutes. Without an index, however, you'd need to go through the table 100,000 times to achieve the same result. This process would take 10,000,000 seconds — more than 115 days. I think you may agree that the difference between waiting almost two minutes for a result and waiting almost 116 days is substantial. That's the difference that indexing can make.

Maintaining an index

After you create an index, something must maintain it. Fortunately, your DBMS maintains your indexes for you by updating them every time you update the corresponding data tables. This process takes a little bit of extra time but not too much. After you create an index and your DBMS is maintaining it, the index is always available to speed your data processing, no matter how many times you need to call on it.

Note: Some DBMS products give you the capability to turn off index maintenance. You may want to do so in some real-time applications where updating indexes is taking a lot of time and you have precious little to spare. You may even elect to update the indexes as a separate operation during off-peak hours.

Clearly, the best time to create an index is at the same time that you create its corresponding data table. If you create the index at the start and begin maintaining it at the same time, you don't need to undergo the pain of building the index later, with the entire operation taking place in a single, very long session. Try to anticipate all the ways that you may want to access your data and then create an index for each such possibility.

Don't fall into the trap of creating an index for retrieval orders that you're unlikely ever to use. A performance penalty is associated with maintaining an index, because index maintenance is an extra operation that the computer must perform every time it modifies the index field or adds or deletes a data table row. For optimal performance, create only those indexes that you really expect to use as retrieval keys — and only for tables containing a large number of rows. Otherwise, indexes can actually degrade performance.

 You may need to compile something such as a monthly or quarterly report that requires the data in an odd order that you don't ordinarily need. Create an index just before running that periodic report, run the report, and then drop the index so that the DBMS isn't burdened with maintaining the index during the long period between reports.

Integrity

A database is valuable only if you're reasonably sure that the data it contains is correct. In medical, aircraft, and spacecraft databases, for example, incorrect data can lead to loss of life. Incorrect data in other applications may have less severe consequences but can still prove damaging. The database designer must do everything possible to ensure that incorrect data never enters the database.

Some problems you can't stop at the database level. The application programmer must intercept these problems before they can damage the database. Everyone responsible for dealing with the database in any way must remain conscious of the threats to data integrity and take appropriate action to nullify those threats.

Databases can experience several distinctly different kinds of integrity — as well as a number of kinds of problems that can affect integrity. In the following sections, I discuss three types of integrity: *entity, domain,* and *referential.* I also look at some of the problems that can threaten database integrity.

Entity integrity

Every table in a database corresponds to an entity in the "real" world. That entity may be physical or conceptual, but in some sense, the entity's existence is independent of the database. A table has *entity integrity* if the table is entirely consistent with the entity that it models. To have entity integrity, a table must have a primary key. The primary key uniquely identifies each row in a table. Without a primary key, you can't be sure that the row retrieved is the one you want.

To maintain entity integrity, you need to specify that the column or group of columns that comprise the primary key are NOT NULL. In addition, you must constrain the primary key to be UNIQUE. Some implementations of SQL enable you to add such a constraint to the table definition. With others, you must apply the constraint later, after you specify how to add, change, or delete data from the table. Perhaps the best way to ensure that your primary key is both NOT NULL and UNIQUE is to give the key the PRIMARY KEY constraint as you create the table, as shown in the following example:

```
CREATE TABLE CLIENT (
    CLIENT_NAME         CHARACTER (30)      PRIMARY KEY,
    ADDRESS_1           CHARACTER (30),
    ADDRESS_2           CHARACTER (30),
    CITY                CHARACTER (25),
    STATE               CHARACTER (2),
    POSTAL_CODE         CHARACTER (10),
    PHONE               CHARACTER (13),
    FAX                 CHARACTER (13),
    CONTACT_PERSON      CHARACTER (30)
    ) ;
```

An alternative is to use NOT NULL in combination with UNIQUE, as shown in the following example:

```
CREATE TABLE CLIENT (
    CLIENT_NAME         CHARACTER (30)      NOT NULL,
    ADDRESS_1           CHARACTER (30),
    ADDRESS_2           CHARACTER (30),
    CITY                CHARACTER (25),
    STATE               CHARACTER (2),
    POSTAL_CODE         CHARACTER (10),
    PHONE               CHARACTER (13),
    FAX                 CHARACTER (13),
    CONTACT_PERSON      CHARACTER (30),
    UNIQUE (CLIENT_NAME) ) ;
```

Domain integrity

You usually can't guarantee that a particular data item in a database is correct, but you can at least determine whether a data item is valid. Many data items have a limited number of possible values. If you make an entry that is not one of the possible values, that entry must be an error. The United States, for example, has 50 states plus the District of Columbia, Puerto Rico, and a few possessions. Each of these areas has a two-character code that the U.S. Postal Service recognizes. If your database has a STATE column, you can enforce *domain integrity* by requiring that any entry into that column be one of the recognized two-character codes. If an operator enters a code that's not on the list of valid codes, that entry breaches domain integrity. If you test for domain integrity, you can refuse to accept any operation that causes such a breach.

Domain integrity concerns arise if you add new data to a table by using either the INSERT or the UPDATE statements. You can specify a domain for a column by using a CREATE DOMAIN statement before you use that column in a CREATE TABLE statement, as shown in the following example:

```
CREATE DOMAIN LEAGUE_DOM CHAR (8)
    CHECK (LEAGUE IN ('American', 'National'));
CREATE TABLE TEAM (
    TEAM_NAME CHARACTER (20) NOT NULL,
    LEAGUE    CHARACTER (8) NOT NULL
    ) ;
```

The domain of the LEAGUE column includes only two valid values: American and National. Your DBMS doesn't enable you to commit an entry or update to the TEAM table unless the LEAGUE column of the row you're adding has a value of either 'American' or 'National'.

Referential integrity

Even if every table in your system has entity integrity and domain integrity, you could still have a problem because of inconsistencies in the way one table relates to another. In most well-designed databases, every table contains at least one column that refers to a column in another table in the database. These references are important for maintaining the overall integrity of the database. The same references, however, make update anomalies possible. (*Update anomalies* are problems that can occur after you update the data in a row of a database table.)

The relationships among tables are generally not bidirectional. One table is usually dependent on the other. Say, for example, that you have a database with a CLIENT table and an ORDERS table. You may conceivably enter a client into the CLIENT table before she makes any orders. You can't, however, enter an order into the ORDERS table unless you already have an entry in the CLIENT table for the client who's making that order. The ORDERS table is dependent on the CLIENT table. This kind of arrangement is often called a *parent-child relationship,* where CLIENT is the parent table and ORDERS is the child table. The child is dependent on the parent. Generally, the primary key of the parent table is the column (or group of columns) that appears in the child table. Within the child table that same column (or group) is a foreign key. A foreign key may contain nulls and need not be unique.

Update anomalies arise in several ways. A client moves away, for example, and you want to delete her from your database. If she's already made some orders, which you recorded in the ORDERS table, deleting her from the CLIENT table could present a problem. You'd have records in the ORDERS (child) table for which you have no corresponding records in the CLIENT (parent) table. Similar problems arise if you add a record to a child table without making a corresponding addition to the parent table. The corresponding foreign keys in all child tables must reflect any changes to the primary key of a row in a parent table; otherwise, an update anomaly results.

You can eliminate most referential integrity problems by carefully controlling the update process. In some cases, you need to cascade deletes from a parent table to its children. If you delete a row from a parent table, therefore, you must perform the same action (delete) on all rows in its child tables that have foreign keys that match the primary key of the deleted row in the parent table. Take a look at the following example:

```
CREATE TABLE CLIENT (
    CLIENT_NAME       CHARACTER (30)     PRIMARY KEY,
    ADDRESS_1         CHARACTER (30),
    ADDRESS_2         CHARACTER (30),
    CITY              CHARACTER (25)     NOT NULL,
    STATE             CHARACTER (2),
    POSTAL_CODE       CHARACTER (10),
    PHONE             CHARACTER (13),
    FAX               CHARACTER (13),
    CONTACT_PERSON    CHARACTER (30)
    ) ;
```

```
CREATE TABLE TESTS (
     TEST_NAME              CHARACTER (30)        PRIMARY KEY,
     STANDARD_CHARGE        CHARACTER (30)
     ) ;

CREATE TABLE EMPLOYEE (
     EMPLOYEE_NAME          CHARACTER (30)        PRIMARY KEY,
     ADDRESS_1              CHARACTER (30),
     ADDRESS_2              CHARACTER (30),
     CITY                   CHARACTER (25),
     STATE                  CHARACTER (2),
     POSTAL_CODE            CHARACTER (10),
     HOME_PHONE             CHARACTER (13),
     OFFICE_EXTENSION       CHARACTER (4),
     HIRE_DATE              DATE,
     JOB_CLASSIFICATION     CHARACTER (10),
     HOUR_SAL_COMM          CHARACTER (1)
     ) ;

CREATE TABLE ORDERS (
     ORDER_NUMBER           INTEGER               PRIMARY KEY,
     CLIENT_NAME            CHARACTER (30),
     TEST_ORDERED           CHARACTER (30),
     SALESPERSON            CHARACTER (30),
     ORDER_DATE             DATE,
     CONSTRAINT NAME_FK FOREIGN KEY (CLIENT_NAME)
          REFERENCES CLIENT (CLIENT_NAME)
               ON DELETE CASCADE,
     CONSTRAINT TEST_FK FOREIGN KEY (TEST_ORDERED)
          REFERENCES TESTS (TEST_NAME)
               ON DELETE CASCADE,
     CONSTRAINT SALES_FK FOREIGN KEY (SALESPERSON)
          REFERENCES EMPLOYEE (EMPLOYEE_NAME)
               ON DELETE CASCADE
     ) ;
```

The constraint NAME_FK names CLIENT_NAME as a foreign key that references the CLIENT_NAME column in the CLIENT table. If you delete a row in the CLIENT table, you also automatically delete all rows in the ORDERS table that have the same value in the CLIENT_NAME column as those in the CLIENT_NAME column of the CLIENT table. The deletion cascades down from the CLIENT table to the ORDERS table. The same is true for the foreign keys in the ORDERS table that refer to the primary keys of the TESTS and EMPLOYEE tables.

You may not want to cascade a deletion. Instead you may want to change the child table's foreign key to a NULL value. Consider the following variant of the previous example:

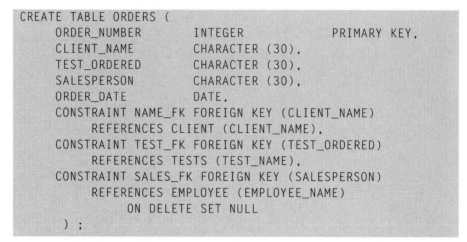

```
CREATE TABLE ORDERS (
     ORDER_NUMBER        INTEGER            PRIMARY KEY,
     CLIENT_NAME         CHARACTER (30),
     TEST_ORDERED        CHARACTER (30),
     SALESPERSON         CHARACTER (30),
     ORDER_DATE          DATE,
     CONSTRAINT NAME_FK FOREIGN KEY (CLIENT_NAME)
          REFERENCES CLIENT (CLIENT_NAME),
     CONSTRAINT TEST_FK FOREIGN KEY (TEST_ORDERED)
          REFERENCES TESTS (TEST_NAME),
     CONSTRAINT SALES_FK FOREIGN KEY (SALESPERSON)
          REFERENCES EMPLOYEE (EMPLOYEE_NAME)
               ON DELETE SET NULL
     ) ;
```

The constraint SALES_FK names the SALESPERSON column as a foreign key that references the EMPLOYEE_NAME column of the EMPLOYEE table. If a salesperson leaves the company, you delete her row in the EMPLOYEE table. New salespeople are eventually assigned to her accounts, but for now, deletion of her name from the EMPLOYEE table causes all her orders in the order table to receive a null value in the SALESPERSON column.

Another way to keep inconsistent data out of a database is to refuse to permit an addition to a child table until a corresponding row exists in its parent table. Yet another possibility is to refuse to permit changes to a table's primary key. If you refuse to permit rows in a child table without a corresponding row in a parent table, you prevent the occurrence of "orphan" rows in the child table. This refusal helps maintain consistency across tables. If you refuse to permit changes to a table's primary key, you don't need to worry about updating foreign keys in other tables that depend on that primary key.

Potential problem areas

Data integrity is subject to assault from a variety of quarters. Some of these problems arise only in multitable databases, while others can happen even in databases that contain only a single table. You want to recognize and minimize all these potential threats.

Bad input data

The source documents or data files that you use to populate your database may contain bad data. This data may not be the data you want at all or it may be a corrupted version of the correct data. Range checks tell you whether the data has domain integrity. This type of check catches some problems but clearly not all. Field values that are within the acceptable range but are nonetheless incorrect aren't identified as problems.

Operator error

Your source data may be correct, but the data entry operator incorrectly transcribes the data. This type of error can lead to the same kinds of problems as bad input data. Some of the solutions are the same, too. Range checks help but aren't a panacea. Another solution is to have another operator independently validate all the data. This approach is costly, because independent validation takes twice the people and twice the time. In some cases, however, the extra effort and expense may prove worthwhile if data integrity is critical.

Mechanical failure

If you experience a mechanical failure, such as a disk crash, while a database table is open, the data in the table can become corrupted. Good backups are your main defense against this problem.

Malice

Consider the possibility that someone may want to intentionally corrupt your data. Your first line of defense is to deny database access to anyone who may have a malicious intent and restrict everyone else's access to what they need. Your second defense is to maintain data backups in a safe place. Periodically reevaluate the security features of your installation. Being just a little paranoid doesn't hurt.

Data redundancy

Data redundancy is a big problem with the hierarchical database model, but the problem can plague relational databases, too. Not only does such redundancy waste storage space and slow down processing, but the problem can also lead to serious data corruption. If you store the same data item in two different tables in a database, the item in one of those tables may change, while the corresponding item in the other table remains the same. This situation generates a discrepancy, and you may have no way of telling which version is correct. A good idea is to hold data redundancy to a minimum. A certain amount of redundancy is necessary for the primary key of one table to serve as a foreign key in another. Try, however, to avoid any redundancy beyond that.

After you eliminate most redundancy from a database design, you may find that performance is now unacceptable. Operators very often purposefully use redundancy to speed up processing. In the previous example, the ORDERS table contains only the client's name to identify the source of each order. If you prepare an order, you must join the ORDERS table with the CLIENT table to get the client's address. If this joining of tables makes the program that prints orders run too slowly, you may decide to store the client's address redundantly in the ORDERS table. This redundancy offers the advantage of printing the orders faster — but at the expense of slowing down and making more complicated any updating of the client's address.

A very common practice is for users to initially design a database with very little redundancy and with high degrees of normalization and then, after finding that important applications run slowly, to selectively add redundancy and denormalize. The key word here is *selectively*. The redundancy that you add back in has a specific purpose, and because you're acutely aware of both the redundancy and the hazard it represents, you take appropriate measures to ensure that the redundancy doesn't cause more problems than it solves.

Constraints

Earlier in this chapter, I talk about constraints as mechanisms for ensuring that data you enter into a table column falls within the domain of that column. A *constraint* is an application rule that the DBMS enforces. After you define a database, you can include constraints (such as NOT NULL) in a table definition. The DBMS makes sure that you can never commit any transaction that violates a constraint.

You have three different kinds of constraints: column constraints, table constraints, and assertions. A *column constraint* imposes a condition on a column in a table. A *table constraint* is a constraint on an entire table. An *assertion* is a constraint that affects more than one table.

Column constraints

An example of a column constraint is shown in the following DDL (Data Definition Language) statement:

```
CREATE TABLE CLIENT (
    CLIENT_NAME        CHARACTER (30)      NOT NULL,
    ADDRESS_1          CHARACTER (30),
    ADDRESS_2          CHARACTER (30),
    CITY               CHARACTER (25),
    STATE              CHARACTER (2),
    POSTAL_CODE        CHARACTER (10),
    PHONE              CHARACTER (13),
    FAX                CHARACTER (13),
    CONTACT_PERSON     CHARACTER (30)
    ) ;
```

The statement applies the constraint NOT NULL to the CLIENT_NAME column specifying that CLIENT_NAME may not assume a null value. UNIQUE is another constraint that you can apply to a column. This constraint specifies that every value in the column must be unique. The CHECK constraint is particularly useful in that it can take any valid expression as an argument. Consider the following example:

```
CREATE TABLE TESTS (
    TEST_NAME           CHARACTER (30)      NOT NULL,
    STANDARD_CHARGE     NUMERIC (6,2)
            CHECK (STANDARD_CHARGE >= 0.0
                AND STANDARD_CHARGE <= 200.0)
    ) ;
```

VetLab's standard charge for a test must always be greater than or equal to zero. And none of the standard tests costs more than $200. The CHECK clause refuses to accept any entries that fall outside the range 0 <= STANDARD_CHARGE <= 200. Another way of stating the same constraint is as follows:

```
CHECK (STANDARD_CHARGE BETWEEN 0.0 AND 200.0)
```

Table constraints

The PRIMARY KEY constraint specifies that the column to which it applies is a primary key. This constraint is thus a constraint on the entire table and is equivalent to a combination of the NOT NULL and the UNIQUE column constraints. You can specify this constraint in a CREATE statement, as shown in the following example:

```
CREATE TABLE CLIENT (
    CLIENT_NAME         CHARACTER (30)      PRIMARY KEY,
    ADDRESS_1           CHARACTER (30),
    ADDRESS_2           CHARACTER (30),
    CITY                CHARACTER (25),
    STATE               CHARACTER (2),
    POSTAL_CODE         CHARACTER (10),
    PHONE               CHARACTER (13),
    FAX                 CHARACTER (13),
    CONTACT_PERSON      CHARACTER (30)
    ) ;
```

Assertions

An *assertion* specifies a restriction that applies to more than one table. In the following example, you use a search condition drawn from two tables to create an assertion.

```
CREATE TABLE ORDERS (
    ORDER_NUMBER          INTEGER             NOT NULL,
    CLIENT_NAME           CHARACTER (30),
    TEST_ORDERED          CHARACTER (30),
    SALESPERSON           CHARACTER (30),
    ORDER_DATE            DATE
    ) ;

CREATE TABLE RESULTS (
    RESULT_NUMBER         INTEGER             NOT NULL,
    ORDER_NUMBER          INTEGER,
    RESULT                CHARACTER(50),
    DATE_REPORTED         DATE,
    PRELIM_FINAL          CHARACTER (1)
    ) ;

CHECK (NOT EXISTS SELECT * FROM ORDERS, RESULTS
    WHERE ORDERS.ORDER_NUMBER = RESULTS.ORDER_NUMBER
    AND ORDERS.ORDER_DATE > RESULTS.DATE_REPORTED) ;
```

This assertion ensures that you receive no reports of any result before you order its corresponding test.

Normalizing the Database

Some ways of organizing data are better than others. Some are more logical. Some are simpler. Some are better at preventing inconsistencies from arising after you start using the database.

A host of different problems (called *modification anomalies*) can potentially plague a database if you don't structure the database correctly. To prevent these problems, you can *normalize* the database structure. Normalization generally entails splitting one database table into two, with each of the resulting tables simpler than the original.

Modification anomalies are so named because they are generated by the addition of, change to, or deletion of data from a database table.

To illustrate how modification anomalies can occur, consider the table shown in Figure 5-2.

SALES

Customer_ID	Product	Price
1001	Laundry detergent	12
1007	Toothpaste	3
1010	Chlorine bleach	4
1024	Toothpaste	3

Figure 5-2:
This SALES table leads to modification anomalies.

Your company sells household cleaning and personal-care products, and you charge all customers the same price for each product. The SALES table keeps track of everything for you. Now assume that customer 1001 moves out of the area and no longer is a customer. You don't care what he's bought in the past, because he's not going to buy again. You want to delete his row from the table. If you do so, however, you lose not only the fact that customer 1001 has bought laundry detergent; you also lose the fact that laundry detergent costs $12. This situation is called a *deletion anomaly*. In deleting one fact (that customer 1001 buys laundry detergent), you inadvertently delete another fact (that laundry detergent costs $12).

You can use the same table to illustrate an insertion anomaly. Say that you want to add stick deodorant to your product line at a price of $2. You can't add this data to the SALES table until you have a customer who buys stick deodorant.

The problem with the SALES table in the figure is that this table deals with more than one thing. The table deals with which products customers buy and also deals with what the products cost. You need to split the SALES table into two tables, each one dealing with only a single theme or idea, as shown in Figure 5-3.

CUST_PURCH

Customer_ID	Product
1001	Laundry detergent
1007	Toothpaste
1010	Chlorine bleach
1024	Toothpaste

PROD_PRICE

Product	Price
Laundry detergent	12
Toothpaste	3
Chlorine bleach	4

Figure 5-3:
The SALES table is split into two tables.

The figure shows that the SALES table is divided into two tables, CUST_PURCH and PROD_PRICE. CUST_PURCH deals with the single idea of customer purchases. PROD_PRICE deals with the single idea of product pricing. You can now delete the row for customer 1001 from CUST_PURCH without losing the fact that laundry detergent costs $12. That fact is now stored in PROD_PRICE. You can also add stick deodorant to PROD_PRICE, whether anyone is currently buying the product or not. You store purchase information elsewhere, in the CUST_PURCH table.

The process of breaking up a table into multiple tables, each of which has a single theme, is called *normalization*.

A normalization operation that solves one problem may not affect others. You may need to perform several successive normalization operations to reduce each of the resulting tables to a single theme. Each table in a database should deal with one — and only one — main theme. Sometimes, determining that a table is really dealing with two or even more themes is difficult.

You can classify tables according to the types of modification anomalies to which they're subject. In E.F. Codd's 1970 paper, the first to describe the relational model, Codd identified three sources of modification anomalies and defined first, second, and third *normal forms* (1NF, 2NF, 3NF) as remedies to those types of anomalies. In the ensuing years, Codd and others discovered additional types of anomalies and specified new normal forms to deal with them. The Boyce-Codd normal form (BCNF), the fourth normal form (4NF), and the fifth normal form (5NF) each afforded a higher degree of protection against modification anomalies. Not until 1981, however, did a paper, written by R. Fagin, describe domain/key normal form (DKNF); using this last normal form enables you to guarantee that a table is free of modification anomalies.

The normal forms are *nested* in the sense that a table that's in 2NF is automatically also in 1NF. Similarly, a table in 3NF is automatically in 2NF, and so on. For most practical applications, putting a database in 3NF is sufficient to ensure a high degree of integrity. To be absolutely sure of its integrity, however, you must put the database into DKNF.

After you normalize a database as much as possible, you may want to make selected denormalizations to improve performance. If you do, be fully aware of the types of anomalies that may now become possible.

First normal form

To be in first normal form (1NF), a table must have the following qualities:

- ✔ The table is a two-dimensional table, with rows and columns.
- ✔ Each row contains data that pertains to some thing or portion of a thing.
- ✔ Each column contains data for a single attribute of the thing it's describing.
- ✔ Each cell (intersection of a row and a column) of the table must have only a single value.
- ✔ Entries in any column must all be of the same kind. If, for example, the entry in one row of a column contains an employee name, all the other rows must contain employee names in that column, too.
- ✔ Each column must have a unique name.
- ✔ No two rows may be identical (that is, each row must be unique).
- ✔ The order of the columns and the order of the rows is not significant.

A table (relation) in first normal form is immune to some kinds of modification anomalies but is still subject to others. The SALES table shown in Figure 5-2 is in first normal form and, as shown, the table is subject to deletion and insertion anomalies. First normal form, therefore, may prove useful in some applications but unreliable in others.

Second normal form

To appreciate second normal form, you must understand the idea of functional dependency.

A *functional dependency* is a relationship between or among attributes. One attribute is functionally dependent on another if the value of the second attribute determines the value of the first attribute. If you know the value of the second attribute, you can determine the value of the first attribute.

Suppose, for example, that a table has attributes (columns) STANDARD_CHARGE, NUMBER_OF_TESTS, and TOTAL_CHARGE, which relate through the following equation:

```
TOTAL_CHARGE = STANDARD_CHARGE * NUMBER_OF_TESTS
```

TOTAL_CHARGE is then functionally dependent on both STANDARD_CHARGE and on NUMBER_OF_TESTS. If you know the values of STANDARD_CHARGE and NUMBER_OF_TESTS, you can determine the value of TOTAL_CHARGE.

Every table in first normal form must have a unique primary key. That key may consist of one or more than one column. A key consisting of more than one column is called a *composite key*. To be in second normal form (2NF), all non-key attributes (columns) must depend on all the key. Thus every relation that is in 1NF, with a single attribute key, is automatically in second normal form. If a relation has a composite key, all non-key attributes must depend on all components of the key. If you have a table where some non-key attributes don't depend on all components of the key, you want to break the table up into two or more tables so that, in each of the new tables, all non-key attributes depend on all the primary key.

All this stuff sound pretty confusing? Take a look at an example to clarify matters. Consider a table similar to the SALES table back in Figure 5-2. Instead of recording only a single purchase for each customer, however, you add a row every time a customer buys a certain item for the first time. An additional difference is that "charter" customers — those with CUSTOMER_ID values of 1001 to 1009 — get a special discount from the normal price. Figure 5-4 shows some of this table's rows.

SALES_TRACK

Customer_ID	Product	Price
1001	Laundry detergent	11
1007	Toothpaste	2.70
1010	Chlorine bleach	4
1024	Toothpaste	3
1010	Laundry detergent	12
1001	Toothpaste	2.70

Figure 5-4: In the SALES_TRACK table, the CUSTOMER_ID and PRODUCT columns constitute a composite key.

Notice that, in this table, CUSTOMER_ID does not uniquely identify a row. You have two rows in which CUSTOMER_ID is 1001 and two in which CUSTOMER_ID is 1010. The combination of the CUSTOMER_ID column and the PRODUCT column, however, does uniquely identify a row. These two columns taken together constitute a composite key.

If not for the fact that some customers qualify for a discount and others don't, the table wouldn't be in second normal form, because PRICE (a non-key attribute) would depend only on part of the key (PRODUCT). Because some customers do qualify for a discount, however, PRICE depends on both CUSTOMER_ID and PRODUCT, and the table is in second normal form.

Third normal form

Tables in second normal form are still subject to some types of modification anomalies. These anomalies arise because transitive dependencies are possible.

A *transitive dependency* is one in which one attribute depends on a second attribute, which, in turn, depends on a third attribute. Deletions in a table with such a dependency can cause unwanted loss of information. A relation in third normal form is a relation in second normal form with no transitive dependencies.

Look again at the SALES table in Figure 5-2, which you know is in first normal form. As long as you constrain entries to permit only one row for each CUSTOMER_ID, you have a single-attribute primary key, and the table is in second normal form. The table is still, however, subject to anomalies. What if customer 1010 is unhappy with the chlorine bleach, for example, and returns the item for a refund? You want to remove the third row from the table, which records the fact that customer 1010 bought chlorine bleach. You have a problem: If you remove that row, you also lose the fact that chlorine bleach has a price of $4. This situation is an example of a transitive dependency. PRICE depends on PRODUCT, which, in turn, depends on the primary key CUSTOMER_ID.

Breaking the SALES table into two tables solves the transitive dependency problem. The two tables shown in Figure 5-3, CUST_PURCH and PROD_PRICE, comprise a database that's in third normal form.

Domain key normal form

After a database is in third normal form, you've eliminated most, but not all, chances of modification anomalies. Normal forms beyond the third are defined to squash those few remaining bugs. Boyce-Codd normal form (BCNF), fourth normal form (4NF), and fifth normal form (5NF) are examples of such forms. Each of these forms eliminates a possible modification anomaly but doesn't guarantee to prevent all possible modification anomalies. Domain/key normal form (DKNF), however, does provide such a guarantee.

A relation is in *domain/key normal form* if every constraint on the relation is a logical consequence of the definition of keys and domains. A *constraint* in this definition is any rule that's precise enough that you can evaluate whether it's true. A *key* is a unique identifier of a row in a table. A *domain* is the set of permitted values of an attribute.

Look again at the database in Figure 5-2, which is in 1NF, to see what you must do to put that database in DKNF.

Table:	SALES (CUSTOMER_ID, PRODUCT, PRICE)
Key:	CUSTOMER_ID
Constraints:	1. CUSTOMER_ID determines PRODUCT
	2. PRODUCT determines PRICE
	3. CUSTOMER_ID must be an integer > 1000

To enforce constraint 3, that CUSTOMER_ID must be an integer greater than 1,000, you can simply define the domain for CUSTOMER_ID to incorporate this constraint. That makes the constraint a logical consequence of the domain of the CUSTOMER_ID column. Because PRODUCT depends on CUSTOMER_ID and CUSTOMER_ID is a key, you have no problem with constraint 1, which is a logical consequence of the definition of the key. Constraint 2, however, *is* a problem. PRICE depends on (that is, it's a logical consequence of) PRODUCT, and PRODUCT is not a key. The solution is to divide the SALES table into two tables, one of which uses CUSTOMER_ID as a key and the other of which uses PRODUCT as a key. This setup is, in fact, what you have in Figure 5-3. The database in Figure 5-3, besides being in 3NF, is also in DKNF.

Design your databases so that they're in domain/key normal form if at all possible. If you do so, enforcing key and domain restrictions causes all constraints to be met. Modification anomalies aren't possible. If a database's structure is such that you can't put it into domain/key normal form, you must build the constraints into the application program that uses the database, because the database doesn't guarantee that the constraints are going to be met.

Abnormal form

Sometimes, being abnormal pays off. You can sometimes get carried away with normalization and go too far. You can break a database up into so many tables that the entire thing becomes unwieldy and inefficient. Performance can plummet. Often, the optimal structure is somewhat denormalized. In fact, practical databases are almost never normalized all the way to DKNF. You want to normalize the databases you design as much as possible, however, to eliminate the possibility of data corruption that results from modification anomalies.

After you normalize the database as far as you can, make some retrievals. If performance isn't satisfactory, examine your design to see whether selective denormalization would improve performance without sacrificing integrity. You probably find that, by carefully adding redundancy in strategic locations and denormalizing, you can arrive at a database that's both efficient and safe from anomalies.

Part III
Retrieving Data

The 5th Wave   By Rich Tennant

"FOR US, IT WAS TOTAL INTEGRATION OR NOTHING. FOR INSTANCE-
AT THIS TERMINAL ALONE I CAN GET DEPARTMENTAL DATA,
PRINTER AND STORAGE RESOURCES, ESPN, HOME SHOPPING
NETWORK AND THE MOVIE CHANNEL."

In this part . . .

SQL provides a rich set of tools for manipulating data in a relational database. As you may expect, SQL has mechanisms for adding new data, updating existing data, retrieving data, and deleting obsolete data. Nothing's particularly extraordinary about these capabilities. Where SQL shines, however, is in its capability to isolate the exact data you want from all the rest and present that data to you in an understandable form. SQL's comprehensive Data Manipulation Language (DML) provides this critically important capability.

In this part, I delve deep into the riches of the DML. You discover how to use SQL tools to massage raw data into a form suitable for your present purposes and then to retrieve the result as useful information.

Chapter 6
Manipulating Database Data

● ●

In This Chapter

▶ Displaying the contents of a table row

▶ Displaying only selected information from one or more tables

▶ Adding a new row to a table

▶ Changing some or all of the data in a table row

▶ Deleting a table row

● ●

As I explain in Chapters 3 and 4, creating a sound database structure is critical. The stuff that you're really interested in, however, is the data itself, not its structure. You want to do four things with data: add it to tables, retrieve and display it, change it, and delete it from tables.

The SQL Data Manipulation Language (DML)

In principle, database manipulation is quite simple. Understanding how to add data to a table isn't difficult. You can add your data either one row at a time or in a batch. Changing, deleting, or retrieving table rows also is easy in practice. The main challenge lies in selecting the rows that you want to change, delete, or retrieve. Sometimes, retrieving data is like trying to put together a jigsaw puzzle with pieces that are mixed in with pieces from a hundred other puzzles. The data that you want may reside in the same database with a much larger volume of data that you don't want. Happily, if you can specify what you want precisely enough by using an SQL SELECT statement, the computer does all the searching for you.

SQL in proprietary tools

Actually, you may not need to use an SQL SELECT statement. If you're interacting with your database through a DBMS, that system probably already has proprietary tools for manipulating data. You can use these tools (many of which are quite intuitive) to add to, delete from, change, or query your database.

In a client-server system, the relational database on the server generally understands only SQL. If you develop a database application by using a DBMS or RAD tool, you can create data-entry screens that contain fields corresponding to database table fields. You can group the fields logically on-screen and explain the fields by using supplemental text. The user, sitting at a client machine, can easily examine or change the data in these fields.

Say that the user changes the value of some fields. The DBMS "front end" on the client takes the input that the user types into the screen form, translates that text into an SQL UPDATE statement, and then sends the UPDATE statement to the server. The DBMS "back end" on the server executes the statement. People who manipulate data on a relational database, therefore, are using SQL whether they realize it or not. These people may use SQL directly or indirectly through a translation process.

Many DBMS front ends give you the choice of using either their proprietary tools or SQL. In some cases, the proprietary tools can't express everything that you can express by using SQL. If you need to perform an operation that the proprietary tool can't handle, you may need to use SQL. So becoming very familiar with SQL is a pretty good idea, even if you do use a proprietary tool most of the time. To successfully perform an operation that's too complex for your proprietary tool, you need a clear understanding of what SQL can do and how SQL works.

Retrieving Data

The data manipulation task that people perform most frequently is retrieving selected information from a database. You may want to retrieve the contents of one specific row out of thousands in a table. You may want to retrieve all the rows that satisfy a condition or a combination of conditions. You may even want to retrieve all the rows in the table. One SQL statement, the SELECT statement, performs all these tasks for you.

The simplest use of the SELECT statement is to retrieve all the data in all the rows of a specified table. To do so, use the following syntax:

```
SELECT *x FROM CUSTOMER ;
```

The asterisk (*) is a wildcard character that means "everything." In this context, the character is a shorthand substitute for listing all the column names of the CUSTOMER table. As a result of this statement, all the data in all the rows and columns of the CUSTOMER table appear on-screen.

SELECT statements can be much more complicated than this example. In fact, some SELECT statements can be so complicated that they're virtually indecipherable. This potential complexity results from the fact that you can tack multiple modifying clauses onto the basic statement. In Chapter 9, I analyze these modifying clauses in detail. In this chapter, I briefly discuss the WHERE clause, which is the method most commonly used to restrict the rows that a SELECT statement returns.

A SELECT statement with a WHERE clause has the following general form:

```
SELECT column_list FROM table_name
   WHERE condition ;
```

The column list specifies which of the columns in the table you want to display. The statement displays only the columns you list. The FROM clause specifies from which table you want to display columns. The WHERE clause excludes rows that do not satisfy a specified condition. The condition may be simple (for example, WHERE CUSTOMER_STATE = 'NH'), or it may be compound (for example, WHERE CUSTOMER_STATE='NH' AND STATUS='Active').

The following example shows what a compound condition looks like inside a SELECT statement:

```
SELECT CUSTOMER_NAME, CUSTOMER_PHONE FROM CUSTOMER
   WHERE CUSTOMER_STATE = "NH"
   AND STATUS = "Active" ;
```

This statement returns the names and phone numbers of all active customers living in New Hampshire. The AND keyword means that, for a row to qualify for retrieval, that row must meet both conditions, CUSTOMER_STATE = 'NH' and STATUS = 'ACTIVE'.

Creating Views

The structure of a database that's designed according to sound principles maximizes the integrity of the data. This structure, however, is often not the best way to look at the data. Several different applications may all make use of the same data, but each application may have a different emphasis. One of the most powerful features of SQL is its capability to display views of the data that are structured differently from how the database tables actually store the data.

The tables that you use as the sources for the columns and rows in a view are the *base tables*.

I talk about views as part of the data definition language (DDL) in Chapter 3. I take another look at views in this chapter in the context of retrieving and manipulating data.

A SELECT statement always returns a result in the form of a virtual table. A view is a special kind of *virtual table*. You can distinguish a view from other virtual tables because the database's metadata holds the definition of a view. This distinction gives a view a degree of persistence that other virtual tables don't possess. You can manipulate a view just as you can manipulate a real table. The difference is that a view's data doesn't have an independent existence. The view derives its data from the table or tables from which you draw the view's columns. Each application can have its own unique views of the same data.

Consider the VetLab database I describe in Chapter 5. That database contains five tables, CLIENT, TESTS, EMPLOYEE, ORDERS, and RESULTS. The national marketing manager wants to see from which states the company's orders are coming. Part of this information lies in the CLIENT table and part lies in the ORDERS table. The quality-control officer wants to compare the order date of a test to the date on which the final test result came in. This comparison requires some data from the ORDERS table and some from the RESULTS table. To satisfy these needs and others that are sure to arise, you can create views that, in each specific case, give you exactly the data you want.

For the marketing manager, you can create the view shown in Figure 6-1 by using the following statement:

```
CREATE VIEW ORDERS_BY_STATE
    (CLIENT_NAME, STATE, ORDER_NUMBER)
  AS SELECT CLIENT.CLIENT_NAME, STATE, ORDER_NUMBER
  FROM CLIENT, ORDERS
  WHERE CLIENT.CLIENT_NAME = ORDERS.CLIENT_NAME ;
```

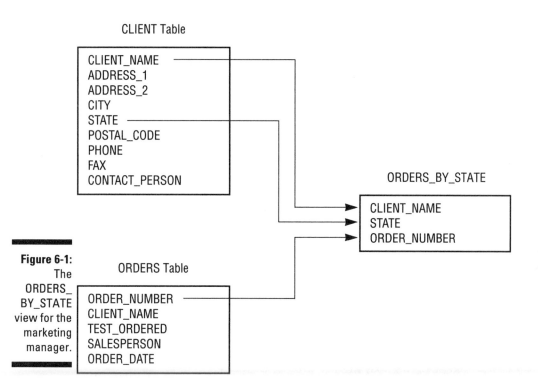

CLIENT Table

CLIENT_NAME
ADDRESS_1
ADDRESS_2
CITY
STATE
POSTAL_CODE
PHONE
FAX
CONTACT_PERSON

ORDERS_BY_STATE

CLIENT_NAME
STATE
ORDER_NUMBER

Figure 6-1:
The
ORDERS_
BY_STATE
view for the
marketing
manager.

ORDERS Table

ORDER_NUMBER
CLIENT_NAME
TEST_ORDERED
SALESPERSON
ORDER_DATE

The new view has three columns, CLIENT_NAME, STATE, and ORDER_NUMBER. CLIENT_NAME appears in both the CLIENT and the ORDERS table and serves as the link between the two tables. The new view draws STATE information from the CLIENT table and takes the ORDER_NUMBER of each order from the ORDERS table. In the preceding example, you explicitly declare the names of the columns in the new view. This declaration is not strictly necessary, however, if the names are the same as the names of the corresponding columns in the source tables. The following example shows a similar CREATE VIEW statement but with the view column names implied rather than explicitly stated.

The quality-control officer requires a different view from the one that the marketing manager uses, as shown by the example in Figure 6-2.

```
CREATE VIEW REPORTING_LAG
    AS SELECT ORDERS.ORDER_NUMBER, ORDER_DATE, DATE_REPORTED
    FROM ORDERS, RESULTS
    WHERE ORDERS.ORDER_NUMBER = RESULTS.ORDER_NUMBER
    AND RESULTS.PRELIM_FINAL = 'F' ;
```

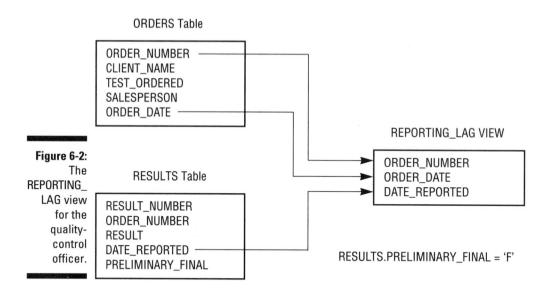

ORDERS Table

Figure 6-2:
The
REPORTING_
LAG view
for the
quality-
control
officer.

RESULTS Table

REPORTING_LAG VIEW

RESULTS.PRELIMINARY_FINAL = 'F'

This view contains order-date information from the ORDERS table and final-report-date information from the RESULTS table. Only rows that have an 'F' in the PRELIM_FINAL column of the RESULTS table appear in the REPORTING_LAG view.

The SELECT clauses in the two previous examples contain only column names. You can, however, include expressions in the SELECT clause as well. Suppose that the owner of VetLab is having a birthday and wants to give all his customers a 10-percent discount to celebrate. He can create a view that he bases on the ORDERS table and the TESTS table. He may construct this table as shown in the following example:

```
CREATE VIEW BIRTHDAY
    (CLIENT_NAME, TEST, ORDER_DATE, BIRTHDAY_CHARGE)
    AS SELECT CLIENT_NAME, TEST_ORDERED, ORDER_DATE,
        STANDARD_CHARGE * .9
    FROM ORDERS, TESTS
    WHERE TEST_ORDERED = TEST_NAME ;
```

Notice that the second column in the BIRTHDAY view, TEST, corresponds to the TEST_ORDERED column in the ORDERS table, which also corresponds to the TEST_NAME column in the TESTS table. Figure 6-3 shows how to create this view.

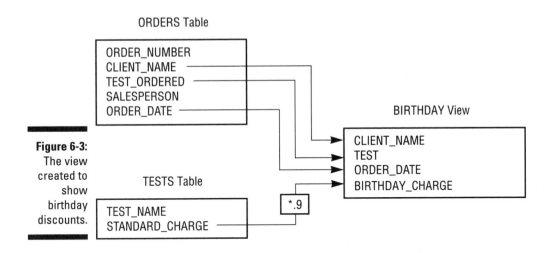

ORDERS Table

BIRTHDAY View

TESTS Table

You can build a view that you base on multiple tables, as shown in the preceding examples, or you can build a view that you base on only one table. If you don't need some of the columns or rows in a table, create a view to remove those elements from sight and then deal with the view rather than the original table. This approach protects the user from confusion or distraction that may result from looking at parts of the table that aren't relevant to the task at hand.

Another reason for creating a view is to provide security for its underlying tables. You may want to make some of the columns in your tables available for inspection while hiding others. You can create a view that includes only the columns that you want to make available and then grant broad access to that view, while restricting access to the tables from which you draw the view. Chapter 12 talks about database security and describes how to grant and revoke data-access privileges.

Updating Views

After you create a table, that table is automatically capable of accommodating insertions, updates, and deletions. Views, on the other hand, don't necessarily exhibit the same capability. If you update a view, you're actually updating its underlying table. Some views, however, may draw components from two or more tables. If you update such a view, which of its underlying tables gets updated? Another problem involves the SELECT list. A view may include an expression for a SELECT list. How do you update an expression? Suppose that you create a view by using the following statement:

```
CREATE VIEW COMP AS SELECT NAME, SALARY+COMM AS PAY
    FROM EMPLOYEE ;
```

Could you then update PAY, by using the following statement?

```
UPDATE COMP SET PAY = PAY + 100 ;
```

No, that approach wouldn't make any sense, because the underlying table has no PAY column. Keep the following rule in mind whenever you consider updating views: You can't update a column of a view unless it corresponds to a column of an underlying base table.

Adding New Data

Every database table starts out empty. After you create a table, either by using SQL's DDL or a RAD tool, that table is nothing but a structured shell, containing no data. To make the table useful, you must put some data into it. You may or may not have that data already stored in digital form.

If your data's not already in digital form, someone will probably have to use a keyboard and monitor to enter the data one record at a time. You can also enter data by using optical scanners and voice recognition systems, but the use of such devices for data entry is still relatively rare. If your data's already in digital form but perhaps not in the format of the database tables you use, you first need to translate the data into the appropriate format and then insert the data into the database. You may also want to transfer data that's already in the correct format to a new database. Depending on the current form of the data, you may be able to transfer it into your database in one operation, or you may need to enter the data one record at a time. Each data record you enter corresponds to a single row in a database table.

Adding data one row at a time

Most DBMSes support form-based data entry. This feature enables you to create a screen form that has a field for every column in a database table. Text on the form enables you to easily determine what data goes into each field. The data-entry operator enters all the data for a single row into the form. After the DBMS accepts the new row, the system clears the form to accept another row. In this way, you can easily add data to a table one row at a time.

Form-based data entry is easy to use and less susceptible to data-entry errors than is a list of comma-delimited values. The main problem with form-based data entry is that it is nonstandard. Each different DBMS has its own method of creating forms. This diversity, however, is no problem for the data-entry operator. You can make the form look much the same from one DBMS to another. The application developer is the one who must return to the bottom of the learning curve every time she changes development tools. Another possible problem with form-based data entry is that some implementations may not permit a full range of validity checks on the data you enter.

The best way to maintain a high level of data integrity in a database is to keep bad data out of the database in the first place. You can prevent the entry of some bad data by applying constraints to the fields on a data-entry form. This approach enables you to make sure that the database accepts only data values of the correct type and that fall within a predefined range. Of course, applying such constraints can't prevent all possible errors, but doing so does at least catch some of them.

If the form-design tool in your DBMS doesn't enable you to apply all the validity checks that you need to ensure data integrity, you may want to build your own screen, accept data entries into variables, and check the entries by using application program code. After you're sure that all the values entered for a table row are valid, you can then set your code to add that row by using the SQL INSERT command.

If you enter the data for a single row into a database table, the INSERT command uses the following syntax:

```
INSERT INTO table_1 [(column_1, column_2, ..., column_n)]
    VALUES (value_1, value_2, ..., value_n) ;
```

As indicated by the square brackets ([ ]), the listing of column names is optional. The default column list order is the order of the columns in the table. If you put the VALUES in the same order as the columns in the table, these elements go into the correct columns, whether you explicitly specify those columns or not. If you want to specify the VALUES in some order other than the order of the columns in the table, you must list the column names, putting the columns in an order that corresponds to the order of the VALUES.

To enter a record into the CUSTOMER table, for example, use the following syntax:

```
INSERT INTO CUSTOMER (CUSTOMER_ID, FIRST_NAME, LAST_NAME,
    STREET, CITY, STATE, ZIPCODE, PHONE)
    VALUES (vcustid, 'David', 'Taylor', '235 Nutley Ave.',
    'Nutley', 'NJ', '07110', '(201) 555-1963') ;
```

The first VALUE, vcustid, is a variable that you increment with your program code after you enter each new row of the table. This approach guarantees that you have no duplication of the CUSTOMER_ID. CUSTOMER_ID is the primary key for this table and, therefore, must remain unique. The rest of the values are data items rather than variables that contain data items. Of course, you could hold the data for these columns in variables, too, if you want. The INSERT statement works equally well either with variables or with an explicit copy of the data itself as arguments of the VALUES keyword.

Adding data only to selected columns

Sometimes you want to note the existence of an object, even though you don't have all the facts on it yet. If you have a database table for such objects, you can insert a row for the new object without filling in the data in all the columns. If you want the table in at least first normal form, you must insert enough data to distinguish the new row from all the other rows in the table. (For a discussion of *first normal form,* see Chapter 5.) Inserting the new row's primary key is sufficient for this purpose. In addition to the primary key, insert any other data about the object that you have. Columns in which you enter no data contain nulls.

The following example shows such a partial row entry:

```
INSERT INTO CUSTOMER (CUSTOMER_ID, FIRST_NAME, LAST_NAME)
    VALUES (vcustid, 'Tyson', 'Taylor') ;
```

You insert only the customer's unique identification number and name into the database table. The other columns in this row contain null values.

Adding a block of rows to a table

Loading a database table one row at a time by using INSERT statements can become awfully tedious, particularly if that's all you do all day. Even entering the data into a carefully human-engineered ergonomic screen form gets tiring after a while. Clearly, if you do have a reliable way to enter the data automatically, you're going to find occasions in which automatic entry is better than having a human sit at a keyboard and type.

Automatic data entry is feasible, for example, if the data already exists in electronic form, because, at some point in the past, somebody somewhere manually entered the data into a computer. If so, you have no compelling reason to repeat history. The transfer of data from one data file to another is a task that a computer can perform with a minimum of human involvement. If you know the characteristics of the source data and the desired form of the destination table, a computer can (in principle) perform the data transfer automatically.

Copying from a foreign data file

Suppose that you're building a database for a new application. Some of the data you need already exists in a computer file. The file may be a flat file or a table in a database that operates in a DBMS different from the one you use. The data may be in ASCII or EBCDIC code or in some arcane proprietary format. What should you do?

The first thing you do is hope and pray that the data you want is in a format that has seen widespread use. If the data's in a popular format, you have a good chance of finding a format conversion utility that can translate the data into one or more other popular formats. Your development environment can probably import at least one of these formats. If you're really lucky, your development environment can handle the data's current format directly. On personal computers, the dBASE and Paradox formats are probably the most widely used. If the data you want is in one of those formats, conversion should prove easy. If the format of the data is something less common, you may need to go through a two-step conversion.

As a last resort, you can always turn to one of the professional data-translation services. These businesses specialize in translating computer data from one format to another. They have the capability of dealing with hundreds of different formats, most of which nobody's ever heard of. Give one of these services a tape or disk containing the data in its original format and you get back the same data translated into whatever format you specify.

Transferring rows from one table to another

A much less severe problem than dealing with foreign data is taking data that already exists in one table in your database and combining that data with the data in another table. This process works great if the structure of the second table is identical to the structure of the first table — that is, every column in the first table has a corresponding column in the second table, and the data types of the corresponding columns match. If so, you can combine the contents of the two tables by using the UNION relational operator. The result is a virtual table containing data from both source tables. I discuss the relational operators, including UNION, in Chapter 10.

Transferring only selected columns and rows from one table to another

More often than not, however, the data in the source table doesn't exactly match the structure of the table into which you want to insert the data. Perhaps only some of the columns match — and these are the columns you want to transfer. By combining SELECT statements with a UNION, you can specify which columns from the source tables to include in the virtual result table. By including WHERE clauses in the SELECT statements, you can restrict the rows that you place into the result table to those that satisfy specific conditions. I cover WHERE clauses extensively in Chapter 9.

Suppose that you have two tables, PROSPECT and CUSTOMER, and you want to list everyone living in the state of Maine who appears in either table. You can create a virtual result table with the desired information by using the following command:

```
SELECT FIRST_NAME, LAST_NAME
    FROM PROSPECT
      WHERE STATE = 'ME'
UNION
SELECT FIRST_NAME, LAST_NAME
    FROM CUSTOMER
      WHERE STATE = 'ME' ;
```

The SELECT statements specify that the columns included in the result table are FIRST_NAME and LAST_NAME. The WHERE clauses restrict the rows included to those with the value 'ME' in the STATE column. The STATE column isn't included in the result table but is present in both the PROSPECT and CUSTOMER tables. The UNION operator combines the results from the SELECT on PROSPECT with the results of the SELECT on CUSTOMER, deletes any duplicate rows, and then displays the result.

Another way to copy data from one table in a database to another is to nest a SELECT statement within an INSERT statement. This method (a subselect) doesn't create a virtual table but instead actually duplicates the selected data. You can take all the rows from the CUSTOMER table, for example, and insert those row into the PROSPECT table. If you later want to isolate those customers who live in Maine, a simple SELECT with one condition in the WHERE clause does the trick, as shown in the following example.

```
INSERT INTO PROSPECT
    SELECT * FROM CUSTOMER
      WHERE STATE = 'ME' ;
```

Even though this operation creates redundant data (you're now storing customer data in both the PROSPECT table and the CUSTOMER table), you may want to do it anyway to improve the performance of retrievals. Be aware of the redundancy, however, and, to maintain data consistency, make sure that you don't insert, update, or delete rows in one table without inserting, updating, or deleting the corresponding rows in the other table.

Updating Existing Data

In this world, the one thing you can count on is change. If you don't like the current state of affairs, just wait a while. Before long, things are different. Because the world is constantly changing, the databases used to model aspects of that world need to change, too. A customer may change his address. The quantity of a product in stock may change (because, you hope, someone buys one now and then). A basketball player's season performance statistics change each time he plays in another game. These are the kinds of typical events that require you to update a database.

SQL provides the UPDATE statement for changing data in a table. By using a single UPDATE, you can change one, some, or all the rows in a table. The UPDATE statement uses the following syntax:

```
UPDATE table_name
    SET column_1 = expression_1, column_2 = expression_2,
    ..., column_n = expression_n
    [WHERE predicates] ;
```

The WHERE clause is optional. This clause specifies the rows that you're updating. If you don't use a WHERE clause, all the rows in the table are updated. The SET clause specifies the new values for the columns that you're changing.

Consider the CUSTOMER table shown in Table 6-1.

Table 6-1		CUSTOMER **Table**	
Name	**City**	**Area-Code**	**Telephone**
Abe Abelson	Springfield	(714)	555-1111
Bill Bailey	Decatur	(714)	555-2222
Chuck Wood	Philo	(714)	555-3333
Don Stetson	Philo	(714)	555-4444
Dolph Stetson	Philo	(714)	555-5555

Customer lists change occasionally, as people move, change their phone number, and so on. Suppose that Abe Abelson moves from Springfield to Kankakee. You can update his record in the table by using the following UPDATE statement:

```
UPDATE CUSTOMER
    SET CITY = 'Kankakee', TELEPHONE = '666-6666'
    WHERE NAME = 'Abe Abelson' ;
```

This statement causes the changes shown in Table 6-2.

Table 6-2	CUSTOMER **Table after** UPDATE **to One Row**		
Name	*City*	*Area-Code*	*Telephone*
Abe Abelson	Kankakee	(714)	666-6666
Bill Bailey	Decatur	(714)	555-2222
Chuck Wood	Philo	(714)	555-3333
Don Stetson	Philo	(714)	555-4444
Dolph Stetson	Philo	(714)	555-5555

You can use a similar statement to update multiple rows. Assume that Philo is experiencing explosive population growth and now requires its own area code. You can change all rows for customers who live in Philo by using a single UPDATE statement, as follows:

```
UPDATE CUSTOMER
   SET AREA_CODE = '(619)'
   WHERE CITY = 'Philo' ;
```

The table now looks like the one shown in Table 6-3.

Table 6-3	CUSTOMER **Table after** UPDATE **to Several Rows**		
Name	*City*	*Area-Code*	*Telephone*
Abe Abelson	Kankakee	(714)	666-6666
Bill Bailey	Decatur	(714)	555-2222
Chuck Wood	Philo	(619)	555-3333
Don Stetson	Philo	(619)	555-4444
Dolph Stetson	Philo	(619)	555-5555

Updating all the rows of a table is even easier than updating only some of the rows. You don't need to use a WHERE clause. Imagine that the city of Rantoul has acquired major political clout and has now annexed not only Kankakee, Decatur, and Philo, but also all the cities and towns in the database. You can update all the rows by using a single statement, as follows:

```
UPDATE CUSTOMER
   SET CITY = 'Rantoul' ;
```

Table 6-4 shows the result.

Table 6-4	CUSTOMER **Table after** UPDATE **to All Rows**		
Name	*City*	*Area-Code*	*Telephone*
Abe Abelson	Rantoul	(714)	666-6666
Bill Bailey	Rantoul	(714)	555-2222
Chuck Wood	Rantoul	(619)	555-3333
Don Stetson	Rantoul	(619)	555-4444
Dolph Stetson	Rantoul	(619)	555-5555

The WHERE clause you use to restrict the rows to which an UPDATE statement applies can contain a subselect. Such a subset enables you to update rows in one table based on the contents of another table.

For an example of a subselect within an UPDATE, say you're a wholesaler and your database includes a VENDOR table containing the names of all the manufacturers from whom you buy products. You also have a PRODUCT table containing the names of all the products you sell and the prices you charge for them. The VENDOR table has columns VENDOR_ID, VENDOR_NAME, STREET, CITY, STATE, and ZIP. The PRODUCT table has PRODUCT_ID, PRODUCT_NAME, VENDOR_ID, and SALE_PRICE.

Your vendor, Cumulonimbus Corporation, decides to raise the prices of all its products by 10 percent. To maintain your own profit margin, you must raise your prices on products you obtain from Cumulonimbus by 10 percent. You can do so by using the following UPDATE statement:

```
UPDATE PRODUCT
   SET SALE_PRICE = (SALE_PRICE * 1.1)
   WHERE VENDOR_ID IN
      (SELECT VENDOR_ID FROM VENDOR
       WHERE VENDOR_NAME = 'Cumulonimbus Corporation') ;
```

The subselect finds the VENDOR_ID that corresponds to Cumulonimbus. You can then use the VENDOR_ID field in the PRODUCT table to find the rows that you need to update. The prices on all Cumulonimbus products increase by 10 percent, while the prices on all other products stay the same. I discuss subselects more extensively in Chapter 11.

Deleting Obsolete Data

As time passes, some data gets old and loses its usefulness. You may want to remove this outdated data from its table. Unneeded data in a table slows performance, consumes memory, and can confuse users. You may want to transfer older data to an archive table and then take the archive offline. That way, in the unlikely event that you ever need to look at that data again, you can recover it. In the meantime, it doesn't slow down your everyday processing. Whether you decide that obsolete data is worth archiving or not, you eventually come to the point where you want to delete that data. SQL provides for the removal of rows from database tables by use of the DELETE statement.

You can delete all the rows in a table by using a single DELETE statement, or you can restrict the deletion to only selected rows by adding a WHERE clause. The syntax is similar to the syntax of a SELECT statement, except that you use no specification of columns. If you delete a table row, you remove all the data in all that row's columns.

As an example, say that your customer David Taylor just moved to Tahiti and isn't going to buy anything from you any more. You can remove him from your CUSTOMER table by using the following statement:

```
DELETE FROM CUSTOMER
    WHERE FIRST_NAME = 'David' AND LAST_NAME = 'Taylor' ;
```

Assuming that you have only one customer named David Taylor, this statement makes the intended deletion. If any chance exists that two of your customers may share the name David Taylor, you can add more conditions to the WHERE clause (such as STREET or PHONE or CUSTOMER_ID) to make sure that you delete only the one you want to remove.

Chapter 7

Specifying Values

● ●

In This Chapter

▶ Using variables to eliminate redundant coding

▶ Maintaining a system activity log

▶ Retrieving information on multiple table rows with a single command

▶ Extracting frequently required information from a database table field

▶ Combining simple values into complex expressions

● ●

*I*n the preceding chapters, I emphasize the importance of database structure for maintaining database integrity. Database structure is very important and often isn't given its due. You must never forget, however, that the most important thing is the data itself. After all, the values held in the fields that form the intersections of the rows and columns of a database table are the raw materials from which you can derive meaningful relationships and trends.

You can represent values in several ways. You can represent them directly, or you can derive them. This chapter describes the various kinds of values, as well as functions and expressions.

Functions look at data and calculate a value based on the data. *Expressions* are combinations of data items that SQL can evaluate to produce a single value.

Values

SQL recognizes several different kinds of values: *row values, literal values, variables, special variables,* and *column references.*

Atoms aren't indivisible either

In the 19th century, scientists believed that an atom was the irreducible smallest possible piece of matter. That is why they named it *atom*, which comes from the Greek word *atomos*, which means indivisible. Now scientists know that atoms aren't indivisible; they're made up of protons, neutrons, and electrons. Protons and neutrons, in turn, are made up of quarks, gluons, and virtual quarks. Even these things may not be indivisible. Who knows?

The value of a field in a database table is called *atomic*, even though many fields aren't indivisible either. A DATE value has components of month, year, and day. A TIMESTAMP value has components of hour, minute, seconds, and so on. A REAL or FLOAT value has components of exponent and mantissa. A CHAR value has components that you can access by using SUBSTRING. So calling database field values *atomic* is true to the analogy of atoms of matter. Neither modern application of the term *atomic*, however, is true to the word's original meaning.

Row values

The most visible values in a database are the *table row values*. These are the values that each row of a database table contains. A row value is typically made up of multiple components, because each column in a row contains a value. A *field* is the intersection of a single column with a single row. A field contains a *scalar,* or *atomic,* value. A value that's scalar or atomic has only a single component.

Literal values

In SQL either a variable or a constant may represent a *value*. Sensibly enough, the value of a *variable* may change from time to time. The value of a *constant* never changes, which is why it's called a constant. An important kind of constant is the *literal value*. You may consider a *literal* to be a *WYSIWYG* value, because *What You See Is What You Get*. The representation is itself the value.

Just as SQL has many different data types, it also has many different types of literals. Table 7-1 shows some examples of literals of the various data types.

Table 7-1	Example Literals of Various Data Types
Data Type	**Example Literal**
INTEGER	186282
SMALLINT	186
NUMERIC	186282.42
DECIMAL	186282.42
REAL	6.02257E-23
DOUBLE PRECISION	3.1415926535897E00
FLOAT	6.02257E-23
CHARACTER(15)	'GREECE '
Note: Fifteen total characters and spaces are between the quote marks above.	
VARCHAR (CHARACTER VARYING)	'lepton'
NATIONAL CHARACTER(15)	'ΕΛΛΑΣ '[1]
Note: Fifteen total characters and spaces are between the quote marks above.	
NATIONAL CHARACTER VARYING	'λεπτον'[2]
BIT(12)	B'100111001110'[3]
BIT(12)	X'9CE'[4]
BIT VARYING(16)	B'1001111000111'
BIT VARYING(16)	X'F7'
DATE	DATE '07-20-1969'
TIME(2)	TIME '13:41:32.50'
TIMESTAMP(0)	TIMESTAMP '04-17-1995 14:18:00'
TIME WITH TIMEZONE(4)	TIME '13:41:32.5000-08:00'
TIMESTAMP WITH TIMEZONE(0)	TIMESTAMP '04-17-1995 14:18:00+02:00'
INTERVAL DAY	INTERVAL '7' DAY

[1]This term is the word Greeks use to name their own country in their own language. (The English equivalent is 'Hellas.')

[2]This term is the word 'lepton' in Greek national characters.

[3]BIT and BIT VARYING values that start with a 'B' are interpreted as binary numbers.

[4]BIT and BIT VARYING values that start with an 'X' are interpreted as hexadecimal numbers.

Notice that single quotes enclose the literals of the nonnumeric types. These marks help to prevent confusion; they can, however, also cause problems.

What if a literal is a character string that itself contains a single quote? In that case, you must type two single quotes to show that one of the quote marks you're typing is a part of the character string and not an indicator of the end of the string. You'd type `'Earth''s atmosphere'`, for example, to represent the character literal `'Earth's atmosphere'`.

Variables

Having the capability to manipulate literals and other kinds of constants while dealing with a database is great. In many cases, you'd need to do a lot more work if you didn't have variables. A *variable,* by the way, is a quantity that has a value that can change. Look at the following example to see why variables are valuable.

Say that you're a retailer who has several classes of customers. You give your high-volume customers the best price, your medium-volume customers the next best price, and your low-volume customers the highest price. You want to index all prices to your cost of goods. For your F-117A product, you decide to charge your best customers (Class C) 1.4 times your cost of goods. You charge your next-best customers (Class B) 1.5 times your cost of goods, and you charge your worst (Class A) customers 1.6 times your cost.

You store your cost of goods and the prices you charge in a table you name PRICING. To implement your new pricing structure, you issue the following SQL commands:

```
UPDATE PRICING
    SET PRICE = COST * 1.4
    WHERE PRODUCT = 'F-117A'
        AND CLASS = 'C' ;
UPDATE PRICING
    SET PRICE = COST * 1.5
    WHERE PRODUCT = 'F-117A'
        AND CLASS = 'B' ;
UPDATE PRICING
    SET PRICE = COST * 1.6
    WHERE PRODUCT = 'F-117A'
        AND CLASS = 'A' ;
```

This code is fine and does what you want it to do for now. But what if aggressive competition begins to eat into your market share? You may need to reduce your margins to remain competitive. You need to enter something along the lines of the following commands:

```
UPDATE PRICING
    SET PRICE = COST * 1.25
    WHERE PRODUCT = 'F-117A'
        AND CLASS = 'C' ;
UPDATE PRICING
    SET PRICE = COST * 1.35
    WHERE PRODUCT = 'F-117A'
        AND CLASS = 'B' ;
UPDATE PRICING
    SET PRICE = COST * 1.45
    WHERE PRODUCT = 'F-117A'
        AND CLASS = 'A' ;
```

If you're in a volatile market, you may need to rewrite your SQL code repeatedly. This task can become very tedious, particularly if prices appear in multiple places in your code. You can minimize this problem if you replace literals (such as 1.45) with variables (such as :multiplierA). Then you can perform your updates as follows:

```
UPDATE PRICING
    SET PRICE = COST * :multiplierC
    WHERE PRODUCT = 'F-117A'
        AND CLASS = 'C' ;
UPDATE PRICING
    SET PRICE = COST * :multiplierB
    WHERE PRODUCT = 'F-117A'
        AND CLASS = 'B' ;
UPDATE PRICING
    SET PRICE = COST * :multiplierA
    WHERE PRODUCT = 'F-117A'
        AND CLASS = 'A'
```

Now whenever market conditions cause you to change your pricing, you need only change the values of the variables :multiplierC, :multiplierB, and :multiplierA. These variables are parameters that pass to the SQL code, which uses the variables to compute new prices.

Sometimes you see variables that you use in this way called *parameters* and, at other times, *host variables*. These variables are called parameters if they're within applications written in SQL module language and host variables if they are used in embedded SQL.

Embedded SQL means that SQL statements are embedded into the code of an application written in a host language. Alternatively, you can use SQL module language to create an entire module of SQL code. The host language application then calls the module. Either method could give you the capabilities you want. The approach you use depends on your particular implementation of SQL.

Special variables

If a user on a client machine connects to a database on a server, this connection establishes a session. If the user connects to several databases, the session associated with the most recent connection is considered the current session; previous sessions are considered dormant. SQL-92 defines several special variables that are valuable on multiuser systems. These variables keep track of the different users. The special variable SESSION_USER, for example, holds a value that's equal to the user authorization identifier of the current SQL session. If you write a program that performs a monitoring function, you can interrogate SESSION_USER to find out who's executing SQL statements.

An SQL module may have a user-specified authorization identifier associated with it. The CURRENT_USER variable stores this value. If a module has no such identifier, CURRENT_USER has the same value as SESSION_USER.

The SYSTEM_USER variable contains the operating system's identifier of a user. This identifier may differ from that user's identifier in an SQL module. A user may log onto the system as LARRY, for example, but identify himself to a module as PLANT_MGR. The value in SESSION_USER is PLANT_MGR. If he makes no explicit specification of the module identifier, CURRENT_USER also contains PLANT_MGR. SYSTEM_USER holds the value LARRY.

One use of the SYSTEM_USER, SESSION_USER, and CURRENT_USER special variables is to track who's using the system. You can maintain a log table and periodically insert into that table the values that SYSTEM_USER, SESSION_USER, and CURRENT_USER contain. The following example shows how:

```
INSERT INTO USAGELOG (SNAPSHOT)
    VALUES ('User ' || SYSTEM_USER ||
        ' with ID ' || SESSION_USER ||
        ' active at ' || CURRENT_TIMESTAMP) ;
```

This statement produces log entries similar to the following example:

```
User LARRY with ID PLANT_MGR active at 04-17-199514:18:00
```

Column references

Columns contain values, one in each row of a table. SQL statements often refer to such values. A fully qualified column reference consists of the table name, a period, and then the column name (for example, PRICING.PRODUCT). Consider the following statement:

```
SELECT PRICING.COST
    FROM PRICING
    WHERE PRICING.PRODUCT = 'F-117A' ;
```

PRICING.PRODUCT is a column reference. This reference contains the value 'F-117A'. PRICING.COST is also a column reference, but you don't know its value until after the preceding SELECT statement executes.

Because it only makes sense to reference columns in the current table, you don't generally need to use fully qualified column references. The following statement, for example, is completely equivalent to the previous one:

```
SELECT COST
    FROM PRICING
    WHERE PRODUCT = 'F-117A' ;
```

At times, however, you may be dealing with more than one table. Two tables in a database may well contain one or more columns with the same name. If so, you must fully qualify column references for those columns to guarantee that the column you get is indeed the one you want.

Say, for example, that your company maintains facilities at Hollis and at Jefferson, and you maintain separate employee records for each site. You name the employee table at Hollis EMP_HOLLIS, and you name the Jefferson employee table EMP_JEFFERSON. You want a list of all employees who work at both sites, so you need to find all employees whose names appear in both tables. The following SELECT gives you what you want:

```
SELECT EMP_HOLLIS.F_NAME, EMP_HOLLIS.L_NAME
    FROM EMP_HOLLIS, EMP_JEFFERSON
    WHERE EMP_HOLLIS.EMP_ID = EMP_JEFFERSON.EMP_ID ;
```

Because the employee's ID number is unique and is the same regardless of work site, you can use this ID as a link between the two tables. This retrieval returns only the names of employees who appear in both tables.

Functions

A *function* is a simple-to-moderately complex operation that the usual SQL commands don't perform but that comes up fairly often in practice. The functions that SQL provides perform tasks that the application code in the host language (within which you embed your SQL statements) would otherwise need to perform. SQL has two main categories of functions: *set* (or *aggregate*) *functions*, and *value functions*.

Summarizing by using set functions

The set functions apply to *sets* of rows in a table rather than to a single row. These functions summarize some characteristic of the current set of rows. The set may include all the rows in the table or a subset of rows that a WHERE clause specifies. (I discuss WHERE clauses extensively in Chapter 9.) Programmers sometimes call set functions aggregate functions, because these functions take information from multiple rows, process that information in some way, and deliver a single-row answer. That answer is an *aggregation* of the information in the rows making up the set.

To illustrate the use of the set functions, consider Table 7-2, a list of nutrition facts for 100 grams of certain selected foods.

Table 7-2	Nutrition Facts for 100 Grams of Selected Foods			
Food	**Calories**	**Protein (grams)**	**Fat (grams)**	**Carbohydrate (grams)**
Almonds, roasted	627	18.6	57.7	19.6
Asparagus	20	2.2	0.2	3.6
Bananas, raw	85	1.1	0.2	22.2
Beef, lean hamburger	219	27.4	11.3	
Chicken, light meat	166	31.6	3.4	
Opossum, roasted	221	30.2	10.2	
Pork, ham	394	21.9	33.3	

Food	Calories	Protein (grams)	Fat (grams)	Carbohydrate (grams)
Beans, lima	111	7.6	0.5	19.8
Cola	39			10.0
Bread, white	269	8.7	3.2	50.4
Bread, whole wheat	243	10.5	3.0	47.7
Broccoli	26	3.1	0.3	4.5
Butter	716	0.6	81.0	0.4
Jelly beans	367		0.5	93.1
Peanut brittle	421	5.7	10.4	81.0

A database table named FOODS stores the information in Table 7-2. Blank fields contain the value NULL. The set functions COUNT, AVG, MAX, MIN, and SUM can tell us important facts about the data in this table.

COUNT

The COUNT function tells us how many rows are in the table or how many rows in the table meet certain conditions. The simplest usage of this function is as follows:

```
SELECT COUNT (*)
   FROM FOODS ;
```

This function yields a result of 15, because it counts all rows in the FOODS table. The following statement produces the same result:

```
SELECT COUNT (CALORIES)
   FROM FOODS ;
```

Because the CALORIES column in every row of the table has an entry, the count is the same. If a column contains nulls, however, the function doesn't count the rows corresponding to those nulls.

The following statement returns a value of 11, because four of the 15 rows in the table contain nulls in the CARBOHYDRATE column.

```
SELECT COUNT (CARBOHYDRATE)
   FROM FOODS ;
```

A field in a database table may contain a null value for a variety of reasons. One common reason is that the actual value is not known or not yet known. Or the value may be known but not yet entered. Sometimes, if a value is known to be zero, the data entry operator doesn't bother entering anything in a field, leaving that field a null. This is not a good practice. Zero is a definite value, and you can include it in computations. Null is *not* a definite value, and SQL does not include null values in computations.

You can also use the COUNT function, in combination with DISTINCT, to determine how many distinct values exist in a column. Consider the following statement:

```
SELECT COUNT (DISTINCT FAT)
   FROM FOODS ;
```

The answer that returns is 13. You can see that 100 grams of asparagus has exactly the same fat content as 100 grams of bananas (0.2 grams) and that 100 grams of lima beans has exactly the same fat content as 100 grams of jelly beans (0.5 grams). Thus the table has a total of only 13 distinct fat values.

AVG

The AVG function calculates and returns the average of the values in the specified column. Of course, you can use the AVG function only on columns that contain numeric data, as in the following example:

```
SELECT AVG (FAT)
   FROM FOODS ;
```

The result is 14.3. This number is so high primarily because of the presence of butter in the database. You may wonder what the average fat content may be if you didn't include butter. To find out, you can add a WHERE clause to your statement, as follows:

```
SELECT AVG (FAT)
   FROM FOODS
   WHERE FOOD <> 'Butter' ;
```

The average fat value drops all the way down to 9.6 grams per 100 grams of food.

MAX

The MAX function returns the maximum value found in the specified column. The following statement returns a value of 81 (the fat content in 100 grams of butter):

```
SELECT MAX (FAT)
   FROM FOODS ;
```

MIN

The MIN function returns the minimum value found in the specified column. The following statement returns a value of 0.4, because the function doesn't treat the nulls as zeros:

```
SELECT MIN (CARBOHYDRATE)
   FROM FOODS ;
```

SUM

The SUM function returns the sum of all the values found in the specified column. The following statement returns 3,924, which is the total calorie content of all 15 foods:

```
SELECT SUM (CALORIES)
   FROM FOODS ;
```

Value functions

A number of operations apply in a wide variety of contexts. Because you need to use these operations so often, incorporating them into SQL as value functions makes a lot of sense. SQL offers relatively few value functions compared to PC database management systems such as Paradox or dBASE, but the few that SQL does have are probably the ones that you want to use most often. SQL uses the following three different types of value functions:

- ✔ String value functions
- ✔ Numeric value functions
- ✔ Datetime value functions

String value functions

String value functions take one character string (or bit string) as an input and produce another character string (or bit string) as an output. SQL has six such functions:

- ✔ SUBSTRING
- ✔ UPPER
- ✔ LOWER

  ✔ TRIM

  ✔ TRANSLATE

  ✔ CONVERT

SUBSTRING

Use the SUBSTRING function to extract a substring from a source string. The source string may be either a character string or a bit string. The extracted substring is of the same type as the source string. If the source string is a character string, for example, the substring is also a character string. Following is the syntax of the SUBSTRING function:

```
SUBSTRING (string_value FROM start [FOR length])
```

The clause in square brackets ([ ]) is optional. The substring extracted from string_value begins with the character (or bit) that start represents and continues for length characters (or bits). If the FOR clause is absent, the substring extracted extends from the start character to the end of the string. Consider the following example:

```
SUBSTRING ('Bread, whole wheat' FROM 8 FOR 7)
```

The substring extracted is 'whole w'. This substring starts with the eighth character of the source string and has a length of seven characters. On the surface, SUBSTRING doesn't seem like a very valuable function. If I have a literal such as 'Bread, whole wheat' I don't need a function to figure out what the 8th through the 14th characters are. SUBSTRING really is a valuable function, however, because the string value doesn't need to be a literal. The value can be any expression that evaluates to a character string. Thus, I could have a variable named fooditem that takes on different values at different times. The following expression would extract the desired substring regardless of what character string the fooditem variable currently represents:

```
SUBSTRING (fooditem FROM 8 FOR 7)
```

All the value functions are similar in that these functions can operate on expressions that evaluate to values as well as on the literal values themselves.

You do need to watch out for a couple of things if you use the SUBSTRING function. Make sure that the substring you specify actually falls within the source string. If you ask for a substring starting at character eight but the source string is only four characters long, you get a null result. You must, therefore, have some idea of the form of your data before you specify a substring function. You also don't want to specify a negative substring length, because the end of a string cannot precede the beginning.

If a column is of the VARCHAR type, you may not know how far the field extends for a particular row. This lack of knowledge, however, doesn't present a problem for the SUBSTRING function. If the length you specify goes beyond the right edge of the field, SUBSTRING returns whatever it finds. It doesn't return an error.

Say that you have the following statement:

```
SELECT * FROM FOODS
   WHERE SUBSTRING (FOOD FROM 8 FOR 7) = 'white' ;
```

This statement returns the row for white bread from the FOODS table, even though the value in the FOOD column ('Bread, white') is less than 14 characters long.

If any operand in the substring function has a null value, SUBSTRING returns a null result.

To extract a substring from a bit string, incorporate a 'B' in the string value argument, such as in the following example:

```
SUBSTRING (B'0111000110101' FROM 4 FOR 6)
```

This example returns a value of B'100011'. The substring starts with the fourth bit of the source string and proceeds for six bits.

UPPER

The UPPER value function converts a character string to all uppercase characters, as in the example shown in the following table.

This statement	Returns
UPPER ('e. e. cummings')	'E. E. CUMMINGS'
UPPER ('Isaac Newton, PhD')	'ISAAC NEWTON, PHD'

The UPPER function doesn't affect a string that's already in all uppercase characters.

LOWER

The LOWER value function converts a character string to all lowercase characters, as in the examples in the following table.

This statement	Returns
LOWER ('TAXES')	'taxes'
LOWER ('E. E. Cummings')	'e. e. cummings'

The LOWER function doesn't affect a string that's already in all lowercase characters.

TRIM

Use the TRIM function to trim off leading or trailing blanks (or other characters for that matter) from a character string. The following examples show how to use TRIM:

This statement	*Returns*
TRIM (LEADING ' ' FROM ' treat ')	'treat '
TRIM (TRAILING ' ' FROM ' treat ')	' treat'
TRIM (BOTH ' ' FROM ' treat ')	'treat'
TRIM (BOTH 't' from 'treat')	'rea'

The default trim character is the blank, so the following syntax also is legal:

```
TRIM (BOTH FROM ' treat ')
```

This syntax gives you the same result as the third example in the table — 'treat'.

TRANSLATE and CONVERT

The TRANSLATE and CONVERT functions take a source string in one character set and transform the original string into a string in another character set. Examples may be English to Kanji or Hebrew to French. The conversion functions that specify these transformations are implementation specific. Consult the documentation of your implementation for details.

If translating from one language to another were as easy as invoking an SQL TRANSLATE function, that would be great. Unfortunately the task is not that easy. All TRANSLATE does is translate a character in the first character set to the corresponding character in the second character set. The function could, for example, translate ''Ελλασ' to 'Ellas'. TRANSLATE can't, however, translate 'Ελλασ' to 'Greece'.

Numeric value functions

Numeric value functions may take data of a variety of types as input, but the output is always a numeric value. SQL has five numeric value functions:

- ✔ POSITION
- ✔ CHARACTER_LENGTH
- ✔ OCTET_LENGTH

✔ BIT_LENGTH

✔ EXTRACT

POSITION

POSITION searches for a specified target string within a specified source string and returns the character position where the target string begins. The syntax is as follows:

```
POSITION (target IN source)
```

The following table shows a few examples.

This statement	Returns
POSITION ('B' IN 'Bread, whole wheat')	1
POSITION ('Bre' IN 'Bread, whole wheat')	1
POSITION ('wh' IN 'Bread, whole wheat')	7
POSITION ('whi' IN 'Bread, whole wheat')	0
POSITION ('' IN 'Bread, whole wheat')	1

If the function doesn't find the target string, the POSITION function returns a zero value. If the target string has zero length (as in the last example), the POSITION function always returns a value of one. If any operand in the function has a null value, the result is a null value.

CHARACTER_LENGTH

The CHARACTER_LENGTH function returns the number of characters in a character string. The following statement, for example, returns 16:

```
CHARACTER_LENGTH ('Opossum, roasted')
```

As I note in regard to the SUBSTRING function (in its section earlier in the chapter), this function is not particularly useful if its argument is a literal such as 'Opossum, roasted'. I can just as easily write 16 as I can CHARACTER_LENGTH ('Opossum, roasted'). In fact, writing 16 is easier. This function becomes more useful if its argument is an expression rather than a literal value.

OCTET_LENGTH

In music, a vocal ensemble made up of eight singers is called an *octet*. Typically, the parts that the ensemble represents are first and second soprano, first and second alto, first and second tenor, and first and second bass. In computer terminology, an ensemble of eight data bits is called a *byte*. The word *byte* is clever in that the term clearly relates to *bit* but implies something larger than a bit. A nice word play — but, unfortunately, nothing in the word *byte* conveys the concept of "eightness." By borrowing the musical term, a more apt description of a collection of eight bits becomes possible.

In practically all modern computers, you use eight bits to represent a single alphanumeric character. More complex character sets (such as Chinese) require 16 bits to represent a single character. The OCTET_LENGTH function counts and returns the number of octets (bytes) in a string. If the string is a bit string, OCTET_LENGTH returns the number of octets you need to hold that number of bits. If the string is an English-language character string (with one octet per character) the function returns the number of characters in the string. If the string is a Chinese-character string, the number the function returns is twice the number of Chinese characters. The following strings offer some examples:

```
OCTET_LENGTH ('Beans, lima') returns 11
OCTET_LENGTH (B'10111010011')   returns 2
```

The second string is 11 bits long, so you'd need two octets to hold the entire string.

Some character sets use a variable number of octets for different characters. In particular, some character sets that support mixtures of Kanji and Latin characters use "escape" characters to switch between the two character sets. A string that contains both Latin and Kanji may have, for example, 30 characters and require 30 octets if all the characters are Latin; 62 characters if all the characters are Kanji (60 characters plus a leading and trailing shift character); and 150 characters if the characters alternate between Latin and Kanji (because each Kanji character needs two octets for the character and one octet each for the leading and trailing shift characters). The OCTET_LENGTH function returns the number of octets you need for the current value of the string.

BIT_LENGTH

If you understand CHARACTER_LENGTH and OCTET_LENGTH, the BIT_LENGTH function ought to be easy for you. BIT_LENGTH returns the length of a bit string. If the string is six bits long, the function returns a 6. If the string is 15 bits long, the function returns a 15. The following statement, for example, returns 8:

```
BIT_LENGTH (B'01100111')
```

EXTRACT

The EXTRACT function extracts a single field from a datetime or an interval. The following statement, for example, returns 4:

```
EXTRACT (MONTH FROM DATE '1995-04-22')
```

Datetime value functions

SQL includes three functions that return information about the current date, current time, or both. CURRENT_DATE returns the current date; CURRENT_TIME returns the current time; and CURRENT_TIMESTAMP returns (surprise!) both the current date and the current time. CURRENT_DATE doesn't take an argument, but CURRENT_TIME and CURRENT_TIMESTAMP both take a single argument. The argument specifies the precision for the seconds part of the time value that the function returns. I describe the *datetime* data types in Chapter 2 and explain the concept of precision there as well.

The following table offers some examples of these datetime value functions.

This statement	Returns
CURRENT_DATE	1997-07-22
CURRENT_TIME (1)	08:36:57.3
CURRENT_TIMESTAMP (2)	1997-07-22 08:36:57.38

The date that CURRENT_DATE returns is DATE type data, not CHARACTER. The time that CURRENT_TIME (p) returns is TIME type data, and the timestamp that CURRENT_TIMESTAMP(p) returns is TIMESTAMP type data. Because SQL retrieves date and time information from your computer's system clock, the information is correct for the time zone in which the computer resides.

In some applications, you may want to deal with dates, times, or timestamps as character strings to take advantage of the functions that operate on character data. You can perform a type conversion by using the CAST expression, which I describe in Chapter 8.

Value Expressions

An expression may be simple or very complex. The expression can contain literal values, column names, parameters, host variables, subqueries, logical connectives, and arithmetic operators. Regardless of its complexity, an expression must reduce to a single value.

For this reason SQL expressions are commonly known as *value expressions*. Combining multiple value expressions into a single expression is possible, as long as the component value expressions reduce to values of compatible data types.

SQL-92 has five different kinds of value expressions:

- ✔ String value expressions
- ✔ Numeric value expressions
- ✔ Datetime value expressions
- ✔ Interval value expressions
- ✔ Conditional value expressions

String value expressions

The simplest *string value expression* is a single string value specification. Other possibilities include a column reference, a set function, a scalar subquery, a CASE expression, a CAST expression, or a complex string value expression. I discuss CASE and CAST value expressions in Chapter 8. Only one operator is possible in a string value expression — the *concatenation operator*. You may concatenate any of the expressions I mention in the bulleted list prior to this paragraph with another expression to create a more complex string value expression. A pair of vertical lines (||) represents the concatenation operator. The following table shows some examples of string value expressions.

Expression	Produces
`'Peanut ' || 'brittle'`	`'Peanut brittle'`
`'Jelly' || ' ' || 'beans'`	`'Jelly beans'`
`FIRST_NAME || ' ' || LAST_NAME`	`'Joe Smith'`
`B'1100111' || B'01010011'`	`B'110011101010011'`
`'' || 'Asparagus'`	`'Asparagus'`
`'Asparagus' || ''`	`'Asparagus'`
`'As' || '' || 'par' || '' || 'agus'`	`'Asparagus'`

As the table shows, if you concatenate a string to a zero-length string, the result is the same as the original string.

Numeric value expressions

In *numeric value expressions,* you can apply the addition, subtraction, multiplication, and division operators to numeric-type data. The expression must reduce to a numeric value. The components of a numeric value expression may be of different data types as long as all are numeric. The data type of the result depends on the data types of the components from which you derive the result. The SQL-92 standard doesn't rigidly specify the type that results from any specific combination of source expression components because of differences among hardware platforms. Check the documentation for your specific platform when mixing numeric data types.

Following are some examples of numeric value expressions:

```
-27
```

```
49+83
```

```
5*(12-3)
```

```
PROTEIN+FAT+CARBOHYDRATE
```

```
FEET/5280
```

```
COST * :multiplierA
```

Datetime value expressions

Datetime value expressions perform operations on data that deal with dates and times. These value expressions can contain components that are of the types DATE, TIME, TIMESTAMP, or INTERVAL. The result of a datetime value expression is always of a datetime type (either DATE, TIME, or TIMESTAMP). The following expression, for example, gives the date of one week from today:

```
CURRENT_DATE + INTERVAL '7' DAY
```

Times are maintained in Universal Coordinated Time (UCT), but you can specify an offset to make the time correct for any particular time zone. For your system's local time zone, you can use the simple syntax given in the following example:

```
TIME '22:55:00' AT LOCAL
```

Alternatively, you could specify this value the long way:

```
TIME '22:55:00' AT TIME ZONE INTERVAL '-08:00' HOUR TO
        MINUTE
```

This expression shows that the time refers to the time zone for Portland, Oregon, which is eight hours earlier than that of Greenwich, England.

Interval value expressions

If you subtract one datetime from another, you get an *interval*. Adding one datetime to another makes no sense, so SQL doesn't permit you to do so. If you add two intervals together or subtract one interval from another interval, the result is an interval. You can also either multiply or divide an interval by a numeric constant.

Recall that SQL has two types of interval: *year-month* and *day-time*. To avoid ambiguities, you must specify which to use in an interval expression. The following expression, for example, gives the interval in years and months until you reach retirement age:

```
(BIRTHDAY_65 - CURRENT_DATE) YEAR TO MONTH
```

The following example, on the other hand, gives an interval of 40 days:

```
INTERVAL '17' DAY + INTERVAL '23' DAY
```

The example that follows approximates the total number of months that a mother of five has been pregnant (assuming that she's not currently expecting number six!):

```
INTERVAL '9' MONTH * 5
```

Intervals can be negative as well as positive and may consist of any value expression or combination of value expressions that evaluates to an interval.

Conditional value expressions

The value of a *conditional value expression* depends on a condition. The conditional value expressions CASE, NULLIF, and COALESCE are significantly more complex than are the other kinds of value expressions. In fact, these three conditional value expressions are so complex that I don't have enough room to talk about them here. I give conditional value expressions extensive coverage, therefore, in Chapter 8.

Chapter 8

Advanced SQL-92 Value Expressions

● ●

In This Chapter

▶ Updating one column in a table row based on the value of another column

▶ Using the CASE expression to avoid computations that lead to errors

▶ Replacing special characters in a database table with nulls

▶ Converting a data item from one data type to another

▶ Saving data entry time by using row value expressions

● ●

*I*n Chapter 2, I describe SQL as a data sublanguage. The sole function of SQL is to operate on data in a database. As such, SQL lacks many of the features of a conventional procedural language. As a result, developers who use SQL must switch back and forth between SQL and its host language to control the flow of execution. This repeated switching complicates matters at development time and negatively affects performance at runtime.

New features added to SQL-92 reduce an application's reliance on its host language. Tasks in older implementations that required a switch back to the host language you can now perform within SQL. One of these new features *(the* CASE *expression)* provides a long-sought conditional structure. A second new feature (CAST) facilitates data conversion in a table, from one type of data to another. A third new feature *(the row value expression)* enables you to operate on a list of values where, previously, only a single value was possible. If, for example, your list of values is a list of columns in a table, you can now perform an operation on all those columns by using a very simple syntax.

CASE Conditional Expressions

Every complete computer language has some kind of conditional statement or command. Most have several. Probably the most common is the IF..THEN..ELSE..ENDIF structure. If the condition following the IF keyword evaluates to True, the block of commands following the THEN keyword executes. If the condition is not True, the block of commands following the ELSE keyword executes. The ENDIF keyword signals the end of the structure. This structure is great for any decision that can go one of two ways. The structure is less applicable, however, to decisions that can have more than two outcomes.

Note: The CASE statement handles situations in which you may want to perform more than two different tasks based on more than two conditions.

SQL's CASE expression is different from the CASE statements that you find in other languages in that CASE is an expression in SQL rather than a statement. In SQL, you can place a CASE expression almost any place where a value is legal. At runtime, a CASE expression evaluates to a value. The CASE statements that you find in other languages don't evaluate to a value but rather execute a block of statements.

The key point to remember is that CASE in SQL is an *expression* and thus only part of a statement — not a statement in its own right.

You can use the CASE expression two different ways. The first way is to use the expression with search conditions. CASE searches for rows in a table where specified conditions are True. If CASE finds a search condition to be True for a table row, the statement containing the CASE expression makes a specified change to that row.

The second way you can use a CASE expression is to compare a table field to a value you specify in the CASE expression. The outcome of the statement containing the CASE expression depends on which of several specified values the table field is equal to for each table row.

Examples in the following sections help make these concepts clearer. First, I give two examples using CASE with search conditions. One example searches a table and makes different changes to table values, based on a condition. This usage is called a *translation-oriented* use of CASE. The second checks the values in the table during the search for conditions that cause errors. This usage is called an *exception avoidance* use of CASE.

The last section on CASE looks at an example of the value form of CASE.

Using CASE with search conditions

One powerful way to use the CASE expression is to search a table for rows in which a specified search condition is True. If you use CASE this way, the expression uses the following syntax:

```
CASE
    WHEN condition₁ THEN result₁
    WHEN condition₂ THEN result₂
    ...
    WHEN conditionₙ THEN resultₙ
    ELSE resultₓ
END
```

CASE examines the first qualifying row (the first row that meets the conditions of the enclosing WHERE clause, if any) to see whether $condition_1$ is True. If it is, the CASE expression receives a value of $result_1$. If $condition_1$ is not True, CASE evaluates the row for $condition_2$. If $condition_2$ is True, the CASE expression receives the value of $result_2$ and so on. If none of the stated conditions are True, the CASE expression receives the value of $result_x$. The ELSE clause is optional. If the expression has no ELSE clause and none of the specified conditions is True, the expression receives a null value. After the SQL statement containing the CASE expression applies itself to the first qualifying row in a table and takes the appropriate action, it processes the next row. This sequence continues until the SQL statement finishes processing the entire table.

Updating values based on a condition

Because you can embed a CASE expression within an SQL statement in almost any place where a value is possible, this expression gives you tremendous flexibility. You can use CASE within an UPDATE statement, for example, to make different changes to table values, based on a certain condition. Consider the following example:

```
UPDATE FOODS
    SET RATING = CASE
                    WHEN FAT < 1
                        THEN 'very low fat'
                    WHEN FAT < 5
                        THEN 'low fat'
                    WHEN FAT < 20
                        THEN 'moderate fat'
                    WHEN FAT < 50
                        THEN 'high fat'
                    ELSE 'heart attack city'
                END
```

This statement evaluates the WHEN conditions in order until the first True, after which the statement ignores the rest of the conditions. For this reason, you don't need to code the preceding example as follows:

```
WHEN FAT < 1
     THEN 'very low fat'
WHEN FAT >= 1 AND FAT < 5
     THEN 'low fat'
WHEN FAT >= 5 AND FAT < 20
     THEN 'moderate fat'
WHEN FAT >= 20 AND < 50
     THEN 'high fat'
ELSE 'heart attack city'
```

Table 7-2 in Chapter 7 shows the fat content of 100 grams of certain selected foods. A database table holding that information could contain a RATING column that gives a quick assessment of the meaning of the fat content. If you run the preceding UPDATE on the FOODS table in Chapter 7, the statement assigns asparagus a value of very low fat, chicken a value of low fat, and puts roasted almonds into the heart attack city category.

Avoiding conditions that cause errors

Another valuable use of CASE is *exception avoidance* — checking for conditions that cause errors.

Consider a case that determines compensation for salespeople. Companies that compensate their salespeople by straight commission often start out a new person by giving the employee a "draw" against commission. In the following example, new salespeople receive a draw against commission that's withdrawn gradually as their commissions rise:

```
UPDATE SALES_COMP
   SET COMP = COMMISSION + CASE
                       WHEN COMMISSION <> 0
                          THEN DRAW/COMMISSION
                       WHEN COMMISSION = 0
                          THEN DRAW
                   END
```

If the salesperson's commission is zero, the structure in this example avoids a division by zero operation, which would surely cause an error. If the salesperson has a nonzero commission, total compensation is the commission plus a draw that's reduced proportionately to the size of the commission.

Note: The THEN expressions in a CASE expression must all be of the same type — all numeric, all character, or all date. The result of the CASE expression is also of the same type.

Using CASE with values

You can use a more compact form of the CASE expression if you're comparing a test value for equality with a series of other values. This form is useful within a SELECT or UPDATE statement if a table contains a limited number of values in a column and you want to associate a corresponding result value to each of those column values. If you use CASE in this way, the expression has the following syntax:

```
CASE value_t
    WHEN value_1 THEN result_1
    WHEN value_2 THEN result_2
    ...
    WHEN value_n THEN result_n
    ELSE result_x
END
```

If the test value ($value_t$) is equal to $value_1$, the expression takes on the value $result_1$. If $value_t$ isn't equal to $value_1$ but is equal to $value_2$, the expression takes on the value $result_2$. The expression tries each comparison value in turn, all the way down to $value_n$, until achieving a match. If none of the comparison values equals the test value, the expression takes on the value $result_x$. Again, if the optional ELSE clause isn't present and none of the comparison values match the test value, the expression receives a null value.

For an actual example of how the value form works, consider a case in which you have a table containing the names and ranks of various military officers. You want to list the names preceded by the correct abbreviation for each rank. The following statement does the job:

```
SELECT CASE RANK
        WHEN 'general'            THEN 'Gen.'
        WHEN 'colonel'            THEN 'Col.'
        WHEN 'lieutenant colonel' THEN 'Lt. Col.'
        WHEN 'major'              THEN 'Maj.'
        WHEN 'captain'            THEN 'Capt.'
        WHEN 'first lieutenant'   THEN '1st. Lt.'
        WHEN 'second lieutenant'  THEN '2nd. Lt.'
        ELSE 'Mr.'
    END,
        LAST_NAME
    FROM OFFICERS ;
```

The result is a list similar to that of the following example:

```
Capt.  Midnight
Col.   Sanders
Gen.   Schwarzkopf
Maj.   Disaster
Mr.    Nimitz
```

Chester Nimitz was an admiral in the United States Navy during World War II. Because his rank isn't one of those listed in the CASE expression, the ELSE clause determines his title.

As another example, say that Captain Midnight gets a promotion to major and you want to update the OFFICERS database accordingly. Assume that the variable officer_last_name contains the value 'Midnight' and that the variable new_rank contains an integer (4) that corresponds to Midnight's new rank, according to the following table.

new_rank	Rank
1	general
2	colonel
3	lieutenant colonel
4	major
5	captain
6	first lieutenant
7	second lieutenant
8	Mr.

You can record the promotion by using the following SQL code:

```
UPDATE OFFICERS
   SET RANK = CASE :new_rank
                WHEN 1 THEN 'general'
                WHEN 2 THEN 'colonel'
                WHEN 3 THEN 'lieutenant colonel'
                WHEN 4 THEN 'major'
                WHEN 5 THEN 'captain'
                WHEN 6 THEN 'first lieutenant'
                WHEN 7 THEN 'second lieutenant'
                WHEN 8 THEN 'Mr.'
             END
   WHERE LAST_NAME = :officer_last_name
```

An alternative syntax for the CASE with values is as follows:

```
CASE
    WHEN value_t = value_1 THEN result_1
    WHEN value_t = value_2 THEN result_2
    ...
    WHEN value_t = value_n THEN result_n
    ELSE result_x
END
```

A special CASE — NULLIF

If you can be sure of one thing in this world, it's change. Sometimes things change from one known state to another. Other times, you think that you know something but later find out that you didn't know it after all. Classical thermodynamics, as well as modern chaos theory, tells us that systems naturally migrate from a well-known, ordered state into a disordered state that no one can predict. Anyone who's ever monitored the status of a teenager's room for a period of a week after the room is cleaned can vouch for the accuracy of these theories.

Database tables have definite values in fields containing known contents. Usually, if the value of a field is unknown, the field contains the null value. In SQL, you can use a CASE expression to change the contents of a table field from a definite value to a null. The null indicates that you no longer know the value of the field. Consider the following example.

Imagine that you own a small airline that offers flights between Southern California and Washington State. Until recently, some of your flights stopped at San Jose International Airport to refuel before continuing on. Unfortunately, you just lost your right to fly into San Jose. From now on, you must make your refueling stop at either San Francisco International or Oakland International. At this point, you don't yet know which flights stop at which airport, but you definitely do know that none of the flights are stopping at San Jose any more. You have a FLIGHT database that contains important information about each of your routes, and now you want to update the database to remove all references to San Jose. One way to do so is as follows:

```
UPDATE FLIGHT
    SET REFUEL_STOP = CASE
                    WHEN REFUEL_STOP = 'San Jose'
                        THEN NULL
                    ELSE REFUEL_STOP
                END ;
```

Because occasions frequently arise in which you want to replace a known value with a null, SQL-92 offers a shorthand notation to accomplish this task. The preceding example, expressed in this shorthand form, appears as follows:

```
UPDATE FLIGHT
   SET REFUEL_STOP = NULLIF(REFUEL_STOP, 'San Jose') ;
```

You can read this expression as, "Update the FLIGHT database by setting column REFUEL_STOP to null if the existing value of REFUEL_STOP is 'San Jose'. Otherwise, make no change."

NULLIF comes in even handier if you're converting data that you originally accumulated for use with a program written in a standard programming language such as COBOL or FORTRAN. Standard programming languages don't have nulls, so a common practice is to represent the "not known" or "not applicable" concept by using special values. A numeric –1 may represent a "not known" value for SALARY, for example, and a character string "***" may represent a "not known" or "not applicable" value for JOBCODE. If you want to represent those "not known" and "not applicable" states in an SQL-compatible database by using nulls, you need to convert the special values to nulls. The following example makes this conversion for an employee table, where some salary values are unknown:

```
UPDATE EMP
   SET SALARY = CASE SALARY
                   WHEN -1 THEN NULL
                   ELSE SALARY
                END ;
```

You can perform this conversion more conveniently by using NULLIF, as follows:

```
UPDATE EMP
   SET SALARY = NULLIF(SALARY, -1) ;
```

Another special CASE — COALESCE

COALESCE, as is NULLIF, is a shorthand form of a particular CASE expression. COALESCE deals with a list of values that may or may not be null. If one of the values in the list is nonnull, the COALESCE expression takes on that value. If more than one value in the list is nonnull, the expression takes on the value of the first nonnull item in the list. If all the values in the list are null, the expression takes on the null value.

A CASE expression with this function has the following form:

```
CASE
    WHEN value₁ IS NOT NULL
        THEN value₁
    WHEN value₂ IS NOT NULL
        THEN value₂
    ...
    WHEN valueₙ IS NOT NULL
        THEN valueₙ
    ELSE NULL
END
```

The corresponding COALESCE shorthand appears as follows:

```
COALESCE(value₁, value₂, ..., valueₙ)
```

You may want to use a COALESCE expression after you perform an OUTER JOIN operation (which I discuss in Chapter 10). In such cases, COALESCE can save you a lot of typing.

CAST Data-Type Conversions

In Chapter 2, I discuss the different data types that SQL recognizes and supports. Ideally, each column in a database table has a perfect choice of data type. In this nonideal world, however, exactly what that perfect choice may be isn't always clear. In defining a database table, you may assign a data type to a column that works perfectly for your current application. Later, however, you may want to expand the scope of your application or write an entirely new application that makes a different use of the data. This new use may require a data type different from the one you originally chose.

You may want to compare a column of one type in one table with a column of a different type in a different table. You may, for example, have dates stored as character data in one table and as date data in another. Even if both columns contain the same things (dates, for example), the fact that the types are different may prevent you from making the comparison. In SQL-86 and SQL-89, type incompatibility could be a big problem. SQL-92, however, offers an easy-to-use solution in the CAST expression.

The CAST expression converts table data or host variables of one type to another type. After you make the conversion, you can proceed with the operation or analysis that you originally envisioned.

Naturally, you do have restrictions in using this expression. You can't just indiscriminately convert data of any type into any other. The data you're converting must be compatible with the new data type. You can, for example, use CAST to convert the CHAR(10) character string '1995-04-26' to the DATE type. You can't, however, use CAST to convert the CHAR(10) character string 'rhinoceros' to the DATE type. You can't convert an INTEGER to the SMALLINT type if the former exceeds the maximum size of a SMALLINT.

You can convert an item of any of the character types to any other type (such as numeric or date), provided that the value of the item has the form of a literal of the new type. Conversely, you can convert an item of any type to any of the character types, provided that the value of the item has the form of a literal of the original type.

The following list describes some additional possible conversions you can make:

- ✔ *Any bit string to a character string.* The bits function as though they're the bits that make up characters.

- ✔ *Any numeric type to any other numeric type.* If converting to a type of less fractional precision, the system rounds or truncates the result.

- ✔ *Any exact numeric to a single component interval,* such as INTERVAL DAY or INTERVAL SECOND.

- ✔ *Any* DATE *to a* TIMESTAMP. The time part of the TIMESTAMP fills in with zeros.

- ✔ *Any* TIME *to a* TIME *with a different fractional-seconds precision or a* TIMESTAMP. The date part of the TIMESTAMP fills in with the current date.

- ✔ *Any* TIMESTAMP *to either a* DATE, *a* TIME, *or a* TIMESTAMP *with a different fractional-seconds precision.*

- ✔ *Any year-month* INTERVAL *to an exact numeric or another year-month* INTERVAL *with different leading-field precision.*

- ✔ *Any day-time* INTERVAL *to an exact numeric or another day-time* INTERVAL *with different leading-field precision.*

Using CAST within SQL

Say that you work for a sales company that keeps track of prospective customers as well as customers who've actually bought something. You list the prospective customers in a table named PROSPECT, and you distinguish each one by a unique Prospect ID number, which you store as a CHAR(5) type. You list the paying customers in a table named CUSTOMER, and you distinguish them by a unique Customer ID number, which is of SMALLINT type. You now want to generate a list of all customers who appear in both tables. You can use CAST to perform the task, as follows:

```
SELECT * FROM CUSTOMER
   WHERE CUSTOMER.CUSTOMER_ID =
      CAST(PROSPECT.PROSPECT_ID AS SMALLINT) ;
```

Using CAST between SQL and the host language

The key use of CAST is to deal with data types that are in SQL but not in the host language you use. The following list offers some examples of such data types:

- ✔ SQL has DECIMAL and NUMERIC, but FORTRAN and Pascal don't.
- ✔ SQL has FLOAT and REAL, but standard COBOL doesn't.
- ✔ SQL has DATETIME, and no other language does.

Suppose that you want to use FORTRAN or Pascal to access tables with DECIMAL(5,3) columns, and you don't want the inaccuracies that result from converting those values to the REAL data type of FORTRAN and Pascal. You can perform this task by CASTing the data to and from character-string host variables. You retrieve a numeric salary of 198.37 as a CHAR(10) value of '0000198.37'. Then if you want to update that salary to 203.74, you can place that value in a CHAR(10) as '0000203.74'. First, you use CAST to change the SQL DECIMAL (5,3) data type to the CHAR (10) type for the specific employee whose ID number you're storing in the host variable :emp_id_var, as follows:

```
SELECT CAST(SALARY AS CHAR(10)) INTO :salary_var
         FROM EMP
         WHERE EMPID = :emp_id_var ;
```

Then the application examines the resulting character string value in :salary_var, possibly sets the string to a new value of '000203.74', and then updates the database by using the following SQL code:

```
UPDATE EMP
   SET SALARY = CAST(:salary_var AS DECIMAL(5,3))
      WHERE EMPID = :emp_id_var;
```

Dealing with character-string values such as '000198.37' is awkward in FORTRAN or Pascal, but you can write a set of subroutines to do the necessary manipulations. You can then retrieve and update any SQL data from any host language and get and set exact values.

The general idea is that CAST is most valuable for converting between host types and the database rather than for converting within the database.

Row Value Expressions

In SQL-86 and SQL-89, most operations deal with a single value or single column in a table row. To operate on multiple values, you must build complex expressions by using logical connectives (which I discuss in Chapter 9).

SQL-92 introduces *row value expressions,* which operate on a list of values or columns rather than a single value or column. A row value expression is a list of value expressions that you enclose in parentheses and separate by commas. You can operate on an entire row at once or on a selected subset of the row.

In Chapter 6, I discuss how to use the INSERT statement to add a new row to an existing table. To do so, the statement uses a row value expression. Consider the following example:

```
INSERT INTO FOODS
    (FOODNAME, CALORIES, PROTEIN, FAT, CARBOHYDRATE)
    VALUES
    ('Cheese, cheddar', 398, 25, 32.2, 2.1);
```

In this example, ('Cheese, cheddar', 398, 25, 32.2, 2.1) is a row value expression. If you use one in an INSERT statement this way, a row value expression can contain null and default values. (A *default value* is the value that a table column assumes if you specify no other value.) The following line, for example, is a legal row value expression:

```
('Cheese, cheddar', 398, NULL, 32.2, DEFAULT)
```

You can add multiple rows to a table by putting multiple row value expressions in the VALUES clause, as follows:

```
INSERT INTO FOODS
    (FOODNAME, CALORIES, PROTEIN, FAT, CARBOHYDRATE)
    VALUES
    ('Lettuce', 14, 1.2, 0.2, 2.5),
    ('Margarine', 720, 0.6, 81.0, 0.4),
    ('Mustard', 75, 4.7, 4.4, 6.4),
    ('Spaghetti', 148, 5.0, 0.5, 30.1);
```

You can use row value expressions to save typing in comparisons. Say that you have two tables of nutritional values, one compiled in English and the other in Spanish. You want to find those rows in the English language table that correspond exactly to rows in the Spanish language table. Without a row value expression, you may need to formulate something such as the following example:

```
SELECT * FROM FOODS
    WHERE FOODS.CALORIES = COMIDA.CALORIA
        AND FOODS.PROTEIN = COMIDA.PROTEINA
        AND FOODS.FAT = COMIDA.GORDO
        AND FOODS.CARBOHYDRATE = COMIDA.CARBOHIDRATO;
```

Row value expressions enable you to code the same logic as follows:

```
SELECT * FROM FOODS
    WHERE (FOODS.CALORIES, FOODS.PROTEIN, FOODS.FAT,
        FOODS.CARBOHYDRATE)
        =

        (COMIDA.CALORIA, COMIDA.PROTEINA, COMIDA.GORDO,
        COMIDA.CARBOHIDRATO);
```

In this example, you don't save much typing. The benefit would be greater if you were comparing more columns, but not much greater. In cases of marginal benefit such as this example, you may be better off sticking with the older syntax because its meaning is clearer.

You do gain one benefit by using a row value expression instead of its coded equivalent; the row value expression is a lot faster. In principle, a very clever implementation can analyze the coded version and implement that version the same as the row-value version, but in practice, this operation is a difficult optimization that no DBMS currently on the market can perform (at least as far as I know).

Chapter 9
Zeroing In on the Data You Want

A database management system has two main functions: storing data and providing easy access to that data. Storing data is nothing special. A file cabinet can perform that chore. The hard part of data management is providing easy access. For data to be useful, you must be able to separate the (usually) small amount you do want from the huge amount you don't want.

SQL enables you to use some characteristic of the data itself to determine whether a particular table row is of interest or not. In particular the SELECT, DELETE, and UPDATE statements need to convey to the database engine (that part of the DBMS that actually interacts with the data) which rows to select, delete, or update and which rows to leave alone. You can accomplish this discrimination by adding modifying clauses to your SELECT, DELETE, and UPDATE statements.

Modifying Clauses

The modifying clauses available in SQL are FROM, WHERE, HAVING, GROUP BY, and ORDER BY. The FROM clause tells the database engine which table or tables to operate on. The WHERE and HAVING clauses specify a characteristic of the data that determines whether to include a particular row in the current operation or not. The GROUP BY and ORDER BY clauses specify how to display the retrieved rows. Table 9-1 provides a summary.

Table 9-1	Modifying Clauses and Functions
Modifying Clause	*Function*
FROM	Specifies from which tables to take data.
WHERE	Filters out rows that don't satisfy the search condition.
GROUP BY	Separates rows into groups, based on the values in the grouping columns.
HAVING	Filters out groups that don't satisfy the search condition.
ORDER BY	Sorts the results of prior clauses to produce final output.

If you have more than one of these clauses, they must appear in the following order:

```
SELECT column_list
   FROM table_list
   [WHERE search_condition]
   [GROUP BY grouping_column]
   [HAVING search_condition]
   [ORDER BY ordering_condition] ;
```

The WHERE clause is a filter that passes rows that meet the search condition and rejects those that don't meet the condition. The GROUP BY clause rearranges the rows that the WHERE clause passes according to the value of the grouping column. The HAVING clause is another filter that takes each group that the GROUP BY clause forms and passes those groups that meet the search condition, rejecting the rest. The ORDER BY clause sorts whatever remains after all the preceding clauses process the table. As the square brackets ([ ]) indicate, the WHERE, GROUP BY, HAVING, and ORDER BY clauses are optional.

SQL evaluates these clauses in the order FROM, WHERE, GROUP BY, HAVING, and finally SELECT, with the clauses operating in a "pipeline" manner in which each clause takes as input the result of the prior clause and produces an output for the next clause. In functional notation, this order of evaluation appears as follows:

```
SELECT(HAVING(GROUP BY(WHERE(FROM...)))))
```

Note: ORDER BY operates after SELECT, which explains why ORDER BY can only reference columns in the SELECT list. ORDER BY can't reference other columns in the FROM table(s).

FROM Clauses

The FROM clause is easy to understand if you specify only one table, as in the following example:

```
SELECT * FROM SALES ;
```

This statement returns all the data in all the rows of every column in the SALES table. You can, however, specify more than one table in a FROM clause. Consider the following example:

```
SELECT *
   FROM CUSTOMER, SALES ;
```

This statement forms a virtual table that combines the data from the CUSTOMER table with the data from the SALES table. Each row in the CUSTOMER table combines with every row in the SALES table to form the new table. The new virtual table that this combination forms, therefore, contains the number of rows in the CUSTOMER table multiplied by the number of rows in the SALES table. If the CUSTOMER table has ten rows and the SALES table has a hundred, the new virtual table has a thousand rows.

This operation is called the *Cartesian product* of the two source tables. The Cartesian product is actually a type of JOIN. I cover JOIN operations in detail in Chapter 10.

In most applications, the majority of the rows that form as a result of taking the Cartesian product of two tables are garbage. In the case of the virtual table that forms from the CUSTOMER and SALES tables, only the rows where the CUSTOMER_ID from the CUSTOMER table matches the CUSTOMER_ID from the SALES table are of interest. You can filter out the rest of the rows by using a WHERE clause.

WHERE Clauses

WHERE clauses appear several times in previous chapters. I use the clause in those places without really explaining it because its meaning and use are so intuitively obvious: A statement performs an operation (such as a SELECT, DELETE, or UPDATE) only on table rows WHERE a stated condition is True. The syntax of the WHERE clause is as follows:

```
SELECT column_list
   FROM table_name
   WHERE condition ;

DELETE FROM table_name
   WHERE condition ;

UPDATE table_name
   SET column₁=value₁, column₂=value₂, ..., columnₙ=valueₙ
   WHERE condition ;
```

In all cases, the condition in the WHERE clause may be simple or arbitrarily complex. You may join multiple conditions together by using the logical connectives AND, OR, and NOT (which I discuss later in this chapter) to create a single condition.

The following statements are examples of typical WHERE clauses:

```
WHERE CUSTOMER.CUSTOMER_ID = SALES.CUSTOMER_ID
WHERE FOODS.CALORIES = COMIDA.CALORIA
WHERE FOODS.CALORIES < 219
WHERE FOODS.CALORIES > 3 * base_value
WHERE FOODS.CALORIES < 219 AND FOODS.PROTEIN > 27.4
```

The conditions that these WHERE clauses express are known as predicates. A *predicate* is an expression that asserts a fact about values.

The predicate FOODS.CALORIES < 219, for example, is True if the value for the current row of the column FOODS.CALORIES is less than 219. If the assertion is True, it satisfies the condition. An assertion may either be True, False, or unknown. The unknown case arises if one or more elements in the assertion are null. The *comparison predicates* (=, <, >, <>, <=, and >=) are the most common, but SQL offers a number of others that greatly increase your capability to distinguish, or "filter out," a desired data item from others in the same column. The following list notes the predicates that give you that filtering capability:

- ✔ Comparison predicates
- ✔ BETWEEN
- ✔ IN [NOT IN]
- ✔ LIKE [NOT LIKE]
- ✔ NULL
- ✔ ALL, SOME, ANY
- ✔ EXISTS

 ✔ UNIQUE
 ✔ OVERLAPS
 ✔ MATCH

I discuss all these predicates in the following sections.

Comparison predicates

The examples in the preceding section show typical uses of comparison predicates, in which you compare one value to another. For every row in which the comparison evaluates to a True value, that value satisfies the WHERE clause and the operation (SELECT, UPDATE, DELETE, or whatever) executes. Consider, for example, the following SQL statement:

```
SELECT * FROM FOODS
   WHERE CALORIES < 219 ;
```

This statement displays all rows from the FOODS table that have a value of less than 219 in the CALORIES column.

Six comparison predicates are listed in Table 9-2.

Table 9-2	SQL's Comparison Predicates
Comparison	*Symbol*
Equal	=
Not equal	<>
Less than	<
Less than or equal	<=
Greater than	>
Greater than or equal	>=

BETWEEN

Sometimes you want to select a row if the value in a column falls within a specified range. One way to make this selection is by using comparison predicates. You can, for example, formulate a WHERE clause to select all the rows in the FOODS table that have a value in the CALORIES column greater than 100 and less than 300, as follows:

```
WHERE FOODS.CALORIES > 100 AND FOODS.CALORIES < 300
```

This comparison doesn't include foods with a calorie count of exactly 100 or 300 — only those values that fall in between these two. To include the end points, you can write the statement as follows:

```
WHERE FOODS.CALORIES >= 100 AND FOODS.CALORIES <= 300
```

Another way of specifying a range that includes the end points is to use a BETWEEN predicate in the following manner:

```
WHERE FOODS.CALORIES BETWEEN 100 AND 300
```

This clause is functionally identical to the preceding example, which uses comparison predicates. As you can see, this formulation saves some typing and is also perhaps a little more intuitive than the one that uses two comparison predicates joined by the logical connective AND.

The BETWEEN keyword may be somewhat confusing because it doesn't tell you explicitly whether the clause includes the end points. In fact, the clause does include these end points. BETWEEN also fails to explicitly tell you that the first term in the comparison must be equal to or less than the second. If, for example, FOODS.CALORIES contains a value of 200, the following clause returns a True value:

```
WHERE FOODS.CALORIES BETWEEN 100 AND 300
```

However, a clause that you'd think is equivalent to the preceding example returns the opposite result, False:

```
WHERE FOODS.CALORIES BETWEEN 300 AND 100
```

If you use BETWEEN, you must be able to guarantee that the first term in your comparison is always equal to or less than the second term.

You can use the BETWEEN predicate with character, bit, and datetime data types as well as with the numeric types. You may see something like the following example:

```
SELECT FIRST_NAME, LAST_NAME
    FROM CUSTOMER
    WHERE CUSTOMER.LAST_NAME BETWEEN 'A' AND 'Mzzz' ;
```

This example returns all customers whose last name is in the first half of the alphabet.

IN and NOT IN

The IN and NOT IN predicates deal with whether a particular set includes their arguments. You may, for example, have a table that lists suppliers of a commodity that your company purchases on a regular basis. You want to know the phone numbers of those suppliers located in the Pacific Northwest. You can find these numbers by using comparison predicates, such as those shown in the following example:

```
SELECT company, phone
   FROM SUPPLIER
   WHERE state = 'OR' OR state = 'WA' OR state = 'ID' ;
```

You can, however, also use the IN predicate to perform the same task, as follows:

```
SELECT company, phone
   FROM SUPPLIER
   WHERE state IN ('OR', 'WA', 'ID') ;
```

This formulation is a little more compact than the one using comparison predicates and logical OR.

The NOT IN version of this predicate works the same way. Say that you have locations in California, Arizona, and New Mexico, and to avoid sales tax, you want to consider suppliers located anywhere except in those states. Use the following construction:

```
SELECT company, phone
   FROM SUPPLIER
   WHERE state NOT IN ('CA', 'AZ', 'NM') ;
```

If you use the IN keyword this way, it saves you a little typing. The more elements you have in the set, the more typing you save by using IN this way. Saving a little typing, however, is not that great an advantage. You can still do the same job by using comparison predicates as shown in the first example of this section.

You may have another good reason to use the IN predicate rather than comparison predicates, even if using IN doesn't save much typing. Your DBMS probably implements the two methods differently, and one of the methods may be significantly faster than the other on your system.

You may want to run a performance comparison on the two ways of expressing inclusion in (or exclusion from) a group and then use the technique that produces the quickest results.

The IN keyword is valuable in another area, too. If IN is part of a subquery, the keyword enables you to pull information from two tables to obtain results that you can't derive from a single table. I cover subqueries in Chapter 11, but following is an example that shows how a subquery uses the IN keyword.

Suppose that you want to display the names of all customers who've bought the F-117A product in the last 30 days. Customer names are in the CUSTOMER table and sales transaction data is in the TRANSACT table. You could use the following query:

```
SELECT FIRST_NAME, LAST_NAME
    FROM CUSTOMER
    WHERE CUSTOMER_ID IN
        (SELECT CUSTOMER_ID
            FROM TRANSACT
            WHERE PRODUCT_ID = 'F-117A'
            AND TRANS_DATE >= (CURRENT_DATE - 30)) ;
```

The inner SELECT of the TRANSACT table nests within the outer SELECT of the CUSTOMER table. The inner SELECT finds the CUSTOMER_ID numbers of all customers who bought the F-117A product in the last 30 days. The outer SELECT displays the first and last names of all customers whose CUSTOMER_ID is retrieved by the inner SELECT.

LIKE and NOT LIKE

You can use the LIKE predicate to compare two character strings for a partial match. Partial matches are valuable if you have some idea of the string for which you're searching but don't know its exact form. You can also use partial matches to retrieve multiple rows that contain similar strings in one of the table's columns.

To identify partial matches, SQL makes use of two wildcard characters. The percent sign (%) can stand for any string of characters, zero or more characters in length. The underscore (_) stands for any single character. Table 9-3 provides some examples showing how to use LIKE.

Table 9-3	SQL's LIKE Predicate
Statement	*Values Returned*
WHERE WORD LIKE 'intern%'	intern
	internal
	international
	internet
	interns
WHERE WORD LIKE '%Peace%'	Justice of the Peace
	Peaceful Warrior
WHERE WORD LIKE 't_p_'	tape
	taps
	tipi
	tips
	tops
	type

The NOT LIKE predicate retrieves all rows that don't satisfy a partial match, including one or more wildcard characters, as in the following example:

```
WHERE PHONE NOT LIKE '503%'
```

This example returns all the rows in the table for which the phone number starts with something other than 503.

You may want to search for a string that includes a percent sign or an underscore. In this case, you want SQL to interpret the percent sign *as* a percent sign and not as a wildcard character. You can conduct such a search by typing an escape character just prior to the character you want SQL to take literally. You can choose any character as the escape character, as long as that character doesn't appear in the string you're testing, as shown in the following example:

```
SELECT QUOTE
   FROM BARTLETTS
   WHERE QUOTE LIKE '20#%%'
      ESCAPE '#' ;
```

The first % character is escaped by the preceding # sign, so the statement actually interprets this symbol as a percent sign. The second % character is not escaped, so SQL interprets that symbol as a wildcard. The preceding query, for example, would find the following quotation in *Bartlett's Familiar Quotations:*

```
20% of the salespeople produce 80% of the results
```

The query would also find the following:

```
20%
```

NULL

The NULL predicate finds all rows where the value in the selected column is null. In the FOODS table in Chapter 7, several rows have null values in the CARBOHYDRATE column. You can retrieve their names by using a statement such as the following:

```
SELECT (FOOD)
   FROM FOODS
   WHERE CARBOHYDRATE IS NULL ;
```

This query returns the following values:

```
Beef, lean hamburger
Chicken, light meat
Opossum, roasted
Pork, ham
```

As you may expect, including the NOT keyword reverses the result, as in the following example:

```
SELECT (FOOD)
   FROM FOODS
   WHERE CARBOHYDRATE IS NOT NULL ;
```

This query returns all the rows in the table except the four that the preceding query returns.

The statement CARBOHYDRATE IS NULL is not the same as CARBOHYDRATE = NULL. To illustrate this point, assume that, in the current row of the FOODS table, both CARBOHYDRATE and PROTEIN are null. From this fact, you can draw the following conclusions:

✔ `CARBOHYDRATE IS NULL` is True.

✔ `PROTEIN IS NULL` is True.

✔ `CARBOHYDRATE IS NULL AND PROTEIN IS NULL` is True.

✔ `CARBOHYDRATE = PROTEIN` is unknown.

✔ `CARBOHYDRATE = NULL` is an illegal expression.

Using the keyword `NULL` in a comparison is meaningless, because the answer always returns as "unknown."

Why is `CARBOHYDRATE = PROTEIN` defined as unknown, even though `CARBOHYDRATE` and `PROTEIN` have the same (null) value? Because `NULL` simply means "I don't know." You don't know what `CARBOHYDRATE` is, and you don't know what `PROTEIN` is; therefore, you don't know whether those (unknown) values are the same. Maybe `CARBOHYDRATE` is 37 and `PROTEIN` is 14, or maybe `CARBOHYDRATE` is 93 and `PROTEIN` is 93. If you don't know either the carbohydrate value or the protein value, you can't say whether the two are the same.

ALL, SOME, ANY

Thousands of years ago, the Greek philosopher Aristotle formulated a system of logic that became the basis for much of Western thought. Its essence is to start with a set of premises that you know to be true, apply valid operations to these premises, and, thereby, arrive at new truths. An example of this procedure is as follows:

ANY can be ambiguous

The original SQL used the word ANY for existential quantification. This usage turned out to be confusing and error prone, because the English language connotations of *any* are sometimes universal and sometimes existential:

✔ "Do any of you people know where Baker Street is?"

✔ "I can eat more eggs than any of you people."

The first sentence is probably asking whether some people know where Baker Street is. *Any* is used as an existential quantifier. The second sentence, however, is a boast that's stating that I can eat more eggs than all you people can eat. In this case, *any* is used as a universal quantifier.

Thus, for the SQL-92 standard, the developers retained the word ANY for compatibility with early products but added the word SOME as a less confusing synonym.

> *Premise 1:* All Greeks are human.
>
> *Premise 2:* All humans are mortal.
>
> *Conclusion:* All Greeks are mortal.

Another example:

> *Premise 1:* Some Greeks are women.
>
> *Premise 2:* All women are human.
>
> *Conclusion:* Some Greeks are human.

Another way of stating the same logical idea of this second example is as follows:

> If any Greeks are women and all women are human, then some Greeks are human.

The first example uses the universal quantifier ALL in both premises, enabling you to make a sound deduction about all Greeks in the conclusion. The second example uses the existential quantifier SOME in one premise, enabling you to make a deduction about some Greeks in the conclusion. The third example uses the existential quantifier ANY, which is a synonym for SOME, to come to the same conclusion you reach in the second example.

Look at how SOME and ALL apply in SQL.

Consider an example in baseball statistics. Baseball is a physically demanding sport, especially for pitchers. A pitcher must throw the baseball from the pitcher's mound to home plate from 90 to 150 times in the course of a game. This effort can be very tiring, and many times, the pitcher becomes ineffective and a relief pitcher must replace him before the game ends. For the pitcher who starts a game to pitch the entire game without relief is an outstanding achievement.

Suppose that you're keeping track of the number of complete games that all major league pitchers pitch. In one table, you list all the American League pitchers, and in another table, you list all National League pitchers. Both tables contain the players' first names, last names, and number of complete games pitched.

The American League permits a designated hitter (DH), who need not play a defensive position, to hit in place of any of the nine players who do play defense. Usually the DH bats for the pitcher, because pitchers are notoriously poor hitters. Say that you have a theory that, on average, American

League starting pitchers throw more complete games than do National League starting pitchers, because designated hitters enable hard-throwing but weak-hitting American League pitchers to stay in close games, while in a close game, a pinch hitter replaces comparable National League pitchers. To test your theory, you formulate the following query:

```
SELECT FIRST_NAME, LAST_NAME
    FROM AMERICAN_LEAGUER
    WHERE COMPLETE_GAMES > ALL
        (SELECT COMPLETE_GAMES
            FROM NATIONAL_LEAGUER) ;
```

The subquery (the inner SELECT) returns a list, showing for every National League pitcher the number of complete games they pitched. The outer query returns the first and last names of all American Leaguers who pitched more complete games than ALL of the National Leaguers. This result is somewhat confusing. The query doesn't return the names of American League pitchers who pitched more complete games than all National League pitchers combined. Instead, the query returns the names of those American League pitchers who pitched more complete games than the pitcher who has thrown the most complete games in the National League.

Consider the following similar statement:

```
SELECT FIRST_NAME, LAST_NAME
    FROM AMERICAN_LEAGUER
    WHERE COMPLETE_GAMES > ANY
        (SELECT COMPLETE_GAMES
            FROM NATIONAL_LEAGUER) ;
```

In this case, you use the existential quantifier ANY instead of the universal quantifier ALL. The subquery (the inner, nested query) is identical to the subquery in the previous example. This subquery retrieves a complete list of the complete game statistics for all the National League pitchers. The outer query returns the first and last names of all American League pitchers who pitched more complete games than ANY National League pitcher. Because you can be virtually certain that at least one National League pitcher hasn't pitched a complete game, the result most probably includes all American League pitchers who have pitched at least one complete game.

If you replace the keyword ANY with the equivalent keyword SOME, the result is the same. If the statement that at least one National League pitcher hasn't pitched a complete game is a true statement, you can then say that SOME National League pitcher hasn't pitched a complete game.

EXISTS

You can use the EXISTS predicate in conjunction with a subquery to determine whether the subquery returns any rows at all. If the subquery returns at least one row, that result satisfies the EXISTS condition and the outer query executes. Consider the following example:

```
SELECT FIRST_NAME, LAST_NAME
  FROM CUSTOMER
  WHERE EXISTS
    (SELECT DISTINCT CUSTOMER_ID
      FROM SALES
      WHERE SALES.CUSTOMER_ID = CUSTOMER.CUSTOMER_ID);
```

The SALES table contains a record of all a company's sales. The table includes the CUSTOMER_ID of the customer who makes each purchase, as well as other pertinent information. The CUSTOMER table contains each customer's first and last names but no information about specific transactions.

The subquery in the preceding example returns a row for every customer who has made at least one purchase. The outer query returns the first and last names of the customers who made the purchases that the SALES table records.

EXISTS is equivalent to a comparison of COUNT with zero, as the following query shows:

```
SELECT FIRST_NAME, LAST_NAME
  FROM CUSTOMER
  WHERE 0 <>
    (SELECT COUNT(*)
      FROM SALES
      WHERE SALES.CUSTOMER_ID = CUSTOMER.CUSTOMER_ID);
```

For every row in the SALES table that contains a CUSTOMER_ID that's equal to a CUSTOMER_ID in the CUSTOMER table, this statement displays the FIRST_NAME and LAST_NAME columns in the CUSTOMER table. For every sale in the SALES table, therefore, the statement displays the name of the customer who made the purchase.

UNIQUE

As you do with the EXISTS predicate, you use the UNIQUE predicate with a subquery. While the EXISTS predicate evaluates to True only if the subquery returns at least one row, the UNIQUE predicate evaluates to True only if no two rows that the subquery returns are identical. In other words, the UNIQUE predicate evaluates to True only if all rows that its subquery returns are unique. Consider the following example:

```
SELECT FIRST_NAME, LAST_NAME
   FROM CUSTOMER
   WHERE UNIQUE
     (SELECT CUSTOMER_ID FROM SALES
        WHERE SALES.CUSTOMER_ID = CUSTOMER.CUSTOMER_ID);
```

This statement retrieves the names of all new customers for whom the SALES table records only one sale.

OVERLAPS

You can use the OVERLAPS predicate to determine whether two intervals of time overlap each other. This predicate is useful in avoiding scheduling conflicts. If the two intervals overlap, the predicate returns a True value. If they don't overlap, the predicate returns a False value.

You can specify an interval in two ways, either as a start time and an end time or as a start time and a duration. Following are a few examples:

```
(TIME '2:55:00', INTERVAL '1' HOUR)
OVERLAPS
(TIME '3:30:00', INTERVAL '2' HOUR)
```

The preceding example returns a True because 3:30 is less than one hour after 2:55.

```
(TIME '9:00:00', TIME '9:30:00')
OVERLAPS
(TIME '9:29:00', TIME '9:31:00')
```

The preceding example returns a True, because you have one minute of overlap between the two intervals.

```
(TIME '9:00:00', TIME '10:00:00')
OVERLAPS
(TIME '10:15:00', INTERVAL '3' HOUR)
```

This preceding example returns a False, because the two intervals don't overlap.

```
(TIME '9:00:00', TIME '9:30:00)
OVERLAPS
(TIME '9:30:00', TIME '9:35:00)
```

This example returns a False, because, even though the two intervals are contiguous, they don't overlap.

MATCH

In Chapter 5, I discuss referential integrity, which involves maintaining consistency in a multitable database. You can lose integrity by adding a row to a child table that doesn't have a corresponding row in the child's parent table. You can cause similar problems by deleting a row from a parent table if rows corresponding to that row exist in a child table.

Say that your business has a CUSTOMER table that keeps track of all your customers and a SALES table that records all sales transactions. You don't want to add a row to SALES until after you enter the customer making the purchase into the CUSTOMER table. You don't want to delete a customer from the CUSTOMER table if that customer made purchases that exist in the SALES table. Before performing an insertion or deletion, you may want to check the candidate row to make sure that inserting or deleting that row doesn't cause integrity problems. The MATCH predicate can perform such a check.

Examine the use of the MATCH predicate through an example that employs the CUSTOMER and SALES tables. CUSTOMER_ID is the primary key of the CUSTOMER table and acts as a foreign key in the SALES table. Every row in the CUSTOMER table must have a unique, nonnull CUSTOMER_ID. CUSTOMER_ID isn't unique in the SALES table, because repeat customers buy more than once. This situation is fine and does not threaten integrity, because CUSTOMER_ID is a foreign key rather than a primary key in that table.

Seemingly, CUSTOMER_ID can be null in the SALES table, because someone can walk in off the street, buy something, and walk out again without enabling you to enter his name and address into the CUSTOMER table. This situation could create a row in the child table with no corresponding row in the parent table. To overcome this problem, you can create a generic customer in the CUSTOMER table and assign all such anonymous sales to that customer.

Say that a customer steps up to the cash register and claims that she bought an F-117A Stealth fighter on April 1, 1997. She now wants to return the plane because it shows up like an aircraft carrier on opponent radar screens. You can verify her claim by searching your SALES database for a match. First, you must retrieve her CUSTOMER_ID into the variable vcustid; then you can use the following syntax:

```
... WHERE (vcustid, F-117A, 04/01/97)
        MATCH
        (SELECT CUSTOMER_ID, PRODUCT_ID, SALE_DATE
            FROM SALES)
```

If a sale exists for that customer ID for that product on that date, the MATCH predicate returns a True value. Give the customer her money back. (**Note:** If any of the values in the first argument of the MATCH predicate are null, a True value always returns.)

SQL's developers added the MATCH predicate and the UNIQUE predicate for the same reason — they provide a way to explicitly perform the tests defined for the implicit referential integrity (RI) and UNIQUE constraints.

The general form of the MATCH predicate is as follows:

```
Row_value MATCH  {UNIQUE | PARTIAL | FULL } Subquery
```

The UNIQUE, PARTIAL, and FULL options relate to rules that come into play if the Row_value has one or more columns that are null. The rules for the MATCH predicate are a copy of corresponding referential integrity rules.

Referential integrity rules

Referential integrity rules require that the values of a column or columns in one table match the values of a column or columns in another table. You refer to the columns in the first table as the *foreign key* and the columns in the second table as the *primary key,* or *unique key.* You may, for example, declare the column EMP_DEPTNO in an EMPLOYEE table as a foreign key that references the DEPTNO column of a DEPT table. This matchup ensures that, if you record an employee in the EMPLOYEE table as working in department 123, a row appears in the DEPT table where DEPTNO is 123.

This situation is fairly straightforward if the foreign key and primary key consist of a single column. The two keys can, however, consist of multiple columns. The DEPTNO value, for example, may be unique only within a LOCATION; so to uniquely identify a DEPT row, you must specify both a LOCATION and a DEPTNO. If, for example, both the Boston and Tampa offices have a department 123, you need to identify the departments as ('Boston', '123') and ('Tampa', '123'). In this case, the EMPLOYEE table needs two columns to identify a DEPT. Call those columns EMP_LOC and EMP_DEPTNO. If an employee works in department 123 in Boston, the EMP_LOC and EMP_DEPTNO values are 'Boston' and '123'. And the foreign key declaration in EMPLOYEE is as follows:

```
FOREIGN KEY (EMP_LOC, EMP_DEPTNO)
   REFERENCES DEPT (LOCATION, DEPTNO)
```

If the values of EMP_LOC and EMP_DEPTNO are both nonnull or both null, the referential integrity rules are the same as for single-column keys with values that are null or nonnull. But if EMP_LOC is null and EMP_DEPTNO is nonnull — or EMP_LOC is nonnull and EMP_DEPTNO is null — you need new rules. What should the rules be if you insert or update the EMPLOYEE table with EMP_LOC and EMP_DEPTNO values of (NULL, '123') or ('Boston', NULL)? You have three main alternatives, FULL, PARTIAL, and UNIQUE. I summarize these alternative classes of rules in the following list:

✔ FULL prohibits partial nulls — for example, values of ('Boston', '123') and (NULL, NULL) are okay, but ('Boston', NULL) and (NULL, '123') are both illegal.

✔ PARTIAL permits partial nulls and validates the nonnull values. — for example, permitting ('Boston', NULL) only if you have at least one DEPT with LOCATION 'Boston' and (NULL, '123') only if you have at least one LOCATION with DEPTNO '123'.

✔ UNIQUE permits partial nulls and specifies that, if any column is null, you must regard the foreign key as completely null — for example, it treats ('Boston', NULL) and (NULL, '123') the same as (NULL, NULL).

The UNIQUE rule initially sounds peculiar. The rule says that you can have an EMPLOYEE row ('Boston', NULL) even though you have no DEPT row with LOCATION 'Boston'. The reason you may want to use this rule is to deal with the following case.

Suppose that you want to insert an employee that you know works in Boston, even though you don't yet know in which department in Boston he works. Moreover, the department he works in may not yet exist. In fact, Boston may not yet have any departments. You can insert the employee with EMP_LOC='Boston' and EMP_DEPTNO=NULL, because UNIQUE is the refential integrity rule, and it always returns a true value if any.

Rule by committee

The SQL-89 version of the standard specified the UNIQUE rule as the default, before anyone proposed or debated the other alternatives. Then during development of the SQL-92 version of the standard, proposals appeared for the other alternatives. Some people strongly preferred the PARTIAL rules and argued that they should be the only rules. These people thought the SQL-89 (UNIQUE) rules so undesirable that they wanted those rules considered a bug and the PARTIAL rules specified as a correction. Other people preferred the UNIQUE rules and thought that the PARTIAL rules were obscure,

error-prone, and inefficient. Still other people preferred the additional discipline of the FULL rules. The issue was finally settled by providing all three keywords so that the user could choose whichever approach she preferred.

Because SQL-89 specified the UNIQUE rules before anyone provided the additional alternatives, the UNIQUE alternative is the default, for compatibility. This specification explains why, if any of the values in the first argument of the MATCH predicate are null, a True value always returns — because UNIQUE is the default, and for UNIQUE, any null value means "don't perform the check."

Logical Connectives

Often, as a number of previous examples show, applying one condition in a query isn't enough to return the rows that you want from a table. In some cases, the rows must satisfy two or more conditions. In other cases, if a row satisfies any of two or more conditions, it qualifies for retrieval. On other occasions, you want to retrieve only rows that don't satisfy a specified condition. To meet these needs, SQL offers the logical connectives AND, OR, and NOT.

AND

If multiple conditions must all be True before you can retrieve a row, use the AND logical connective. Consider the following example:

```
SELECT INVOICE_NO, SALE_DATE, SALESPERSON, TOTAL_SALE
   FROM SALES
   WHERE SALE_DATE >= 05/01/97
      AND SALE_DATE <= 05/07/97 ;
```

The WHERE clause must meet the following two conditions:

- ✔ SALE_DATE must be greater than or equal to May 1, 1997.
- ✔ SALE_DATE must be less than or equal to May 7, 1997.

Only rows that record sales occurring during the week of May 1 meet both conditions. The query returns only these rows.

Notice that the AND connective is strictly logical. This restriction can sometimes be confusing, because people commonly use the word *and* with a looser meaning. Suppose, for example, that your boss says to you, "I'd like to see the sales for Ferguson and Ford." He said, "Ferguson and Ford," so you may write the following SQL query:

```
SELECT *
   FROM SALES
   WHERE SALESPERSON = 'Ferguson'
      AND SALESPERSON = 'Ford';
```

Well, don't take that answer back to your boss. The following query is more what he had in mind:

```
SELECT *
   FROM SALES
   WHERE SALESPERSON IN ('Ferguson', 'Ford') ;
```

OR

If any one of two or more conditions must be True to qualify a row for retrieval, use the OR logical connective, as in the following example:

```
SELECT INVOICE_NO, SALE_DATE, SALESPERSON, TOTAL_SALE
   FROM SALES
      WHERE SALESPERSON = 'Ford'
         OR TOTAL_SALE > 200 ;
```

This query retrieves all of Ford's sales, regardless of how large, as well as all sales of more than $200, regardless of who made the sales.

NOT

The NOT connective negates a condition. If the condition normally returns a True value, adding NOT causes the same condition to return a False value. If a condition normally returns a False value, adding NOT causes the condition to return a True value. Consider the following example:

```
SELECT INVOICE_NO, SALE_DATE, SALESPERSON, TOTAL_SALE
    FROM SALES
        WHERE NOT (SALESPERSON = 'Ford') ;
```

This query returns rows for all sales transactions that salespeople other than Ford completed.

In using AND, OR, or NOT, sometimes the scope of the connective isn't clear. To be safe, use parentheses to make sure that SQL applies the connective to the predicate you want. In the preceding example, the NOT connective applies to the entire predicate (SALESPERSON = 'Ford').

GROUP BY Clauses

If you retrieve rows from a table by using a SELECT statement, the rows return in the order in which they appear in their source table. Usually, this order isn't the most meaningful. Often, you want to group related rows together so that you can get a sense of the overall content of each group. The GROUP BY clause enables you to specify a column (or several columns) as a grouping column. The output table groups together all rows with an identical value in the grouping column.

Suppose that you're a sales manager and you want to look at sales performance for a particular week, with the information grouped by salesperson. The following example shows one way to do it:

```
SELECT INVOICE_NO, SALE_DATE, SALESPERSON, TOTAL_SALE
    FROM SALES
    WHERE SALE_DATE >= 05/01/97
        AND SALE_DATE <= 05/07/97
    GROUP BY SALESPERSON ;
```

The result of this example is as follows:

```
INVOICE_NO     SALE_DATE     SALESPERSON     TOTAL_SALE
----------     ---------     -----------     ----------
         1     05/01/97      Ferguson              1.98
         3     05/02/97      Ferguson            249.00
         5     05/03/97      Ferguson              4.95
         7     05/04/97      Ferguson             12.95
         4     05/02/97      Ford                  7.50
         9     05/07/97      Ford                  2.50
        10     05/07/97      Ford                  2.49
         2     05/01/97      Podolocek             3.50
         6     05/04/97      Podolocek             3.50
         8     05/05/97      Podolocek             5.00
```

The physical order of the SALES table is by INVOICE_NO, but the GROUP BY clause in the SELECT statement reorders the rows in the virtual table. Rows now group by salesperson, sorted in ascending alphabetical order. Some implementations give you the option of sorting the groups in descending alphabetical order. No reordering is possible within a group.

HAVING Clauses

A HAVING clause is a filter that places a further restriction on the virtual table that a GROUP BY clause creates. Just as a WHERE clause weeds out unwanted individual rows in a query, a HAVING clause weeds out unwanted groups.

Taking the example from the preceding section, say that the sales manager wants to focus on the performance of Ford and Podolocek, disregarding the performance of all the other salespeople. She can do so by adding a HAVING clause to the previous query, as follows:

```
SELECT INVOICE_NO, SALE_DATE, SALESPERSON, TOTAL_SALE
   FROM SALES
   WHERE SALE_DATE >= 05/01/97
      AND SALE_DATE <= 05/07/97
   GROUP BY SALESPERSON
   HAVING SALESPERSON = 'Ford'
      OR SALESPERSON = 'Podolocek' ;
```

The result is as follows:

```
INVOICE_NO   SALE_DATE   SALESPERSON   TOTAL_SALE
----------   ---------   -----------   ----------
         4    05/02/97   Ford              7.50
         9    05/07/97   Ford              2.50
        10    05/07/97   Ford              2.49
         2    05/01/97   Podolocek         3.50
         6    05/04/97   Podolocek         3.50
         8    05/05/97   Podolocek         5.00
```

The argument of the HAVING clause must contain a condition that compares the value of a grouping column to a constant value.

ORDER BY Clauses

Use the ORDER BY clause to display the output table of a query in either ascending or descending alphabetical order. While the GROUP BY clause gathers rows into groups and sorts the groups into alphabetical order, ORDER BY sorts individual rows. The ORDER BY clause must be the last clause that you specify in a query. If the query also contains a GROUP BY clause, the clause first arranges the output rows into groups. The ORDER BY clause then sorts the rows within each group. If you have no GROUP BY clause, the statement considers the entire table as a group and the ORDER BY clause sorts all its rows according to the column (or columns) that the ORDER BY clause specifies.

To illustrate this point, consider the data in the sales table. The SALES table contains columns for INVOICE_NO, SALE_DATE, SALESPERSON, and TOTAL_SALE. If you simply use the following example, you see all of the SALES data, but in an arbitrary order:

```
SELECT * FROM SALES ;
```

On one implementation this order may be the one in which you inserted the rows in the table, and on another implementation the order may be that of the most recent updates. The order can also change unexpectedly if anyone physically reorganizes the database. So most of the time, you want to specify the order in which you want the rows. You may, for example, want to see the rows in order by the SALE_DATE, as follows:

```
SELECT * FROM SALES ORDER BY SALE_DATE ;
```

This example returns all the rows in the SALES table, in order by SALE_DATE.

For rows with the same SALE_DATE, the default order depends on the implementation. You can, however, specify how to sort the rows that share the same SALE_DATE. You may, for example, want to see the SALES for each SALE_DATE in order by INVOICE_NO, as follows:

```
SELECT * FROM SALES ORDER BY SALE_DATE, INVOICE_NO ;
```

This example first orders the SALES by SALE_DATE; then, for each SALE_DATE, it orders the SALES by INVOICE_NO. Don't confuse that example, however, with the following query:

```
SELECT * FROM SALES ORDER BY INVOICE_NO, SALE_DATE ;
```

This query first orders the SALES by INVOICE_NO; then, for each different INVOICE_NO, the query orders the SALES by SALE_DATE.

The following query is another example of how SQL can return data:

```
SELECT * FROM SALES ORDER BY SALESPERSON, SALE_DATE ;
```

This example first orders by SALESPERSON and then by SALE_DATE. After you look at the data in that order, you may want to invert it, as follows:

```
SELECT * FROM SALES ORDER BY SALE_DATE, SALESPERSON ;
```

This example orders the rows first by SALE_DATE and then by SALESPERSON.

All these ordering examples are ascending (ASC), which is the default sort order. The last SELECT shows earlier SALES first and, within a given date, shows SALES for 'Adams' before 'Baker'. If you prefer descending (DESC) order, you can specify this order for one or more of the order columns, as follows:

```
SELECT * FROM SALES
ORDER BY SALE_DATE DESC, SALESPERSON ASC ;
```

This example specifies a descending order for sales date, showing the more recent sales first, but an ascending order for salespeople, putting them in normal alphabetical order.

Chapter 10

Relational Operators

● ●

In This Chapter

▶ Combining tables with similar structures

▶ Combining tables with different structures

▶ Deriving meaningful data from multiple tables

● ●

SQL was designed as a query language for relational databases. In chapters before this one, I present simple databases, and in most cases my examples have dealt with only one table. It's now time to grow up and put the *relational* in relational database. After all, relational databases are so named because they consist of multiple, related tables.

Because the data in a relational database is distributed across multiple tables, a query sometimes must draw data from more than one table. In fact, this is usually the case. SQL-92 has operators that combine data from multiple sources into a single result table. These are the UNION, INTERSECTION, and EXCEPT operators, as well as a family of JOIN operators. Each combines data from multiple tables in a different way.

UNION

The UNION operator is the SQL implementation of relational algebra's union operator. It is useful when you want to draw information from two or more tables that all have the same structure.

By *the same structure* I mean that the tables must all have the same number of columns, and that corresponding columns all have identical data types and lengths. When these criteria are met, the tables are union compatible. The union of two tables returns all the rows that appear in either table, eliminating duplicates.

I introduce a baseball statistics database in Chapter 9. Say that it contains two union-compatible tables named AMERICAN and NATIONAL. Both tables have three columns and corresponding columns are all of the same type. In fact, corresponding columns have identical column names (this is not required for union compatibility).

NATIONAL tells you the names and number of complete games pitched by National League pitchers. AMERICAN gives you the same information about pitchers in the American League. The UNION of the two tables gives you a virtual result table containing all the rows in the first table plus all the rows in the second table. For this example, I put just a few rows in each table to illustrate the operation.

```
SELECT * FROM NATIONAL
FIRST_NAME   LAST_NAME   COMPLETE_GAMES
----------   ---------   --------------

Sal          Maglie              11
Don          Newcombe             9
Sandy        Koufax              13
Don          Drysdale            12

SELECT * FROM AMERICAN

FIRST_NAME   LAST_NAME   COMPLETE_GAMES
----------   ---------   --------------
Whitey       Ford                12
Don          Larson              10
Bob          Turley               8
Allie        Reynolds            14

SELECT * FROM NATIONAL
UNION
SELECT * FROM AMERICAN

FIRST_NAME   LAST_NAME   COMPLETE_GAMES
----------   ---------   --------------
Allie        Reynolds            14
Bob          Turley               8
Don          Drysdale            12
Don          Larson              10
Don          Newcombe             9
Sal          Maglie              11
Sandy        Koufax              13
Whitey       Ford                12
```

I've been using the asterisk (*) as shorthand for all the columns in a table. This is fine most of the time, but it can get you into trouble when you are using relational operators in embedded or module-language SQL. What if you add one or more new columns to one table and not to another, or you add different columns to the two tables? The two tables are then no longer union compatible, and your program will be invalid the next time it is recompiled. Even if the same new columns are added to both tables, so that they are still union compatible, your program is probably not prepared to deal with this additional data. So, explicitly listing the columns that you want rather than relying on the "*" shorthand is generally a good idea. When you are entering ad hoc SQL from the console, the asterisk is probably all right because you can quickly display table structure to verify union compatibility if your query is not successful.

The UNION operation normally eliminates any duplicate rows that result from its operation. Most of the time, this is the desired behavior. Sometimes, however, you may want to preserve duplicate rows. On those occasions, use UNION ALL.

Referring to the example, suppose that "Bullet" Bob Turley had been traded in midseason from the New York Yankees in the American League to the Brooklyn Dodgers in the National League. Suppose further that during the season he pitched eight complete games for each team. The ordinary UNION displayed in the example throws away one of the two lines containing Turley's data. Whereas he seemingly pitched only eight complete games in the season, he in fact hurled a remarkable 16 complete games. The following query gives you the true facts:

```
SELECT * FROM NATIONAL
UNION ALL
SELECT * FROM AMERICAN
```

You can sometimes form the UNION of two tables even if they are not union compatible. If the columns you want in your result table are present and compatible in both tables, you can perform a UNION CORRESPONDING operation. Only the specified columns are considered, and they are the only columns displayed in the result table.

Baseball statisticians keep entirely different statistics on pitchers from the ones they keep on outfielders. Some information is common to both, however. In both cases, first name, last name, putouts, errors, and fielding percentage are recorded. Outfielders, of course, do not have a won/lost record, a saves record, or a number of other things that pertain only to pitching. You can still perform a UNION that takes data from the OUTFIELDER table and from the PITCHER table to give you some overall information about defensive skill.

```
SELECT *
   FROM OUTFIELDER
UNION CORRESPONDING
   (FIRST_NAME, LAST_NAME, PUTOUTS, ERRORS, FIELD_PCT)
SELECT *
   FROM PITCHER ;
```

The result table holds the first and last names of all the outfielders and pitchers, along with the number of putouts, errors, and the fielding percentage of each player. As with the simple UNION, duplicates are eliminated. Thus, if a player spent some time in the outfield as well as being a pitcher, the UNION CORRESPONDING operation loses some of his statistics.

Each column name in the list following the CORRESPONDING keyword must be a name that exists in both of the unioned tables. If you omit this list of names, an implicit list of all names that appear in both tables is used. This implicit list of names may change, however, when new columns are added to one or both of the tables, so explicitly listing the column names is better.

INTERSECT

The UNION operation produces a result table containing all rows that appear in any of the source tables. If you want only rows that appear in all the source tables, you can use the INTERSECT operation, which is the SQL implementation of relational algebra's intersect operation. I illustrate INTERSECT here by returning to the fantasy world in which Bob Turley was traded to the Dodgers in midseason.

```
SELECT * FROM NATIONAL;
FIRST_NAME   LAST_NAME   COMPLETE_GAMES
----------   ---------   --------------

Sal          Maglie             11
Don          Newcombe            9
Sandy        Koufax             13
Don          Drysdale           12
Bob          Turley              8

SELECT * FROM AMERICAN;
```

```
FIRST_NAME    LAST_NAME    COMPLETE_GAMES
----------    ---------    --------------
Whitey        Ford                     12
Don           Larson                   10
Bob           Turley                    8
Allie         Reynolds                 14
```

Only rows that appear on all source tables show up in the INTERSECT operation's result table.

```
SELECT *
    FROM NATIONAL
INTERSECT
SELECT *
    FROM AMERICAN;
FIRST_NAME    LAST_NAME    COMPLETE_GAMES
----------    ---------    --------------
Bob           Turley                    8
```

The result table tells us that Bob Turley was the only pitcher to throw the same number of complete games in both leagues. A rather obscure distinction for old Bullet Bob.

The ALL and CORRESPONDING keywords function in an INTERSECT operation the same way they do in a UNION operation. If you use ALL, duplicates are retained in the result table. If you use CORRESPONDING, the intersected tables need not be union compatible, although the corresponding columns need to have matching types and lengths.

Consider another example. A municipality keeps track of the pagers carried by police officers, fire fighters, street sweepers, and other city employees. A database table called PAGERS contains data on all pagers in active use. Another table named OUT, with an identical structure, contains data on all pagers that for one reason or another have been taken out of service. No pager should ever exist in both tables. With an INTERSECT operation, you can test to see whether such an unwanted duplication has occurred:

```
SELECT *
    FROM PAGERS
INTERSECT CORRESPONDING (PAGER_ID)
SELECT *
    FROM OUT
```

If the result table contains any rows at all, you know you have a problem. You should investigate any PAGER_ID entries that appear in the result table. The corresponding pager is either active or out of service. It cannot be both. After you detect the problem, you can perform a DELETE operation on one of the two tables to restore database integrity.

EXCEPT

The UNION operation acts on two source tables and returns all rows that appear in either table. The INTERSECT operation returns all rows that appear in both the first and the second table. In contrast, the EXCEPT operation returns all rows that appear in the first table that do not also appear in the second table.

Returning to the municipal pager database example, say that a group of pagers that had been declared out of service and returned to the vendor for repairs have now been fixed and placed back into service. The PAGERS table was updated to reflect the returned pagers, but for some reason the returned pagers were not removed from the OUT table as they should have been. You can display the Pager ID numbers of the pagers in the OUT table, with the reactivated ones eliminated, using an EXCEPT operation.

```
SELECT *
    FROM OUT
EXCEPT CORRESPONDING (PAGER_ID)
SELECT *
    FROM PAGERS;
```

This returns all the rows in the OUT table whose PAGER_ID is not also present in the PAGERS table.

JOINS

The UNION, INTERSECT, and EXCEPT operators are valuable in multitable databases in which the tables are union compatible. In many cases, however, you want to draw data from multiple tables that have very little in common. JOINs are powerful relational operators that combine data from multiple tables into a single result table. The source tables may have little (or even nothing) in common with each other.

SQL-92 supports a number of different types of JOINs. The best one to choose in a given situation depends on what result you are trying to achieve.

Basic JOIN

Any multitable query is a type of join. The source tables are joined in the sense that the result table includes information taken from all of the source tables. The simplest JOIN is a two-table SELECT that has no WHERE clause qualifiers. Every row of the first table is joined to every row of the second table. The result table is the Cartesian product of the two source tables. (I discuss the notion of Cartesian product in Chapter 9, in connection with the FROM clause.) The number of rows in the result table is equal to the number of rows in the first source table multiplied by the number of rows in the second source table.

For example, imagine that you are the personnel manager for a company and part of your job is to maintain records on the employees. Most of the data for an employee, such as home address and telephone number, is not particularly sensitive. Some data, however, such as current salary, should be available only to authorized personnel. To maintain security of the sensitive information, you keep it in a separate table that is password protected. Consider the following pair of tables:

```
EMPLOYEE                        COMPENSATION
--------                        ------------
EMP_ID                          EMPLOY
F_NAME                          SALARY
L_NAME                          BONUS
CITY
PHONE
```

Fill the tables with some sample data:

EMP_ID	F_NAME	L_NAME	CITY	PHONE
1	Whitey	Ford	Orange	555-1001
2	Don	Larson	Newark	555-3221
3	Sal	Maglie	Nutley	555-6905
4	Bob	Turley	Passaic	555-8908

EMPLOY	SALARY	BONUS
1	33000	10000
2	18000	2000
3	24000	5000
4	22000	7000

Create a virtual result table with the following query:

```
SELECT *
   FROM EMPLOYEE, COMPENSATION ;
```

producing:

EMP_ID	F_NAME	L_NAME	CITY	PHONE	EMPLOY	SALARY	BONUS
1	Whitey	Ford	Orange	555-1001	1	33000	10000
1	Whitey	Ford	Orange	555-1001	2	18000	2000
1	Whitey	Ford	Orange	555-1001	3	24000	5000
1	Whitey	Ford	Orange	555-1001	4	22000	7000
2	Don	Larson	Newark	555-3221	1	33000	10000
2	Don	Larson	Newark	555-3221	2	18000	2000
2	Don	Larson	Newark	555-3221	3	24000	5000
2	Don	Larson	Newark	555-3221	4	22000	7000
3	Sal	Maglie	Nutley	555-6905	1	33000	10000
3	Sal	Maglie	Nutley	555-6905	2	18000	2000
3	Sal	Maglie	Nutley	555-6905	3	24000	5000
3	Sal	Maglie	Nutley	555-6905	4	22000	7000
4	Bob	Turley	Passaic	555-8908	1	33000	10000
4	Bob	Turley	Passaic	555-8908	2	18000	2000
4	Bob	Turley	Passaic	555-8908	3	24000	5000
4	Bob	Turley	Passaic	555-8908	4	22000	7000

The result table, which is the Cartesian product of the EMPLOYEE and the COMPENSATION tables, contains considerable redundancy. Furthermore, it doesn't make much sense. It combines every row of EMPLOYEE with every row of COMPENSATION. Of these, the only rows that convey meaningful information are those in which the EMP_ID number that came from EMPLOYEE matches the EMPLOY number that came from COMPENSATION. In those rows, an employee's name and address are associated with that same employee's compensation.

When you are trying to get useful information out of a multitable database, the Cartesian product produced by a basic JOIN is almost never what you want. It is almost always the first step toward what you want, however. By applying constraints to the JOIN with a WHERE clause, you can filter out the unwanted rows. The most common JOIN that uses the WHERE clause filter is the equi-join.

Equi-join

An *equi-join* is a basic join with a WHERE clause containing a condition specifying that the value in one column in the first table must be equal to the value of a corresponding column in the second table. Applying an equi-join to the example tables from the previous section brings a much more meaningful result:

```
SELECT *
   FROM EMPLOYEE, COMPENSATION
   WHERE EMPLOYEE.EMP_ID = COMPENSATION.EMPLOY ;
```

producing:

EMP_ID	F_NAME	L_NAME	CITY	PHONE	EMPLOY	SALARY	BONUS
1	Whitey	Ford	Orange	555-1001	1	33000	10000
2	Don	Larson	Newark	555-3221	2	18000	2000
3	Sal	Maglie	Nutley	555-6905	3	24000	5000
4	Bob	Turley	Passaic	555-8908	4	22000	7000

In this result table, the salaries and bonuses on the right apply to the employees named on the left. The table still has some redundancy, however, because the EMP_ID column duplicates the EMPLOY column. You can fix this problem with a slight reformulation of the query.

```
SELECT EMPLOYEE.*,COMPENSATION.SALARY,COMPENSATION.BONUS
   FROM EMPLOYEE, COMPENSATION
   WHERE EMPLOYEE.EMP_ID = COMPENSATION.EMPLOY ;
```

This produces:

EMP_ID	F_NAME	L_NAME	CITY	PHONE	SALARY	BONUS
1	Whitey	Ford	Orange	555-1001	33000	10000
2	Don	Larson	Newark	555-3221	18000	2000
3	Sal	Maglie	Nutley	555-6905	24000	5000
4	Bob	Turley	Passaic	555-8908	22000	7000

This table tells you what you want to know and doesn't burden you with any extraneous data. The query was somewhat tedious to write, however. To avoid ambiguity, qualifying the column names with the names of the tables they came from is a good practice. Writing those table names repeatedly provides good exercise for the fingers but has no merit otherwise.

You can cut down on the amount of typing by using aliases (or correlation names). An *alias* is a short name that stands for a table name. If you use aliases in recasting the preceding query, it comes out like this:

```
SELECT E.*, C.SALARY, C.BONUS
   FROM EMPLOYEE E, COMPENSATION C
   WHERE E.EMP_ID = C.EMPLOY ;
```

In this example, E is the alias for EMPLOYEE and C is the alias for COMPENSATION. The alias is local to the statement it is in. After you declare an alias (in the FROM clause), you must use it throughout the statement. You can't use both the alias and the long form of the table name.

The reason for not mixing the long form of table names with aliases is to avoid confusion. Consider the following very confusing example:

```
SELECT T1.C, T2.C
    FROM T1 T2, T2 T1
    WHERE T1.C > T2.C ;
```

In this example, the alias for T1 is T2 and the alias for T2 is T1. Admittedly, this is not a very smart selection of aliases, but it is not forbidden by the rules. If you could mix aliases with long form table names, you couldn't tell which table was which.

The preceding example with aliases is equivalent to the following SELECT with no aliases:

```
SELECT T2.C, T1.C
    FROM T1 , T2
    WHERE T2.C > T1.C ;
```

SQL-92 allows you to join more than two tables; the maximum number varies from one implementation to another. The syntax is analogous to the two-table case:

```
SELECT E.*, C.SALARY, C.BONUS, Y.TOTAL_SALES
    FROM EMPLOYEE E, COMPENSATION C, YTD_SALES Y
    WHERE E.EMP_ID = C.EMPLOY
        AND C.EMPLOY = Y.EMPNO ;
```

This statement performs an equi-join on three tables, pulling data from corresponding rows of each one to produce a result table showing the salespeople's names, the amount of sales they are responsible for, and their compensation. The sales manager can quickly see whether compensation is in line with production.

You may wonder why storing a salesperson's year-to-date sales in a separate YTD_SALES table is desirable instead of keeping that data in the EMPLOYEE table. The reasons pertain to performance and reliability. The data in the EMPLOYEE table is relatively static. A person's name, address, and telephone number do not change very often. In contrast, the year-to-date sales change very frequently indeed (you hope). Because YTD_SALES has fewer columns than EMPLOYEE, it can be updated more quickly. If in the course of updating sales totals you do not touch the EMPLOYEE table, you lessen the risk of accidentally modifying EMPLOYEE information that should stay the same.

Cross join

SQL-92 introduces the new keyword CROSS JOIN for the basic join without a WHERE clause that previous versions of SQL supported. Thus,

```
SELECT *
FROM EMPLOYEE, COMPENSATION ;
```

can now also be written:

```
SELECT *
FROM EMPLOYEE CROSS JOIN COMPENSATION ;
```

The result is the Cartesian product (also called cross product) of the two source tables. As I said when discussing the basic JOIN, the CROSS JOIN rarely gives you the final result you want, but it can be useful as the first step in a chain of data manipulation operations that ultimately produce the desired result.

Natural join

The *natural join* is a special case of an equi-join. In the WHERE clause of an equi-join, a column from one source table is compared with a column of a second source table for equality. The two columns must be of the same type and length. This is all true of a natural join, but in addition, the columns being compared must have the same name. In fact, in a natural join, all columns in one table that have the same names as corresponding columns in the second table are compared for equality.

Imagine that the COMPENSATION table from the preceding example has columns EMP_ID, SALARY, and BONUS rather than EMPLOY, SALARY, and BONUS. In that case, you could perform a natural join of the COMPENSATION table with the EMPLOYEE table. The traditional JOIN syntax would look like this:

```
SELECT E.*, C.SALARY, C.BONUS
   FROM EMPLOYEE E, COMPENSATION C
   WHERE E.EMP_ID = C.EMP_ID ;
```

This is a natural join. SQL-92 introduces a new syntax for the same operation:

```
SELECT E.*, C.SALARY, C.BONUS
   FROM EMPLOYEE E NATURAL JOIN COMPENSATION C ;
```

Implementations that do not yet support the new syntax still successfully perform a natural join the old-fashioned way.

Condition join

A *condition join* is like an equi-join, except the condition being tested does not have to be equality (although it could be). It can be any well-formed predicate. If the condition is satisfied, the corresponding row becomes part of the result table. The syntax is a little different from what you have seen so far, in that the condition is contained in an ON clause rather than a WHERE clause.

As an example, say that a baseball statistician wants to know which National League pitchers have pitched exactly the same number of complete games as at least one American League pitcher. This is a job for an equi-join, which can also be expressed with condition join syntax.

```
SELECT *
   FROM NATIONAL JOIN AMERICAN
   ON NATIONAL.COMPLETE_GAMES = AMERICAN.COMPLETE_GAMES ;
```

The question now arises, "What National League pitchers have pitched a number of complete games that no American League pitcher has pitched? Inquiring minds want to know." The condition join that does the job is similar to the preceding one:

```
SELECT *
   FROM NATIONAL JOIN AMERICAN
   ON NATIONAL.COMPLETE_GAMES <> AMERICAN.COMPLETE_GAMES ;
```

Column-name join

The column-name join is like a natural join, but it is more flexible. In a natural join, all columns in the source tables that have the same name are compared against each other for equality. With the column-name join, you select which same-name columns are to be compared and which are not. You can choose them all if you wish, making the column-name join effectively a natural join. Or you may choose fewer than all same-name columns. In this way, you have a great degree of control over which cross product rows qualify to be placed into your result table.

Look at an everyday example. Say that you are a chess set manufacturer who has one inventory table to keep track of your stock of white pieces and another table to keep track of black pieces. The tables contain data as follows:

```
WHITE                              BLACK
-----                              -----

Piece   Quant  Wood         Piece   Quant  Wood
-----   -----  ----         -----   -----  ----
King     502   Oak          King     502   Ebony
Queen    398   Oak          Queen    397   Ebony
Rook    1020   Oak          Rook    1020   Ebony
Bishop   985   Oak          Bishop   985   Ebony
Knight   950   Oak          Knight   950   Ebony
Pawn     431   Oak          Pawn     453   Ebony
```

For each type of piece, the number of white pieces should match the number of black pieces. If they do not match, some chessmen are being lost or stolen and you need to tighten up security measures. A natural join compares all columns with the same name for equality. In this case, a result table with no rows is produced because no rows in the WOOD column in the WHITE table match any of the rows in the WOOD column in the BLACK table. This result table doesn't help you determine whether any merchandise is missing. Instead, do a column-name join that excludes the WOOD column from consideration. It can take the following form:

```
SELECT *
    FROM WHITE JOIN BLACK
    USING (PIECE, QUANT) ;
```

The result table shows only the rows for which the number of white pieces in stock equals the number of black pieces.

```
Piece   Quant  Wood         Piece   Quant  Wood
-----   -----  ----         -----   -----  ----
King     502   Oak          King     502   Ebony
Rook    1020   Oak          Rook    1020   Ebony
Bishop   985   Oak          Bishop   985   Ebony
Knight   950   Oak          Knight   950   Ebony
```

The shrewd person can deduce that Queen and Pawn are missing from the list, indicating a shortage somewhere for those piece types.

Inner join

By now you are probably getting the idea that joins are pretty esoteric and that it takes an uncommon level of spiritual discernment to deal with them adequately. You may have even heard of the mysterious inner join and speculated that it probably represents the very core or essence of relational operations. Well, ha! The joke is on you. There is nothing mysterious about inner joins at all. In fact, all the joins covered so far in this chapter are inner joins. I could have formulated the column-name join in the last example as an inner join by using the following syntax:

```
SELECT *
    FROM WHITE INNER JOIN BLACK
    USING (PIECE, QUANT) ;
```

The result is exactly the same.

The inner join is so named to distinguish it from the outer join. An inner join discards all rows from the result table that do not have corresponding rows in both source tables. An outer join preserves unmatched rows. That is the difference. There is nothing metaphysical about it.

Outer join

When you are joining two tables, the first one (call it the one on the left) may have rows that do not have matching counterparts in the second table (the one on the right). Conversely, the table on the right may have rows that do not have matching counterparts in the table on the left. If you perform an inner join on those tables, all the unmatched rows are excluded from the output. Outer joins do not exclude them. Actually, outer joins come in three types: the left outer join, the right outer join, and the full outer join.

Left outer join

In a query that includes a join, the left table is the one that precedes the keyword JOIN and the right table is the one that follows it. The left outer join preserves unmatched rows from the left table but discards unmatched rows from the right table.

To understand outer joins, consider a corporate database that maintains records of the company's employees, departments, and locations. The following contains the database's example data.

LOCATION

LOCATION_ID	CITY
1	Boston
3	Tampa
5	Chicago

DEPT

DEPT_ID	LOCATION_ID	NAME
21	1	Sales
24	1	Admin
27	5	Repair
29	5	Stock

EMPLOYEE

EMP_ID	DEPT_ID	NAME
61	24	Kirk
63	27	McCoy

Now suppose that you want to see all the data for all employees, including department and location. You get this with an equi-join:

```
SELECT *
    FROM LOCATION L, DEPT D, EMPLOYEE E
    WHERE L.LOCATION_ID = D.LOCATION_ID
        AND D.DEPT_ID = E.DEPT_ID ;
```

This statement produces the following result:

```
1      Boston    24    1     Admin    61    24    Kirk
5      Chicago   27    5     Repair   63    27    McCoy
```

This result table gives all the data for all the employees, including their location and department. The equi-join works because every employee has a location and a department.

Suppose now that you want the data on the locations, with the related department and employee data. This is a different problem because a location without any associated departments may exist. To get what you want, you have to use an outer join, as in the following example:

```
SELECT *
    FROM LOCATION L LEFT OUTER JOIN DEPT D
        ON (L.LOCATION_ID = D.LOCATION_ID)
    LEFT OUTER JOIN EMPLOYEE E
        ON (D.DEPT_ID = E.DEPT_ID);
```

This join pulls data from three tables. First, the LOCATION table is joined to
the DEPT table. The resulting table is then joined to the EMPLOYEE table.
Rows from the table on the left of the LEFT OUTER JOIN operator that have
no corresponding row in the table on the right are included in the result.
Thus, in the first join, all locations are included, even if no department
associated with them exists. In the second join, all departments are included, even if no employee associated with them exists. The result is as
follows:

1	Boston	24	1	Admin	61	24	Kirk
5	Chicago	27	5	Repair	63	27	McCoy
3	Tampa	NULL	NULL	NULL	NULL	NULL	NULL
5	Chicago	29	5	Stock	NULL	NULL	NULL
1	Boston	21	1	Sales	NULL	NULL	NULL

The first two rows are the same as the two result rows in the previous
example. The third row (3 Tampa) has nulls in the department and employee
columns because no departments are defined for Tampa and no employees
are stationed there. The fourth and fifth rows (5 Chicago and 1 Boston) have
data about the Stock and the Sales departments, but the employee columns
for these rows contain nulls because these two departments have no
employees. This outer join tells you everything that the equi-join told you
plus the following:

✔ All the company's locations, whether they have any departments or not

✔ All the company's departments, whether they have any employees
or not

The rows returned in the preceding example are not guaranteed to be in the
order you want. The order may vary from one implementation to the next.
To make sure that the rows returned are in the order you want, add an
ORDER BY clause to your SELECT statement, like this:

```
SELECT *
    FROM LOCATION L LEFT OUTER JOIN DEPT D
        ON (L.LOCATION_ID = D.LOCATION_ID)
    LEFT OUTER JOIN EMPLOYEE E
        ON (D.DEPT_ID = E.DEPT_ID)
    ORDER BY L.LOCATION_ID, D.DEPT_ID, E.EMP_ID;
```

The left outer join language may be abbreviated as LEFT JOIN because there is no such thing as a left inner join.

Right outer join

I bet you have figured out how the right outer join will behave. Right! The right outer join preserves unmatched rows from the right table but discards unmatched rows from the left table. You can use it on the same tables and get the same result by reversing the order in which you present tables to the join:

```
SELECT *
    FROM EMPLOYEE E RIGHT OUTER JOIN DEPT D
        ON (D.DEPT_ID = E.DEPT_ID)
    RIGHT OUTER JOIN LOCATION L
        ON (L.LOCATION_ID = D.LOCATION_ID) ;
```

In this formulation, the first join produces a table that contains all departments, whether they have an associated employee or not. The second join produces a table that contains all locations, whether they have an associated department or not.

The right outer join language can be abbreviated as RIGHT JOIN because there is no such thing as a right inner join.

Full outer join

The full outer join combines the functions of the left outer join and the right outer join. It retains the unmatched rows from both the left and the right tables. Consider the most general case of the company database used in the preceding examples. It could have:

✔ Locations that have no departments

✔ Departments with no locations

✔ Departments with no employees

✔ Employees with no departments

To show all locations, departments, and employees, regardless of whether they have corresponding rows in the other tables, use a full outer join in the following form:

```
SELECT *
    FROM LOCATION L FULL JOIN DEPT D
        ON (L.LOCATION_ID = D.LOCATION_ID)
    FULL JOIN EMPLOYEE E
        ON (D.DEPT_ID = E.DEPT_ID) ;
```

The full outer join language can be abbreviated as FULL JOIN because there is no such thing as a full inner join.

Union join

Unlike the other kinds of join, the union join makes no attempt to match a row from the left source table with any of the rows in the right source table. It creates a new virtual table that contains the union of all the columns in both source tables. In the virtual result table, the columns that came from the left source table contain all the rows that were in the left source table. For those rows, the columns that came from the right source table all have the null value. Similarly, the columns that came from the right source table contain all the rows that were in the right source table. For those rows, the columns that came from the left source table all have the null value. Thus, the table resulting from a union join contains all the columns of both source tables, and the number of rows that it contains is the sum of the number of rows in the two source tables.

The result of a union join by itself is not immediately useful in most cases. It produces a result table with a lot of nulls in it. You can use it, however, in conjunction with the COALESCE expression I discuss in Chapter 8 to give you useful information. Look at an example.

Suppose that you work for a company that designs and builds experimental rockets. You have several projects in the works. You also have several design engineers who have skills in multiple areas. As a manager, you want to know which employees, having which skills, have worked on which projects. Currently, this data is scattered among the EMPLOYEE table, the PROJECTS table, and the SKILLS table.

The EMPLOYEE table carries data about employees, and EMPLOYEE.EMP_ID is its primary key. The PROJECTS table has a row for each project that an employee has worked on. PROJECTS.EMP_ID is a foreign key referencing the EMPLOYEE table. The SKILLS table shows the expertise of each employee. SKILLS.EMP_ID is a foreign key referencing the EMPLOYEE table.

The EMPLOYEE table has exactly one row for each employee; the PROJECTS table and the SKILLS table have zero or more rows.

Tables 10-1, 10-2, and 10-3 show example data in the three tables.

Table 10-1	EMPLOYEE Table
EMP_ID	*NAME*
1	Ferguson
2	Frost
3	Toyon

Table 10-2	PROJECTS Table
PROJECT_NAME	*EMP_ID*
X-63 Structure	1
X-64 Structure	1
X-63 Guidance	2
X-64 Guidance	2
X-63 Telemetry	3
X-64 Telemetry	3

Table 10-3	SKILLS Table
SKILL	*EMP_ID*
Mechanical Design	1
Aerodynamics	1
Analog Design	2
Gyroscope Design	2
Digital Design	3
R/F Design	3

From the tables, you can see that Ferguson has worked on X-63 and X-64 structure design and has expertise in mechanical design and aerodynamic loading.

Now suppose that, as a manager, you want to see all the information about all the employees. You decide to apply an equi-join to the EMPLOYEE, PROJECTS, and SKILLS tables:

```
SELECT *
    FROM EMPLOYEE E, PROJECTS P, SKILLS S
    WHERE E.EMP_ID = P.EMP_ID
        AND E.EMP_ID = S.EMP_ID ;
```

You can express this same operation as an inner join using the following syntax:

```
SELECT *
    FROM EMPLOYEE E INNER JOIN PROJECTS P
        ON (E.EMP_ID = P.EMP_ID)
    INNER JOIN SKILLS S
        ON (E.EMP_ID = S.EMP_ID ;
```

Both formulations give the same result, as shown in Table 10-4.

Table 10-4			Result of Inner Join		
E.EMP_ID	*E.NAME*	*P.EMP_ID*	*PROJECT_NAME*	*S.EMP_ID*	*S.SKILL*
1	Ferguson	1	X-63 Structure	1	Mechanical Design
1	Ferguson	1	X-63 Structure	1	Aerodynamic Loading
1	Ferguson	1	X-64 Structure	1	Mechanical Design
1	Ferguson	1	X-64 Structure	1	Aerodynamic Loading
2	Frost	2	X-63 Guidance	2	Analog Design
2	Frost	2	X-63 Guidance	2	Gyroscope Design
2	Frost	2	X-64 Guidance	2	Analog Design
2	Frost	2	X-64 Guidance	2	Gyroscope Design
3	Toyon	3	X-63 Telemetry	3	Digital Design
3	Toyon	3	X-63 Telemetry	3	R/F Design
3	Toyon	3	X-64 Telemetry	3	Digital Design
3	Toyon	3	X-64 Telemetry	3	R/F Design

This arrangement of the data is not particularly enlightening. The employee ID numbers are triplicated and the projects and skills are duplicated for each employee. The inner joins are not well suited to answering this type of question. You can put the union join to work here, along with some strategically chosen SELECT statements, to produce a more suitable result. You begin with the basic union join:

```
SELECT *
    FROM EMPLOYEE E UNION JOIN PROJECTS P
        UNION JOIN SKILLS S ;
```

Notice that the union join has no ON clause. It does no filtering of the data and so does not need an ON clause. This statement produces the result shown in Table 10-5.

Table 10-5			Result of UNION JOIN		
E.EMP_ID	*E.NAME*	*P.EMP_ID*	*P.PROJECT_NAME*	*S.EMP_ID*	*S.SKILL*
1	Ferguson	NULL	NULL	NULL	NULL
NULL	NULL	1	X-63 Structure	NULL	NULL
NULL	NULL	1	X-64 Structure	NULL	NULL
NULL	NULL	NULL	NULL	1	Mechanical Design
NULL	NULL	NULL	NULL	1	Aerodynamic Loading
2	Frost	NULL	NULL	NULL	NULL
NULL	NULL	2	X-63 Guidance	NULL	NULL
NULL	NULL	2	X-64 Guidance	NULL	NULL
NULL	NULL	NULL	NULL	2	Analog Design
NULL	NULL	NULL	NULL	2	Gyroscope Design
3	Toyon	NULL	NULL	NULL	NULL
NULL	NULL	3	X-63 Telemetry	NULL	NULL
NULL	NULL	3	X-64 Telemetry	NULL	NULL
NULL	NULL	NULL	NULL	3	Digital Design
NULL	NULL	NULL	NULL		R/F Design

Each table has been extended to the right or left with nulls, and those null-extended rows have been unioned. The order of the rows is arbitrary and depends on the implementation. Now you can "massage" the data to put it in a more useful form.

First, notice that the table has three ID columns, only one of which is non-null in any row. You can improve the display by coalescing the ID columns. As I note in Chapter 8, the COALESCE expression takes on the value of the first nonnull value in a list of values. In the present case, it takes on the value of the only nonnull value in a column list.

```
SELECT COALESCE (E.EMP_ID, P.EMP_ID, S.EMP_ID) AS ID,
     E.NAME, P.PROJECT_NAME, S.SKILL
  FROM EMPLOYEE E UNION JOIN PROJECTS P
     UNION JOIN SKILLS S
  ORDER BY ID ;
```

The FROM clause is the same as in the previous example, but now you are coalescing the three EMP_ID columns into a single column named ID. You are also ordering the result by ID. Table 10-6 shows the result.

Table 10-6   Result of Union Join with COALESCE Expression

ID	E.NAME	P.PROJECT_NAME	S.SKILL
1	Ferguson	X-63 Structure	NULL
1	Ferguson	X-64 Structure	NULL
1	Ferguson	NULL	Mechanical Design
1	Ferguson	NULL	Aerodynamic Loading
2	Frost	X-63 Guidance	NULL
2	Frost	X-64 Guidance	NULL
2	Frost	NULL	Analog Design
2	Frost	NULL	Gyroscope Design
3	Toyon	X-63 Telemetry	NULL
3	Toyon	X-64 Telemetry	NULL
3	Toyon	NULL	Digital Design
3	Toyon	NULL	R/F Design

Each row in this result has data about a project or a skill, but not both. When you read the result, you have to first determine what type of information is in each row (project or skill). If the PROJECT_NAME column has a non-null value, the row names a project the employee has worked on. If the SKILL column is nonnull, the row names one of the employee's skills.

You can make the result a little clearer by adding another COALESCE to the SELECT statement, as follows:

```
SELECT COALESCE (E.EMP_ID, P.EMP_ID, S.EMP_ID) AS ID,
    E.NAME, COALESCE (P.TYPE, S.TYPE) AS TYPE,
    PROJECT_NAME, S.SKILL
  FROM EMPLOYEE E
    UNION JOIN (SELECT "Project" AS TYPE, P.*
                    FROM PROJECTS) P
    UNION JOIN (SELECT "Skill" AS TYPE, S.*
                    FROM SKILLS) S
  ORDER BY ID, TYPE ;
```

In the union join the PROJECTS table has been replaced with a nested SELECT that appends a column named P.TYPE with a constant value "Project" to the columns coming from the PROJECTS table. Similarly, the SKILLS table has been replaced with a nested SELECT that appends a column named S.TYPE with a constant value "Skill" to the columns coming from the SKILLS table. In each row, P.TYPE will either be null or will be "Project", and S.TYPE will either be null or "Skill".

The outer SELECT list specifies a COALESCE of those two TYPE columns into a single column named TYPE. You then specify TYPE in the ORDER BY clause, which sorts the rows that all have the same ID so that all projects are first, followed by all the skills. The result is shown in Table 10-7.

Table 10-7	Refined Result of Union Join with COALESCE Expressions			
ID	**E.NAME**	**TYPE**	**PROJECT_NAME**	**SKILL**
1	Ferguson	Project	X-63 Structure	NULL
1	Ferguson	Project	X-64 Structure	NULL
1	Ferguson	Skill	NULL	Mechanical Design
1	Ferguson	Skill	NULL	Aerodynamic Loading
2	Frost	Project	X-63 Guidance	NULL
2	Frost	Project	X-64 Guidance	NULL
2	Frost	Skill	NULL	Analog Design
2	Frost	Skill	NULL	Gyroscope Design
3	Toyon	Project	X-63 Telemetry	NULL
3	Toyon	Project	X-64 Telemetry	NULL
3	Toyon	Skill	NULL	Digital Design
3	Toyon	Skill	NULL	R/F Design

The result table now presents a very readable account of the project experience and the skill sets of all the employees in the EMPLOYEE table.

Considering the number of different JOIN operations available, relating data from different tables should not be a problem, regardless of the structure of those tables. Have faith that if the raw data exists in your database, SQL-92 has the means to get it out and display it in a meaningful form.

ON Versus WHERE

The function of the ON and WHERE clauses in the various types of joins is potentially confusing. Here are some facts that may help you keep things straight.

- The ON clause is part of the inner, left, right, and full joins. The cross join and union join don't have an ON clause because neither of them does any filtering of the data.

- The ON clause in an inner join is logically equivalent to a WHERE clause; the same condition could be specified either in the ON clause or a WHERE clause.

- The ON clauses in outer joins (left, right, and full joins) are very different from WHERE clauses. The WHERE clause simply filters the rows that are returned by the FROM clause. Rows that are rejected by the filter are simply not included in the result. The ON clause in an outer join first filters the rows of a cross product and then includes the rejected rows, extended with nulls.

Chapter 11

Delving Deep with Nested Queries

. . . .

In This Chapter

▶ Pulling data from multiple tables with a single SQL statement

▶ Finding data items by comparing a value taken from one table with a set of values taken from another table

▶ Finding data items by comparing a value taken from one table with a single value SELECTed from another table

▶ Finding data items by comparing a value taken from one table with all the corresponding values in another table

▶ Making queries that correlate rows in one table with corresponding rows in another table

▶ Determining which rows to update, delete, or insert by using a subquery

. . . .

*I*n Chapter 5, I point out that one of the best ways to protect the integrity of your data is to avoid modification anomalies by normalizing your database. *Normalization* involves breaking up a single table into multiple tables, each of which has a single theme. You don't want product information in the same table with customer information, even if the customers have bought products.

If you normalize a database properly, the data is scattered across multiple tables. Most queries that you want to make need to pull data from two or more tables. One way to do this, as I note in Chapter 10, is to use a JOIN operator or one of the other relational operators (UNION, INTERSECT, EXCEPT). The relational operators take information from multiple tables and combine it all into a single table. Different operators combine the data in different ways. Another way to pull data from two or more tables is to use a nested query.

In SQL, a *nested query* is one in which an outer enclosing statement contains within it a subquery. That subquery may itself serve as an enclosing statement for a lower-level subquery that is nested within it. No theoretical limit exists to the number of nesting levels that a nested query may have, although implementation-dependent practical limits do exist.

Subqueries are invariably SELECT statements, but the outermost enclosing statement could also be an INSERT, UPDATE, or DELETE.

Because a subquery can operate on a different table than the table operated on by its enclosing statement, nested queries give you another way to extract information from multiple tables.

For example, suppose that you want to query your corporate database to find all departments whose managers are more than 50 years old. With the JOINs I discuss in Chapter 10, you may use a query like this:

```
SELECT D.DEPTNO, D.NAME, E.NAME, E.AGE
   FROM DEPT D, EMPLOYEE E
   WHERE D.MANAGER_ID = E.ID AND E.AGE > 50 ;
```

D is the alias for the DEPT table and E is the alias for the EMPLOYEE table. The EMPLOYEE table has an ID column that is the primary key, and the DEPT table has a column MANAGER_ID that is the ID value of the employee who is the manager of the department. I use a simple join (the list of tables in the FROM clause) to pair related tables, and a WHERE clause to filter all rows except those that meet the criterion. Note that the SELECT statement's parameter list includes the DEPTNO and NAME columns from the DEPT table and the NAME and AGE columns from the EMPLOYEE table.

Next, suppose that you are interested in the same set of DEPT rows but you want only the columns from the DEPT table — in other words, you are interested in the departments whose manager is 50 or older, but you don't care who that manager is or exactly how old he or she is. You could then write the query with a *subquery* rather than a join:

```
SELECT D.DEPTNO, D.NAME
   FROM DEPT D
   WHERE EXISTS (SELECT * FROM EMPLOYEE E
                WHERE E.ID = D.MANAGERID AND E.AGE > 50) ;
```

This query has two new elements: the EXISTS keyword and the SELECT * in the WHERE clause of the first SELECT. The second SELECT is a subquery (or subselect), and the EXISTS keyword is one of several tools for use with a subquery that I describe in this chapter.

What Subqueries Do

Subqueries are located within the WHERE clause of their enclosing statement. Their function is to set the search conditions for the WHERE clause. Different kinds of subqueries produce different results. Some subqueries produce a list of values that is then used as input by the enclosing statement. Other subqueries produce a single value that the enclosing statement then evaluates with a comparison operator. A third kind of subquery returns a value of True or False.

Why Use a Subquery?

In many instances, you can accomplish the same result with a subquery as you can with a JOIN. In most cases, the complexity of the subquery syntax is comparable to the complexity of the corresponding JOIN operation. It comes down to a matter of personal preference. Some people find formulating a retrieval in terms of join operations easier, whereas others prefer nested queries. Sometimes, however, obtaining the results that you want is not possible by using JOIN. In those cases, you must either use a nested query or break the problem up into multiple SQL statements and execute them one at a time.

Nested Queries that Return Sets of Rows

To illustrate how a nested query returns a set of rows, suppose that you work for a system integrator of computer equipment. Your company, Zetec Corporation, assembles systems from components that you buy, and then it sells them to companies and government agencies. You keep track of your business with a relational database. The database consists of many tables, but right now you are concerned with only three of them: the PRODUCT table, the COMP_USED table, and the COMPONENT table. The PRODUCT table (shown in Table 11-1) contains a list of all your standard products. The COMPONENT table (shown in Table 11-2) lists components that go into your products, and the COMP_USED table (shown in Table 11-3) tracks which components go into each product. The tables are defined as follows:

Table 11-1		PRODUCT Table
Column	*Type*	*Constraints*
MODEL	Char (6)	NOT NULL, PRIMARY KEY
PRODNAME	Char (35)	
PRODDESC	Char (31)	
LISTPRICE	Numeric (9,2)	

Table 11-2	COMPONENT Table	
Column	*Type*	*Constraints*
COMPID	CHAR (6)	NOT NULL, PRIMARY KEY
COMPTYPE	CHAR (10)	
COMPDESC	CHAR (31)	

Table 11-3	COMP_USED Table	
Column	*Type*	*Constraints*
MODEL	CHAR (6)	FOREIGN KEY (for PRODUCT)
COMPID	CHAR (6)	FOREIGN KEY (for COMPONENT)

A component may be used in multiple products, and a product can contain multiple components (a many-to-many relationship). This situation could cause integrity problems. To circumvent the problems, the user creates the linking table COMP_USED to relate COMPONENT to PRODUCT. A component may appear in many COMP_USED rows, but each COMP_USED row references only one component (a one-to-many relationship). Similarly, a product may appear in many COMP_USED rows, but each COMP_USED row references only one product (another one-to-many relationship). By adding the linking table, a troublesome many-to-many relationship has been transformed into two relatively simple one-to-many relationships. This process of reducing the complexity of relationships is one example of normalization.

Subqueries introduced by the keyword IN

One form of a nested query compares a single value with the set of values returned by a SELECT. It uses the IN predicate with the following syntax:

```
SELECT column_list
   FROM table
   WHERE expression IN (subquery) ;
```

The expression in the WHERE clause evaluates to a value. If that value is IN the list returned by the subquery, then the WHERE clause returns a True value and the specified columns from the table row being processed are added to the result table. The subquery may reference the same table referenced by the outer query, or it may reference a different table.

I use Zetec's database to demonstrate this type of query. Assume that a shortage of computer monitors exists. When you run out of monitors, you can no longer deliver products that include them. You want to know which products are affected. Enter the following query:

```
SELECT MODEL
    FROM COMP_USED
    WHERE COMPID IN
        (SELECT COMPID
            FROM COMPONENT
            WHERE COMPTYPE = 'Monitor') ;
```

SQL processes the innermost query first, so it processes the COMPONENT table, returning the value of COMPID for every row where COMPTYPE is 'Monitor'. The result is a list of the ID numbers of all monitors. The outer query then compares the value of COMPID in every row in the COMP_USED table against the list. If the comparison is successful, the value of the MODEL column for that row is added to the outer SELECT's result table. The result is a list of all product models that include a monitor. The following shows what happens when you actually run the query.

```
MODEL
- - - - -
CX3000
CX3010
CX3020
MB3030
MX3020
MX3030
```

You now know which products will soon be out of stock. It's time to go to the sales force and tell them to slow down on promoting these particular products.

When you use this form of nested query, the subquery must specify a single column, and the data type of that column must match the data type of the argument preceding the IN keyword.

Subqueries introduced by the keyword NOT IN

Just as you can introduce a subquery with the IN keyword, you can do the opposite and introduce it with the NOT IN keyword. In fact, now is a great time for the management of Zetec to make such a query. By using the query in the preceding section, Zetec management learned what products not to sell. That is valuable information, but it doesn't pay the rent. What Zetec management really wants to know is what products to sell. Management wants to emphasize the sale of products that do not contain monitors. A nested query featuring a subquery introduced by the NOT IN keyword provides the requested information.

```
SELECT MODEL
    FROM COMP_USED
    WHERE MODEL NOT IN
        (SELECT MODEL
            FROM COMP_USED
            WHERE COMPID IN
                (SELECT COMPID
                    FROM COMPONENT
                    WHERE COMPTYPE = 'Monitor')) ;
```

This query produces the following result:

```
MODEL
-----
PX3040
PB3050
PX3040
PB3050
```

A couple of things are worth noting here. First, this query has two levels of nesting. The two subqueries are identical to the previous query statement. The only difference is that a new enclosing statement has been wrapped around them. The enclosing statement takes the list of products that contain monitors and applies a SELECT introduced by the NOT IN keyword to that list. The result is another list that contains all product models except those that have monitors.

Second, the result table does contain duplicates. The duplication occurs because a product containing several components that are not monitors has a row in the COMP_USED table for each component. The query creates an entry in the result table for each of those rows.

In my example, the number of rows is not much of a problem because the result table is short. In the real world, however, such a result table may have hundreds or thousands of rows. To avoid confusion, you need to eliminate the duplicates. You can do so easily by adding the DISTINCT keyword to the query. Only rows that are distinct (different) from all previously retrieved rows are then added to the result table.

```
SELECT DISTINCT MODEL
   FROM COMP_USED
   WHERE MODEL NOT IN
      (SELECT MODEL
         FROM COMP_USED
         WHERE COMPID IN
            (SELECT COMPID
               FROM COMPONENT
               WHERE COMPTYPE = 'Monitor')) ;
```

As expected, the result is as follows:

```
MODEL
- - - -
PX3040
PB3050
```

Nested Queries that Return a Single Value

You can introduce a subquery with one of the six comparison operators (=, <>, <, <=, >, >=), and doing so is often useful. In such a case, the expression preceding the operator evaluates to a single value and the subquery following the operator must also evaluate to a single value. An exception is the case of the quantified comparison operator, which is a comparison operator followed by a quantifier (ANY, SOME, or ALL).

To illustrate a case in which a subquery returns a single value, look at another piece of Zetec Corporation's database. It contains a CUSTOMER table that holds information about the companies that buy Zetec products. It also contains a CONTACT table that holds personal data about individuals at each of Zetec's customer organizations. The tables are structured as shown in Tables 11-4 and 11-5.

Table 11-4	**CUSTOMER Table**	
Column	*Type*	*Constraints*
CUSTID	INTEGER	NOT NULL, PRIMARY KEY
COMPANY	CHAR (40)	

(continued)

Table 11-4 *(continued)*

Column	Type	Constraints
CUSTADDRESS	CHAR (30)	
CUSTCITY	CHAR (20)	
CUSTSTATE	CHAR (2)	
CUSTZIP	CHAR (10)	
CUSTPHONE	CHAR (12)	
MODLEVEL	INTEGER	

Table 11-5   CONTACT Table

Column	Type	Constraints
CUSTID	INTEGER	(Foreign Key)
CONTFNAME	CHAR (10)	
CONTLNAME	CHAR (16)	
CONTPHONE	CHAR (12)	
CONTINFO	CHAR (50)	

Say that you want to look at the contact information for Olympic Sales, but you don't remember that company's CUSTID. Use a nested query like this one to recover the information you want:

```
SELECT *
   FROM CONTACT
      WHERE CONTID =
         (SELECT CONTID
            FROM CUSTOMER
               WHERE COMPANY = 'Olympic Sales') ;
```

The result looks something like this:

```
CUSTID CONTFNAME  CONTLNAME     CONTPHONE    CONTINFO
------ ---------  ---------     ---------    --------
   118 Jerry      Attwater      505-876-3456 Will play
                                             major role in
                                             coordinating
                                             the
                                             information
                                             superhighway.
```

You can now call Jerry at Olympic and tell him about this month's special sale on fax/modems.

When you use a subquery in an "=" comparison, the SELECT list of the subquery must specify a single column (CONTID in the example). When the subquery is executed, it must return a single row in order to have a single value for the comparison.

In this example, I assume that the CUSTOMER table has only one row with a COMPANY value of 'Olympic Sales'. If the CREATE TABLE statement for CUSTOMER specified a UNIQUE constraint for COMPANY, such a statement guarantees that the subquery in the preceding example returns a single value (or no value). Subqueries like the one in the example, however, are commonly used on columns that are not specified to be UNIQUE. In such cases, you are relying on some other reasons for believing that the column has no duplicates.

If it turns out that more than one CUSTOMER has a value of 'Olympic Sales' in the COMPANY column (perhaps in different states), then the subquery raises an error.

On the other hand, if no CUSTOMER with such a company name exists, then the subquery is treated as if it were null, and the comparison becomes "unknown." In this case, the WHERE clause returns no row (because it returns only rows with the condition True and filters rows with condition False or "unknown"). This would probably happen, for example, if someone misspelled the COMPANY as 'Olumpic Sales'.

Although the equals operator (=) may be the most common, you can use any of the other five comparison operators in a similar structure. For every row in the table specified in the enclosing statement's FROM clause, the single value returned by the subquery is compared to the expression in the enclosing statement's WHERE clause. If the comparison gives a True value, a row is added to the result table.

You can guarantee that a subquery will return a single value if you include an aggregate function in it. Aggregate functions always return a single value. (Aggregate functions are described in Chapter 3.) Of course, this way of returning a single value is helpful only if you want the result of an aggregate function. Here's an example.

Say that you are a Zetec salesperson and, because of bills coming due, you need to earn a big commission check this week. You decide that the best way to do that is to concentrate on selling Zetec's most expensive product. You can find out what that product is with a nested query.

```
SELECT MODEL, PRODNAME, LISTPRICE
    FROM PRODUCT
        WHERE LISTPRICE =
            (SELECT MAX(LISTPRICE)
                FROM PRODUCT) ;
```

This is an example of a nested query where both the subquery and the enclosing statement operate on the same table. The subquery returns a single value: the maximum list price in the PRODUCT table. The outer query retrieves all rows from the PRODUCT table that have that list price.

The next example shows a comparison subquery that uses a comparison operator other than =.

```
SELECT MODEL, PRODNAME, LISTPRICE
    FROM PRODUCT
        WHERE LISTPRICE <
            (SELECT AVG(LISTPRICE)
                FROM PRODUCT) ;
```

The subquery returns a single value: the average list price in the PRODUCT table. The outer query retrieves all rows from the PRODUCT table that have a list price less than the average list price.

In the original SQL standard and in most current products, a comparison could have only one subquery and it had to be on the right side of the comparison. SQL-92 allows either or both operands of the comparison to be subqueries.

The ALL, SOME, and ANY Quantifiers

Another way to make sure that a subquery returns a single value is to introduce it with a quantified comparison operator. The universal quantifier ALL and the existential quantifiers SOME and ANY, when combined with a comparison operator, process the list returned by a subquery, reducing it to a single value.

How these quantifiers affect a comparison is best described through examples. Here's another look at the baseball pitchers complete game database from Chapter 10.

The contents of the two tables are given by the following two queries:

```
SELECT * FROM NATIONAL

FIRST_NAME    LAST_NAME    COMPLETE_GAMES
---------     ---------    --------------
Sal           Maglie                   11
Don           Newcombe                  9
Sandy         Koufax                   13
Don           Drysdale                 12
Bob           Turley                    8

SELECT * FROM AMERICAN

FIRST_NAME    LAST_NAME    COMPLETE_GAMES
---------     ---------    --------------
Whitey        Ford                     12
Don           Larson                   10
Bob           Turley                    8
Allie         Reynolds                 14
```

The theory is that the pitchers with the most complete games should be in the American league, because of the presence of designated hitters in that league. One way to verify this theory is to build a query that returns all American League pitchers who have thrown more complete games than all the National League pitchers. The query could be formulated as follows:

```
SELECT *
    FROM AMERICAN
    WHERE COMPLETE_GAMES > ALL
        (SELECT COMPLETE_GAMES FROM NATIONAL) ;
```

This is the result:

```
FIRST_NAME    LAST_NAME    COMPLETE_GAMES
---------     --------     --------------
              Allie        Reynolds                 14
```

The subquery (SELECT COMPLETE_GAMES FROM NATIONAL) returns the values in the COMPLETE_GAMES column for all National League pitchers. The > ALL quantifier says to return only those values of COMPLETE_GAMES in the AMERICAN table that are greater than each of the values returned by the subquery. This condition translates into "greater than the highest value returned by the subquery." In this case, the highest value returned by the subquery is 13 (Sandy Koufax). The only row in the American table higher than that is Allie Reynolds' record, with 14 complete games.

What if your initial assumption was wrong? What if the major league leader in complete games was a National League pitcher, in spite of the fact that the NL has no designated hitter? If that were the case, the query

```
SELECT *
    FROM AMERICAN
    WHERE COMPLETE_GAMES > ALL
        (SELECT COMPLETE_GAMES FROM NATIONAL) ;
```

returns a warning stating that no rows satisfy the conditions of the query, meaning that no American League pitcher has thrown more complete games than the pitcher who has thrown the most complete games in the National League.

Nested Queries that Are an Existence Test

A query returns data from all table rows that satisfy the conditions of the query. Sometimes many rows are returned; sometimes only one. Sometimes none of the rows in the table satisfy the conditions and no rows are returned. You can use the EXISTS and NOT EXISTS predicates to introduce a subquery. That structure tells you whether any rows in the table located in the subquery's FROM clause meet the conditions in its WHERE clause.

Subqueries introduced with EXISTS and NOT EXISTS are fundamentally different from the subqueries looked at so far in this chapter. In all the previous cases, SQL first executes the subquery and then applies the result of that operation to the enclosing statement. EXISTS and NOT EXISTS subqueries are examples of correlated subqueries.

A *correlated subquery* first finds the table and row specified by the enclosing statement and then executes the subquery on the row in the subquery's table that correlates with the current row of the enclosing statement's table.

The subquery either returns one or more rows or it returns none. If it returns at least one row, the EXISTS predicate succeeds, and the enclosing statement performs its action. In the same circumstances, the NOT EXISTS predicate fails and the enclosing statement does not perform its action. After one row of the enclosing statement's table is processed, the same operation is performed on the next row. This action is repeated until every row in the enclosing statement's table has been processed.

EXISTS

Say that you are a salesperson for Zetec Corporation and you want to call your primary contact people at all Zetec's customers in California. Try the following query:

```
SELECT *
   FROM CONTACT
   WHERE EXISTS
     (SELECT *
        FROM CUSTOMER
        WHERE CUSTSTATE = 'CA'
          AND CONTACT.CUSTID = CUSTOMER.CUSTID) ;
```

Notice the reference to CONTACT.CUSTID, which is referencing a column from the outer query and comparing it with a column, CUSTOMER.CUSTID from the inner query. That's the way such queries are defined and evaluated: For each candidate row of the outer query, you evaluate the inner query, by using the CUSTID value from the current CONTACT row of the outer query for the evaluation of the inner query.

The CUSTID column links the CONTACT table to the CUSTOMER table. SQL looks at the first record in the CONTACT table, finds the row in the CUSTOMER table that has the same CUSTID, and checks that row's CUSTSTATE field. If CUSTOMER.CUSTSTATE = 'CA', the current CONTACT row is added to the result table. The next CONTACT record is then processed in the same way, and so on until the entire CONTACT table has been processed.

NOT EXISTS

In the previous example, the Zetec salesperson wanted to know the names and numbers of the contact people of all the customers located in California. Imagine that a second salesperson is responsible for all of the U.S. except California. She can retrieve her contact people by using NOT EXISTS in a query similar to the preceding one:

```
SELECT *
   FROM CONTACT
   WHERE NOT EXISTS
     (SELECT *
        FROM CUSTOMER
        WHERE CUSTSTATE = 'CA'
          AND CONTACT.CUSTID = CUSTOMER.CUSTID) ;
```

Every row in CONTACT for which the subquery does not return a row is added to the result table.

Other Correlated Subqueries

As noted in a previous section of this chapter, subqueries introduced by IN or by a comparison operator need not be correlated queries, but they can be.

Subqueries introduced with IN

One section earlier in this chapter deals with how a noncorrelated subquery can be used with the IN predicate. To show how a correlated subquery may use the IN predicate, you can ask the same question that came up with the EXISTS predicate. "What are the names and phone numbers of the contacts at all of Zetec's customers in California?" You can answer this question with a correlated IN subquery:

```
SELECT *
    FROM CONTACT
    WHERE 'CA' IN
        (SELECT CUSTSTATE
            FROM CUSTOMER
            WHERE CONTACT.CUSTID = CUSTOMER.CUSTID) ;
```

The statement is evaluated for each record in the CONTACT table. If, for that record, the CUSTID numbers in CONTACT and CUSTOMER match, the value of CUSTOMER.CUSTSTATE is compared to 'CA'. The result of the subquery is a list that contains at most one element. If that one element is 'CA', the WHERE clause of the enclosing statement is satisfied and a row is added to the query's result table.

Subqueries introduced with comparison operators

A correlated subquery can also be introduced by one of the six comparison operators. A look at another aspect of Zetec's database system illustrates how.

Zetec pays bonuses to its salespeople based on their total monthly sales volume. The higher the volume, the higher the bonus percentage. The bonus percentage list is kept in a table named BONUSRATE:

MIN_AMOUNT	MAX_AMOUNT	BONUS_PCT
0.00	24999.99	0.
25000.00	49999.99	0.001
50000.00	99999.99	0.002
100000.00	249999.99	0.003
250000.00	499999.99	0.004
500000.00	749999.99	0.005
750000.00	999999.99	0.006

If a person's monthly sales are between $100,000.00 and $249,999.99, the bonus is 0.3 percent of sales.

Sales are recorded in a transaction master table named TRANSMASTER:

```
TRANSMASTER
-----------

Column          Type        Constraints
------          ----        -----------
TRANSID         INTEGER     NOT NULL, PRIMARY KEY
CUSTID          INTEGER     FOREIGN KEY
EMPID           INTEGER     FOREIGN KEY
TRANSDATE       DATE
NET_AMOUNT      NUMERIC
FREIGHT         NUMERIC
TAX             NUMERIC
INVOICETOTAL    NUMERIC
```

Sales bonuses are based on the sum of the NET_AMOUNT field for all of a person's transactions in the month. You can find any particular person's bonus rate with a correlated subquery that uses comparison operators:

```
SELECT BONUS_PCT
    FROM BONUSRATE
        WHERE MIN_AMOUNT <
            (SELECT SUM (NET_AMOUNT)
                FROM TRANSMASTER
                    WHERE EMPID = 133)
            AND MAX_AMOUNT >
                (SELECT SUM (NET_AMOUNT)
                    FROM TRANSMASTER
                        WHERE EMPID = 133) ;
```

This query is interesting in that it contains two subqueries, making use of the logical connective AND. The subqueries use the SUM aggregate operator, which returns a single value — the total monthly sales of employee number 133. That value is then compared against the MIN_AMOUNT and the MAX_AMOUNT columns in the BONUSRATE table, producing the bonus rate for that employee.

If you had not known the EMPID but had known the name of the person in question, you could have arrived at the same answer with a slightly more complex query:

```
SELECT BONUS_PCT
   FROM BONUSRATE
      WHERE MIN_AMOUNT <
         (SELECT SUM (NET_AMOUNT)
            FROM TRANSMASTER
               WHERE EMPID =
                  (SELECT EMPID
                      FROM EMPLOYEE
                         WHERE EMPLNAME = 'Coffin'))
         AND MAX_AMOUNT >
            (SELECT SUM (NET_AMOUNT)
               FROM TRANSMASTER
                  WHERE EMPID =
                     (SELECT EMPID
                         FROM EMPLOYEE
                            WHERE EMPLNAME = 'Coffin'));
```

This example uses subqueries nested within subqueries, which in turn are nested within an enclosing query, to arrive at the bonus rate for the employee named Coffin. This structure works only if you know for sure that the company has one and only one employee whose last name is Coffin. If more than one employee is named Coffin, all the Coffins' sales are added together, and the BONUS_PCT calculated is too high. If you know that more than one employee is named Coffin, you can add terms to the WHERE clause of the innermost subquery until you are sure that only one row of the EMPLOYEE table is selected.

Subqueries in a HAVING clause

You can have a correlated subquery in a HAVING clause just as you can in a WHERE clause. As I mention in Chapter 9, a HAVING clause is normally preceded by a GROUP BY clause. The HAVING clause acts as a filter to restrict the groups created by the GROUP BY clause. Groups that do not satisfy the condition of the HAVING clause are not included in the result. When used in this way, the HAVING clause is evaluated for each group created by the GROUP BY clause. In the absence of a GROUP BY clause, the HAVING clause is evaluated for the set of rows passed by the WHERE clause, which is considered to be a single group. If neither a WHERE clause nor a GROUP BY clause is present, the HAVING clause is evaluated for the entire table:

```
SELECT TM1.EMPID
   FROM TRANSMASTER TM1
      GROUP BY TM1.EMPID
      HAVING MAX (TM1.NET_AMOUNT) >= ALL
         (SELECT 2 * AVG (TM2.NET_AMOUNT)
            FROM TRANSMASTER TM2
            WHERE TM1.EMPID <> TM2.EMPID) ;
```

This query uses two aliases for the same table, allowing you to retrieve the employee ID number of all salespeople who had a sale at least twice the average sale of all the other salespeople.

The query works as follows:

1. The outer query groups TRANSMASTER rows by the EMPID. This is done with the SELECT, FROM, and GROUP BY clauses.

2. The HAVING clause filters these groups. For each group, it calculates the MAX of the NET_AMOUNT column for the rows in that group.

3. The inner query evaluates twice the average NET_AMOUNT from all rows of TRANSMASTER whose EMPID is different from the EMPID of the current group of the outer query. Note that in the last line you need to reference two different EMPID values, so in the FROM clauses of the outer and inner queries you use different aliases for TRANSMASTER.

4. You then use those aliases in the comparison of the last line of the query to indicate that you are referencing both the EMPID from the current row of the inner subquery (TM2.EMPID) and the EMPID from the current group of the outer subquery (TM1.EMPID).

UPDATE, DELETE, and INSERT Statements

In addition to SELECT statements, UPDATE, DELETE, and INSERT statements can also include WHERE clauses. Those WHERE clauses can contain subqueries in the same way that SELECT statement WHERE clauses do.

For example, Zetec has just signed a volume purchase agreement with Olympic Sales and wants to retroactively provide a 10 percent credit to Olympic for all its purchases in the last month. You can provide this credit with a single UPDATE statement:

```
UPDATE TRANSMASTER
    SET NET_AMOUNT = NET_AMOUNT * 0.9
    WHERE CUSTID =
        (SELECT CUSTID
            FROM CUSTOMER
            WHERE COMPANY = 'Olympic Sales') ;
```

You can also have a correlated subquery within an UPDATE statement. Suppose that the CUSTOMER table has a column LAST_MONTHS_MAX, and that Zetec wants to give such a credit for all purchases that exceed LAST_MONTHS_MAX for the customer:

```
UPDATE TRANSMASTER TM
    SET NET_AMOUNT = NET_AMOUNT * 0.9
    WHERE NET_AMOUNT >
        (SELECT LAST_MONTHS_MAX
            FROM CUSTOMER C
            WHERE C.CUSTID = TM.CUSTID) ;
```

Note that this subquery is correlated: The WHERE clause in the last line references both the CUSTID of the CUSTOMER row from the subquery as well as the CUSTID of the current TRANSMASTER row that is a candidate for being updated.

A subquery in an UPDATE statement can also reference the table that is being updated. Suppose that Zetec wants to give a 10 percent credit to customers whose purchases have exceeded $10,000:

```
UPDATE TRANSMASTER TM1
    SET NET_AMOUNT = NET_AMOUNT * 0.9
    WHERE 10000 < (SELECT SUM(NET_AMOUNT)
        FROM TRANSMASTER TM2
            WHERE TM1.CUSTID = TM2.CUSTID);
```

The inner subquery is calculating the SUM of the NET_AMOUNT column for all TRANSMASTER rows for the same customer. But what does this mean? Suppose that customer with CUSTID 37 has four rows in TRANSMASTER with the following values for NET_AMOUNT: 3000, 5000, 2000, and 1000. The SUM of NET_AMOUNT for this CUSTID is 11000.

Note that the order in which the UPDATE statement processes the rows is implementation defined and is generally not predictable. It may be the same each day or it may differ depending on the way that the rows are actually arranged on the disk. Assume that the implementation processes the rows for this CUSTID in the following order: first the TRANSMASTER with NET_AMOUNT 3000; then the one with NET_AMOUNT 5000; and so on. After the first three rows for CUSTID 37 have been updated, their NET_AMOUNT values will be 2700 (90 percent of 3000), 4500 (90 percent of 5000), and 1800 (90 percent of 2000). Then when you process the last TRANSMASTER row for CUSTID 37, whose NET_AMOUNT is 1000, the SUM returned by the subquery would seem to be 10000, that is, the SUM of the new NET_AMOUNT values of the first three rows for CUSTID 37, and the old NET_AMOUNT value of the last row for CUSTID 37. Thus it would seem that last row for CUSTID 37 won't be updated, because the comparison with that SUM is not True (10000 is not less than SELECT SUM(NET_AMOUNT). But that is not the way the UPDATE statement is defined when a subquery references the table that is being updated. The rule is that all evaluations of subqueries in an UPDATE statement reference the old values of the table that is being updated. Thus, in the preceding UPDATE for CUSTID 37, the subquery will return 11000 — that is, the original SUM.

As you can see, the subquery in a WHERE clause operates exactly the same, whether it is in a SELECT statement or an UPDATE statement. The same holds true for DELETE and INSERT. To delete all of Olympic's transactions, you can use this statement:

```
DELETE TRANSMASTER
   WHERE CUSTID =
      (SELECT CUSTID
          FROM CUSTOMER
          WHERE COMPANY = 'Olympic Sales') ;
```

As with UPDATE, DELETE subqueries can also be correlated and can also reference the table being deleted. The rules are similar to the rules for UPDATE subqueries. Consider a case in which you want to delete all rows from TRANSMASTER for customers whose total NET_AMOUNT is larger than $10,000:

```
DELETE TRANSMASTER TM1
   WHERE 10000 < (SELECT SUM(NET_AMOUNT)
      FROM TRANSMASTER TM2
          WHERE TM1.CUSTID = TM2.CUSTID) ;
```

This deletes all rows from TRANSMASTER that have CUSTID 37, as well as any other customers with purchases exceeding $10,000. All references to TRANSMASTER in the subquery denote the contents of TRANSMASTER before any deletes by the current statement. So, even when you are deleting the last TRANSMASTER row for CUSTID 37, the subquery is evaluated on the original TRANSMASTER table, and returns 11000.

Whenever you update, delete, or insert database records, you take a chance that you will change one table's data in such a way that it becomes inconsistent with one or more other tables in the database. Such an inconsistency is called a *modification anomaly,* a problem I discuss in Chapter 5. Specifically, if you delete TRANSMASTER records and you have a TRANSDETAIL table that depends on TRANSMASTER, you must delete the corresponding records from TRANSDETAIL, too. This operation is called a *cascading delete,* because the deletion of a parent record must cascade to all of its associated child records. Otherwise, the undeleted child records become orphans. In this case, they would be invoice detail lines that are in limbo because they are no longer connected to an invoice record.

The INSERT command can include a SELECT clause. A typical use for this is in filling up "snapshot" tables. If you want to have a table with the contents of TRANSMASTER as of May 27, you can do it as follows:

```
CREATE TABLE TRANSMASTER_0527
   (TRANSID INTEGER, TRANSDATE DATE,
   ...) ;
INSERT INTO TRANSMASTER_0527
   (SELECT * FROM TRANSMASTER
            WHERE TRANSDATE = 1997-05-27) ;
```

Or you may want to save rows only for large NET_AMOUNTs:

```
INSERT INTO TRANSMASTER_0527
   (SELECT * FROM TRANSMASTER TM
   WHERE TM.NET_AMOUNT > 10000
            AND TRANSDATE = 1997-05-27) ;
```

Part IV

Controlling Operations

The 5th Wave   By Rich Tennant

"DO YOU WANT ME TO CALL THE COMPANY AND HAVE THEM SEND ANOTHER REVIEW COPY OF THEIR DATABASE SOFTWARE SYSTEM, OR DO YOU KNOW WHAT YOU'RE GOING TO WRITE?"

In this part . . .

After you create a database and fill it with data, you want to protect your new database from harm or misuse. In this part, I discuss in detail SQL's tools for maintaining the safety and integrity of your data. SQL's Data Control Language (DCL) enables you to protect your data from misuse by selectively granting or denying access to the data. You can protect your database from other threats — such as interference from simultaneous access by multiple users — by using SQL's transaction-processing facilities. You can use constraints to help keep users from entering bad data in the first place. SQL can't defend you against bad application design. If you take full advantage of the tools that SQL provides, however, using SQL *can* protect your data from most problems.

Chapter 12
Providing Database Security

● ●

● ●

*I*n preceding chapters, I discuss those parts of SQL that create databases and then manipulate the data in those databases. In Chapter 3, I briefly mention SQL's facilities for protecting databases from harm or misuse. In this chapter, I go into more depth on the subject of misuse. The person in charge of a database has the power to determine who can access that database as well as the level of access that a user receives. That person can selectively grant and revoke access to certain aspects of the system and can even grant to and revoke from someone else the right to grant and revoke such access privileges. If you use them correctly, the security tools that SQL provides are powerful protectors of important data. Used incorrectly, these same tools can act as frustrating impediments to the efforts of legitimate users trying to do their jobs.

Databases often contain sensitive information that you shouldn't make available to everyone. SQL provides different levels of access — from complete to none, with several levels in between. By controlling exactly which operations each authorized user can perform, the person in charge of a database can make sure that people have all the data they need to do their jobs but can't access other parts of the database, which they have no business seeing or changing.

It's a tough job, but . . .

You're probably wondering how you can become a DBA (DataBase Administrator) and accrue for yourself all the status and admiration that goes with the title. The obvious answer is to kiss up to the boss in the hope that he awards you this plum assignment. Demonstrating competence, integrity, and reliability in the performance of your everyday duties may even help. (Actually, the key requisite is that you're sucker enough to take the job. I was kidding when I said that stuff about status and admiration. Mostly, the DBA gets the blame if anything goes wrong with the database — and invariably, sooner or later, something does.)

The SQL Data Control Language (DCL)

Those SQL statements that you use to create databases form a group known as the *Data Definition Language (DDL)*. After you create a database, you can use another set of SQL statements, known collectively as the *Data Manipulation Language (DML),* to add, change, and remove data from the database. SQL includes additional statements that do not fall into either of these categories. Programmers sometimes refer to these statements collectively as the *Data Control Language (DCL)*. DCL statements primarily protect the database from unauthorized access, from harmful interaction among multiple database users, and from power failures and equipment malfunctions. In this chapter, I discuss protection from unauthorized access. In Chapter 13, I look at the other DCL functions.

User Access Levels

SQL-92 provides controlled access to six database management functions: creating, seeing, modifying, deleting, referencing, and using. *Creating, seeing, modifying,* and *deleting* correspond to the INSERT, SELECT, UPDATE, and DELETE operations that I discuss in Chapter 6. *Referencing* — that is, using the REFERENCES keyword (which I discuss in Chapters 3 and 5) — involves applying referential integrity constraints to a table that depends on another table in the database. *Using,* which you specify by use of the USAGE keyword, pertains to domains, character sets, collations, and translations. (I define domains, character sets, collations, and translations in Chapter 5.)

The database administrator

The supreme authority for a database is the *database administrator (DBA)*. The DBA has all rights and privileges to all aspects of the database. Being a DBA can give you a real feeling of power, but the position is also a great responsibility. With all that power at your disposal, you can easily mess up your database and destroy thousands of hours of work. DBAs must think clearly and carefully about the consequences of every action they perform.

Not only does the DBA have all rights to the database, but the DBA also controls the rights that other users can have. This way, highly trusted individuals can access more functions — and, perhaps, more tables — than can the majority of users.

The best way to become a DBA is to install the database-management system yourself. If you do, the installation manual gives you an account, or *login,* and a password. That login identifies you as a specially privileged user. Sometimes the system calls this privileged user the DBA, sometimes the *system administrator,* and sometimes the *super user.* In any case, as your first official act after logging in, you want to change your password. If you don't change the password, anyone who reads the manual can also log in with full DBA privileges. This situation may not prove very healthy for your database. After you change the password, only people who know the new password can log in as DBA.

I suggest that you share the new DBA password with a small number of highly trusted people. After all, a falling meteorite could strike you tomorrow; you could win the lottery; or you may become unavailable to the company in some other way. Your colleagues must be able to carry on in your absence. Anyone who knows the DBA login and password becomes the DBA after the person uses that information to access the system.

If you have DBA privileges, I suggest that you log in as DBA only if you need to perform a specific task that requires DBA privileges. After you finish, log out. For routine work, log in by using your own personal login ID and password. This approach may save you from making mistakes that have serious consequences for other users' tables as well as for your own.

Database object owners

Another class of privileged user, along with the DBA, is the *database object owner.* Tables and views, for example, are database objects. Any user who creates such an object, therefore, is considered its owner. A table owner enjoys every possible privilege associated with that table, including the privilege to grant access to the table to other people. Because you can base views on underlying tables, someone other than a table's owner can actually create a view based on that owner's table. In such a case, however, the view owner receives only the same privileges for the view as that user normally does for the underlying table. The bottom line, therefore, is that a user can't circumvent the protection on another user's table simply by creating a view based on that table.

The public

"The public" consists of all users who aren't specially privileged users (either DBAs or object owners) and to whom a privileged user hasn't specifically granted access rights. If a privileged user grants certain access rights to PUBLIC, everyone who can access the system gains those rights.

A hierarchy of user privilege exists, in which the DBA stands at the highest level and the public at the lowest. Figure 12-1 illustrates the privilege hierarchy.

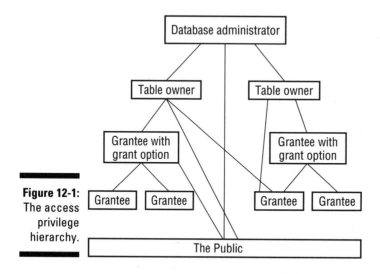

Figure 12-1:
The access
privilege
hierarchy.

Granting Privileges to Users

The DBA, by virtue of his position, has all privileges on all objects in the database. The owner of an object has all privileges with respect to that object. No one else has any privileges with respect to any object, unless someone who already has those privileges and the authority to pass them on specifically grants those privileges to another person. You grant privileges to someone else by using the GRANT statement, which has the following syntax:

```
GRANT privilege-list
   ON object
   TO user-list
   [WITH GRANT OPTION]
```

In this statement, *privilege-list* is defined as follows:

```
privilege [, privilege] ...
```

or ALL PRIVILEGES

Here *privilege* is defined as follows:

```
SELECT
| DELETE
| INSERT [(column-name [, column-name]...)]
| UPDATE [(column-name [, column-name]...)]
| REFERENCES [(column-name [, column-name]...)]
| USAGE
```

In the original statement, *object* is defined as follows:

```
[TABLE] table-name
| DOMAIN domain-name
| CHARACTER SET character-set-name
| COLLATION collation-name
| TRANSLATION translation-name
```

And *user-list* in the statement is defined as follows:

```
login-ID [, login-ID]...
| PUBLIC
```

The preceding syntax considers a view to be a table. The SELECT, DELETE, INSERT, UPDATE, and REFERENCES privileges apply to tables and views only. The USAGE privilege applies to domains, character sets, collations, and translations. The following sections give examples of the various ways you can use the GRANT statement and the results of those uses.

Inserting data

To grant someone the privilege of adding data to a table, follow this example:

```
GRANT INSERT
    ON CUSTOMER
    TO SALES_CLERK ;
```

This privilege enables the clerk in the sales department to add new customer records to the CUSTOMER table.

Looking at data

To enable someone to view the data in a table, use the following example:

```
GRANT SELECT
    ON PRODUCT
    TO PUBLIC ;
```

This privilege enables anyone with access to the system (PUBLIC) to view the contents of the PRODUCT table.

Actually, this statement can be dangerous. Columns in the PRODUCT table may contain information that not everyone should see, such as COST_OF_GOODS. To provide access to most information while withholding access to sensitive information, define a view on the table that doesn't include the sensitive columns. Then grant SELECT privileges on the view rather than on the underlying table. The following example shows the syntax for this procedure:

```
CREATE VIEW MERCHANDISE AS
    SELECT MODEL, PRODNAME, PRODDESC, LISTPRICE
        FROM PRODUCT ;
GRANT SELECT
    ON MERCHANDISE
    TO PUBLIC ;
```

Using the MERCHANDISE view, the public doesn't get to see the PRODUCT table's COST_OF_GOODS column or any other column except the four listed in the CREATE VIEW statement.

Modifying table data

In any active organization, table data changes over time. You need to grant to some people the right and power to make changes and to prevent everyone else from doing so. To grant change privileges, follow this example:

```
GRANT UPDATE (BONUSPCT)
   ON BONUSRATE
   TO SALES_MGR ;
```

The sales manager can adjust the bonus rate that salespeople receive for sales (the BONUSPCT column), based on changes in market conditions. The sales manager can't, however, modify the values in the MINAMOUNT and MAXAMOUNT columns that define the ranges for each step in the bonus schedule. To enable updates to all columns, you must either specify all column names or not specify any column names at all, as shown in the following example:

```
GRANT UPDATE
   ON BONUSRATE
   TO VP_SALES ;
```

Deleting obsolete rows from a table

Customers go out of business or stop buying for some other reason. Employees quit, retire, are laid off, or die. Products become obsolete. Life goes on, and things that you tracked in the past may no longer be of interest to you. Someone needs to remove obsolete records from their tables. On the other hand, you want to carefully control who can remove which records. Regulating such privileges is another job for the GRANT statement, as shown in the following example:

```
GRANT DELETE
   ON EMPLOYEE
   TO PERSONNEL_MGR ;
```

The personnel manager can remove records from the EMPLOYEE table. So can the DBA and the person who creates the EMPLOYEE table (who's probably the DBA also). No one else can remove personnel records (unless another GRANT statement gives that person the power to do so).

Referencing related tables

If one table includes a second table's primary key as a foreign key, information in the second table becomes available to users of the first table. This situation potentially creates a dangerous "back door" through which unauthorized users can extract confidential information. In such a case, a user doesn't need access rights to a table to discover something about its contents. If the user has access rights to a table that references the target table, those rights are often enough to enable him to access the target table as well.

Suppose, for example, that the table LAYOFF_LIST contains the names of the employees who are to be laid off next month. Only authorized management people have SELECT access to the table. An unauthorized employee, however, deduces that the table's primary key is EMPID. The employee then creates a new table SNOOP, which has EMPID as a foreign key, enabling him to reference LAYOFF_LIST. (I describe how to create a foreign key with a REFERENCES clause in Chapter 5.)

```
CREATE TABLE SNOOP
    (EMPID INTEGER REFERENCES LAYOFF_LIST) ;
```

Now all the employee needs to do is try to INSERT rows corresponding to the employee ID numbers of all employees into SNOOP. The inserts that the table accepts are those for the employees on the layoff list. All rejected inserts are for employees not on the list.

SQL-92 prevents this kind of security breach by requiring that a privileged user explicitly grant any reference rights to other users, as shown in the following example:

```
GRANT REFERENCES (EMPID)
    ON LAYOFF_LIST
    TO PERSONNEL_CLERK ;
```

Using domains, character sets, collations, and translations

Domains, character sets, collations, and translations also have an effect on security issues. Domains, in particular, must be watched closely when created to avoid their use as a way to undermine your security measures.

You can define a domain that encompasses a set of columns; in doing so, you want all of these columns to have the same type and to share the same constraints. The columns you create in your CREATE DOMAIN statement inherit the type and constraints of the domain. You can override these characteristics for specific columns, if you want, but domains provide a convenient way to apply numerous characteristics to multiple columns with a single declaration.

Domains come in handy if you have multiple tables that all contain columns with similar characteristics. Your business database, for example, may consist of several tables, each of which contains a PRICE column that should have a type of DECIMAL(10,2) and values that are nonnegative and no greater than 10,000. Before you create the tables that hold these columns, you need to create a domain that specifies the columns' characteristics, as does the following example:

```
CREATE DOMAIN PRICE_TYPE_DOMAIN  DECIMAL (10,2)
    CHECK (VALUE >= 0 AND VALUE <= 10000) ;
```

Perhaps you identify your products in multiple tables by PRODUCT_CODE, which is always of type CHAR (5), with a first character of X, C, or H and a last character of either 9 or 0. You can create a domain for these columns, too, as in the following example:

```
CREATE DOMAIN PRODUCT_CODE_DOMAIN CHAR (5)
    CHECK (SUBSTR (VALUE, 1,1) IN ("X", "C", "H")
    AND SUBSTR (VALUE, 5, 1) IN ("9", "0") ) ;
```

With the domains in place, you can now proceed to create tables, as follows:

```
CREATE TABLE PRODUCT
    (PRODUCT_CODE PRODUCT_CODE_DOMAIN,
    PRODUCT_NAME CHAR (30),
    PRICE PRICE_TYPE_DOMAIN) ;
```

In the table definition, instead of giving the data type for PRODUCT_CODE and PRICE, specify the appropriate domain instead. This action gives those columns the correct type and also applies the constraints you specify in your CREATE DOMAIN statements.

Certain security implications go with the use of domains. What if someone else wants to use the domains you create — may such use cause problems? Yes. What if someone creates a table with a column that has a domain of PRICE_TYPE_DOMAIN. That person can assign progressively larger values to that column until it rejects a value. By doing so, the person can determine the upper bound on PRICE_TYPE that you specify in the CHECK clause of your CREATE DOMAIN statement. If you consider that upper bound private information, you don't want to enable others to use the PRICE_TYPE domain. To protect you in situations such as this example, SQL enables only those to whom the domain owner explicitly grants permission to use domains. Thus only the user who creates the domain (as well as the DBA, of course) can grant such permission. You can grant such permission by using a statement such as that shown in the following example:

```
GRANT USAGE ON PRICE_TYPE DOMAIN TO SALES_MGR ;
```

Different security problems may arise if you DROP domains. Tables that contain columns that you define in terms of a domain cause problems if you try to DROP the domain. You may need to DROP all such tables first. Or you may find yourself unable to DROP the domain. How a domain DROP is handled may vary from one implementation to another. SQL Server may do it one way, whereas Oracle does it another. At any rate, you may want to restrict who can DROP domains. The same applies to character sets, collations, and translations.

Granting the Power to Grant Privileges

The DBA can grant any privileges to anyone. An object owner can grant any privileges on that object to anyone. Users who receive privileges this way, however, can't in turn grant those privileges to someone else. This restriction helps the DBA or table owner retain a good measure of control. Only people the DBA or object owner empowers to do so can gain access to the object in question.

From a security standpoint, limiting a person's ability to delegate access privileges makes a lot of sense. Many occasions arise, however, in which users need such delegation authority. Work can't come to a screeching halt every time someone is ill, on vacation, or out to lunch. You can trust *some* users with the power to delegate their access rights to reliable designated alternates. To pass such a right of delegation to a user, the GRANT statement uses the WITH GRANT OPTION clause. The following statement shows one example of how you can use this clause:

```
GRANT UPDATE (BONUSPCT)
    ON BONUSRATE
    TO SALES_MGR
    WITH GRANT OPTION ;
```

Now the sales manager can delegate the UPDATE privilege by issuing the following statement:

```
GRANT UPDATE (BONUSPCT)
   ON BONUSRATE
   TO ASST_SALES_MGR ;
```

After the execution of this statement, the assistant sales manager can make changes to the BONUSRATE table — a power he didn't have before.

A tradeoff exists between security and convenience. The owner of the BONUSRATE table relinquishes considerable control in granting the UPDATE privilege to the sales manager by using the WITH GRANT OPTION. One hopes that the sales manager takes his responsibility seriously and is careful how he passes on the privilege.

Taking Privileges Away

If you have a way to give access privileges to people, you'd better have a way of taking those privileges away, too. People's job functions change, and with the change, their need for access to data changes. People may even leave the organization to join a competitor. You should probably revoke all the access privileges of such people. SQL provides for the removal of access privileges by using the REVOKE statement. This statement acts just as the GRANT statement does, except in reverse. The syntax for this statement is as follows:

```
REVOKE [GRANT OPTION FOR] privilege-list
   ON object
   FROM user-list [RESTRICT|CASCADE] ;
```

You can use this structure to revoke specified privileges while leaving others intact. The principal difference between the REVOKE statement and the GRANT statement is the presence of the optional RESTRICT or CASCADE keyword in the REVOKE statement. If you used WITH GRANT OPTION to grant the privileges you're revoking, using CASCADE in the REVOKE statement revokes privileges for the grantee and also for anyone to whom that person granted those privileges as a result of the WITH GRANT OPTION clause. On the other hand, the REVOKE statement with the RESTRICT option works only if the grantee hasn't delegated the specified privileges. In the latter case, the REVOKE statement revokes the grantee's privileges. If the grantee passed on the specified privileges, the REVOKE statement with the RESTRICT option doesn't revoke anything but instead returns an error.

You can use a REVOKE statement with the optional GRANT OPTION FOR clause to revoke only the grant option for specified privileges while enabling the grantee to retain those privileges for himself. If the GRANT OPTION FOR clause and the CASCADE keyword are both present, you revoke all privileges that the grantee granted, along with the grantee's right to bestow such privileges — as if you'd never granted the grant option in the first place. If the GRANT OPTION FOR clause and the RESTRICT clause are both present, one of two things happens. If the grantee didn't grant to anyone else any of the privileges you're revoking, the REVOKE executes and removes the grantee's ability to grant privileges. If the grantee's already granted at least one of the privileges you're revoking, the REVOKE doesn't execute but returns an error instead.

The fact that you can grant privileges by using WITH GRANT OPTION, combined with the fact that you can also selectively revoke privileges, makes system security a lot more complex than the concept appears at first glance. Multiple grantors, for example, can conceivably grant a privilege to any single user. If one of those grantors then revokes the privilege, the user still retains that privilege because of the still-existing grant from another grantor. If a privilege passes from one user to another by way of the WITH GRANT OPTION, this situation creates a *chain of dependency,* in which one user's privileges depend on those of another user. If you're a DBA or object owner, always remain aware that, after you grant a privilege by using the WITH GRANT OPTION, that privilege may show up in unexpected places. Revoking the privilege from unwanted users while letting legitimate users retain the same privilege may prove challenging. In general, the GRANT OPTION and CASCADE clauses encompass numerous subtleties. If you use these clauses, check both the SQL-92 standard and your product documentation carefully to ensure that you understand how the clauses work.

Using GRANT and REVOKE Together Saves Time and Effort

Often, you want to grant multiple privileges to multiple users only on selected columns of a table. This type of setup may require a lot of typing. Consider the following example from Zetec Corporation. The vice president of sales wants everyone in the sales department to see everything in the CUSTOMER table. Only sales managers, however, should have the capability to update, delete, or insert rows — and *nobody* should have the capability to update the CUSTID field. The sales managers' names are Tyson, Keith, and David. You can grant appropriate privileges to these three managers by using a series of GRANT statements, as follows:

```
GRANT SELECT, INSERT, DELETE
   ON CUSTOMER
   TO TYSON, KEITH, DAVID ;
GRANT UPDATE
   ON CUSTOMER (COMPANY, CUSTADDRESS, CUSTCITY,
      CUSTSTATE, CUSTZIP, CUSTPHONE, MODLEVEL)
   TO TYSON, KEITH, DAVID ;
GRANT SELECT
   ON CUSTOMER
   TO JENNY, VALERIE, MELODY, NEIL, ROBERT, SAMMY,
      PRESTON, BRANDON, MICHELLE_T, ALLISON, ANDREW,
      SCOTT, MICHELLE_B, JAIME, LINLEIGH, MATT, AMANDA;
```

That statement should do the trick. Everyone now has SELECT rights on the CUSTOMER table. The sales managers have full INSERT and DELETE rights on the table, and they also have the right to update any column except the CUSTID column. This approach works. You do, however, have an easier way to accomplish the same result. Try the following example:

```
GRANT SELECT
   ON CUSTOMER
   TO PUBLIC ;
GRANT INSERT, DELETE, UPDATE
   ON CUSTOMER
   TO TYSON, KEITH, DAVID ;
REVOKE UPDATE
   ON CUSTOMER (CUSTID)
   FROM TYSON, KEITH, DAVID ;
```

You still take three statements in this example to accomplish the same protection that you achieve by using the three statements of the preceding example. No one may change data in the CUSTID column, and only Tyson, Keith, and David have INSERT, DELETE, and UPDATE privileges. These latter three statements, however, are significantly shorter than those in the preceding example, because you don't need to name all the users in the sales department, and you don't need to name all the columns in the table.

Chapter 13

Protecting Data

● ●

In This Chapter

▶ Avoiding database damage

▶ Understanding the problems caused by concurrent operation

▶ Dealing with concurrency problems through SQL mechanisms

▶ Tailoring protection to your needs with `SET TRANSACTION`

▶ Protecting your data without paralyzing operations

● ●

*E*veryone has heard of Murphy's Law, which is usually stated, "If anything can go wrong, it will go wrong." We joke about this pseudo law because most of the time things go fine. At times we seem to be among the lucky few who remain untouched by one of the basic laws of the universe. Usually, when unexpected problems arise, we recognize what has happened and deal with it.

In a very complex structure, however, the potential for unanticipated problems rises approximately as the square of the complexity. This is why large software projects are almost always delivered late and are often loaded with bugs. A nontrivial, multiuser DBMS application is a large, complex structure. In the course of operation, a number of things can go wrong. Methods have been developed for minimizing the impact of these problems, but the problems can never be eliminated completely. This is good news for professional database maintenance and repair people, because automating them out of a job will probably never be possible.

Threats to Data Integrity

Data can be damaged or corrupted in a variety of ways. In Chapter 5, I discuss problems resulting from bad input data, operator error, deliberate destruction, and concurrent access. Poorly formulated SQL statements and improperly designed applications can also damage your data, and figuring out how doesn't take much imagination. Two threats that I haven't mentioned yet are platform instability and equipment failure. I discuss these briefly in this chapter and give more extensive coverage to the problems that can be caused by concurrent access.

Platform instability

Platform instability is a category of problem that shouldn't even exist, but alas, it does. It is most prevalent when you are running one or more new and relatively untried components in your system. Problems can lurk in a new DBMS release, a new operating system version, or new hardware. Conditions or situations that have never arisen before come up while you are running a critical job. Your system locks up and your data is damaged. To remedy the problem, you may direct a few choice words at your computer and the people who built it. Beyond that there is not much you can do except hope that your latest backup was a good one.

Never put important production work on a system that has any unproven components. Resist the temptation to get the beta release of the newest, most function-laden version of your DBMS or operating system and to put your bread-and-butter work on it. If you feel you must gain some hands-on experience with something new, make sure that you do so on a machine that is completely isolated from your production network.

Equipment failure

Even well-proven, highly reliable equipment fails sometimes. Everything physical wears out eventually — even modern, solid-state computers. If such a failure happens while your database is open and active, you can lose data. Even worse, you can lose data and not realize it. Be assured that such a failure will happen sooner or later. If Murphy's Law is in operation that day, it happens at the worst possible time.

One way to protect against equipment failure is redundancy. Keep extra copies of everything. For maximum safety, have duplicate hardware configured exactly the same as your production system. Have backups of your database and applications that can be loaded and run on your backup hardware when needed.

Cost constraints may keep you from duplicating everything (which effectively doubles your costs), but at least make sure that your database and applications are backed up frequently enough that an unexpected failure does not require you to reenter a large amount of data.

Another way to avoid the worst consequences of equipment failure is to use transaction processing. This important topic is covered later in this chapter.

A *transaction* is an indivisible unit of work. Either the entire transaction is executed or none of it is. The worst problems arise when only part of a series of database operations is processed.

Concurrent access

Assume that you are running on proven hardware and software, your data is good, your application is bug free, and your equipment is inherently reliable. Problems can still arise from *contention* — when multiple people try to use the same database table at the same time. Multiple-user database systems must be able to handle concurrent access to data.

Consider an example of a case when interaction between concurrent users may cause problems. Suppose that you are writing an order-processing application that involves four tables: ORDER_MASTER, CUSTOMER, LINE_ITEM, and INVENTORY. ORDER_MASTER has ORDER_NUMBER as a primary key, CUSTOMER_NUMBER as a foreign key referencing the CUSTOMER table, as well as other columns that do not concern you here. The LINE_ITEM table has LINE_NUMBER as a primary key, ITEM_NUMBER as a foreign key referencing the INVENTORY table, and QUANTITY. The INVENTORY table has ITEM_NUMBER as a primary key, QUANTITY_ON_HAND, and other columns.

Your company policy is to ship each order completely or not at all. No partial shipments or back orders are allowed. The ORDER_PROCESSING application processes each order in ORDER_MASTER and determines whether shipping *all* of the line items is possible. If so, it writes the order, decrements the QUANTITY_ON_HAND column of the INVENTORY table as required, and deletes the affected entries from the ORDER_MASTER and LINE_ITEM tables.

More than one way is available to perform the order processing function. One way (Method 1) is to process the INVENTORY row corresponding to each row in the LINE_ITEM table. If QUANTITY_ON_HAND is large enough, decrement it. If QUANTITY_ON_HAND is not large enough, roll back the transaction to restore all of the inventory reductions made to other LINE_ITEMs in this order.

A second way of accomplishing the same result (Method 2) is to check the INVENTORY row corresponding to each row in an order's LINE_ITEMs. If they are *all* big enough, then process those items by decrementing them.

Method 1 is more efficient when you succeed in processing the order, and Method 2 is more efficient when you fail. Thus, if most orders can be filled most of the time, you are better off using Method 1. If most orders cannot be filled most of the time, you are better off with Method 2.

How would this example application be affected on a multiuser system in the absence of adequate concurrency control? Assume that User 1 was processing an order using Method 1. Ten pieces of Item 1 are in stock, and User 1's order takes them all. The order processing is in progress and the quantity of Item 1 is decremented to zero. At this point, User 2 processes a small order for one piece of Item 1 and finds that not enough are in stock to fill the order. User 2's order is rolled back because it cannot be filled.

Meanwhile, User 1 tries to order five pieces of Item 37, but only four are in stock. User 1's order is rolled back because it cannot be completely filled. The INVENTORY table is now back to the state it was in before either user started operating. Neither order is filled, even though User 2's order could be.

If a situation similar to this had occurred on a system using Method 2, there could still be a problem, although a different one. User 1 could check all the items ordered and decide that all the items ordered were available. If User 2 comes in and processes an order for one of those items before User 1 performs the decrement operation, however, User 1's transaction could fail.

No conflict occurs if transactions are executed serially rather than concurrently. In the first example, if User 1's transaction was completed before User 2's transaction started, the ROLLBACK after User 1 failed to process all items makes the item ordered by User 2 available during User 2's transaction. In the second example, User 2 has no opportunity to change the quantity of any item until User 1's transaction is complete. User 1's transaction completes successfully.

If transactions are executed serially, one after the other, they have no chance of interacting destructively. Execution of concurrent transactions is termed *serializable* if the result is the same as it would be if the transactions were executed serially.

Trade-offs exist between performance and protection from harmful interactions. The higher the isolation level, the more time it takes to perform a function. Be aware of what the trade-offs are so that you can configure your system for adequate protection — but not more protection than you need. Too strict control of concurrent access can kill overall system performance.

Reducing Vulnerability to Data Corruption

You can take precautions at several levels to reduce the chances of losing data through some mishap or unanticipated interaction. Some of these precautions are taken by your DBMS. Like guardian angels, they protect you from harm. Also like guardian angels, you don't see them and probably don't even know they are helping you. Your database administrator (DBA) takes other precautions, and you may or may not be aware of these activities. Finally, you, the developer, can take some precautions yourself. Form the habit of doing these things automatically so that they are always included in your code or in your interactions with your database. You can avoid a lot of grief by adhering to a few simple principles whenever you interact with a database.

Using SQL transactions

The transaction is one of SQL's main tools for maintaining database integrity. An SQL transaction encapsulates all the SQL statements that can have an effect on the database. An SQL transaction is completed with either a COMMIT or a ROLLBACK statement. If the transaction is completed with a COMMIT, the effects of all the statements in the transaction are applied to the database in one rapid-fire sequence. If it is completed with a ROLLBACK, the effects of all the statements are "rolled back" and the database is returned to the state it was in before the transaction began.

In this discussion I use the term *application* to mean either an execution of a program (in COBOL, C, or some other programming language) or a series of actions performed at a terminal during a single logon. An application can include a series of SQL transactions. The first SQL transaction begins when the application begins; the last SQL transaction ends when the application ends. Each COMMIT or ROLLBACK that the application performs ends one SQL transaction and begins the next SQL transaction. For example, an application with three SQL transactions would have the form:

```
Start of the application
    Various SQL statements (SQL transaction-1)
COMMIT or ROLLBACK
    Various SQL statements (SQL transaction-2)
COMMIT or ROLLBACK
    Various SQL statements  (SQL transaction-3)
End of the application
```

I refer to "SQL transaction" because the application could be using other facilities, such as for network access, that do other sorts of transactions. In the following discussion I simply say "transaction" to mean "SQL transaction."

A transaction has an access mode that is either READ-WRITE or READ-ONLY, and it has an isolation level that is either SERIALIZABLE, REPEATABLE READ, READ COMMITTED, or READ UNCOMMITTED. I describe these transaction characteristics shortly. The default characteristics are READ-WRITE and SERIALIZABLE. If you want any other characteristics, specify them with a SET TRANSACTION statement, such as

```
SET TRANSACTION READ ONLY ;
```

or

```
SET TRANSACTION READ ONLY REPEATABLE READ ;
```

or

```
SET TRANSACTION READ COMMITTED ;
```

You can have multiple SET TRANSACTION statements in an application, but you can specify only one of them in each transaction, and it must be the first SQL statement executed in the transaction. If you want to use a SET TRANSACTION statement, then execute it either at the beginning of the application or after a COMMIT or ROLLBACK. You must perform a SET TRANSACTION at the beginning of every transaction for which you want nondefault properties, because each new transaction after a COMMIT or ROLLBACK is automatically given the default properties.

A SET TRANSACTION statement can also specify a DIAGNOSTICS SIZE, which determines the number of error conditions about which the implementation should be prepared to save information (because an implementation can detect more than one error during a statement). The default for this is implementor-defined, and that default is almost always adequate.

The default transaction

The default transaction has characteristics that are satisfactory for most users most of the time. On those few occasions when you require transaction characteristics other than those provided by the default transaction, you can specify different characteristics with a SET TRANSACTION statement, as described in the previous section. (I discuss this statement in more detail later in the chapter as well.)

The default transaction sets the mode to READ-WRITE, which, as you may expect, allows you to issue statements that change the database. It sets isolation level to SERIALIZABLE, which is the highest level of isolation possible, and thus the safest. The default diagnostics size is implementation-dependent. You need to look at your SQL documentation to see what it is for your system.

Isolation levels

Ideally, the work that the system is performing for your transaction is completely isolated from anything being done by other transactions that happen to be executing concurrently with yours. On a real-world, multiuser system, however, complete isolation is not always feasible. It may exact too large a performance penalty. The question then arises, "How much isolation do you really want, and how much are you willing to pay for it in terms of performance?"

The weakest level of isolation is called READ UNCOMMITTED, which allows the sometimes problematic dirty read. A *dirty read* is a situation in which a change made by one user can be read by a second user before the first user COMMITs, or finalizes, the change. The problem arises when the first user aborts and rolls back his transaction. The second user's subsequent operations are now based on a wrong value. The classic example of this is in an inventory application, where the first user decrements inventory and the second user reads the new lower value. The first user then rolls back his transaction, restoring the inventory to its initial value. The second user, thinking inventory is low, orders more stock, possibly creating a severe overstock situation.

Don't use the READ UNCOMMITTED isolation level unless you don't care very much about the accuracy of your results, and performance of your system is terrible because it's loaded beyond capacity.

You can use READ UNCOMMITTED when you want approximate statistical data, such as:

- ✔ The maximum delay in filling orders
- ✔ The average age of salespeople who don't make quota
- ✔ The average age of new employees

In many such cases, approximate information is quite sufficient, and the extra (performance) cost of the concurrency control that is required to give an exact result for some point in time isn't worthwhile.

The next highest level of isolation is READ COMMITTED, in which a change made by another transaction does not become visible to your transaction until the other user has COMMITted the other transaction. This is better than the previous case but is still subject to a serious problem — the nonrepeatable read. To illustrate the nonrepeatable read phenomenon, I return to the inventory example. User 1 queries the database to see how many of a particular product are in stock. The number is ten. At almost the same time, User 2 starts and then COMMITs a transaction that records an order for ten units of that same product, decrementing the inventory, leaving none. Now User 1, having seen that ten are available, tries to order five of them. Five are no longer left, however. User 1's initial read of the quantity available is not repeatable. The quantity has changed, so assumptions made on the basis of the initial read are not valid.

An isolation level of REPEATABLE READ guarantees that the nonrepeatable read problem doesn't happen. This isolation level, however, is still subject to the *phantom read* — a problem that arises when a user issues a command whose search condition (the WHERE clause or HAVING clause) selects a set of rows. Immediately afterward, User 2 performs and commits an operation that changes data in some rows. Those data used to meet the search condition, but now they no longer do. Other rows that originally did not meet the search condition now do meet it. User 1, whose transaction is still active, issues another SQL statement with the same search conditions as her first one. She expects to retrieve the same rows. Instead, unknown to her, her second operation is performed on a different set of rows from those that her first operation used.

An isolation level of SERIALIZABLE is not subject to any of these problems. At this level, concurrent transactions can, in principle, be run serially, or one after the other, rather than in parallel, and the results are the same. If you are running at this isolation level, hardware or software problems can still cause your transaction to fail, but at least you don't have to worry about the validity of your results if you know that your system is functioning properly. Table 13-1 shows the four isolation levels and the problems they solve.

Table 13-1	Isolation Levels and Problems Solved
Isolation Level	*Problems Solved*
READ UNCOMMITTED	None
READ COMMITTED	Dirty read
REPEATABLE READ	Dirty read
	Nonrepeatable read
SERIALIZABLE	Dirty read
	Nonrepeatable read
	Phantom read

The implicit transaction-starting statement

Some implementations of SQL require that you signal the beginning of a transaction with an explicit statement, such as BEGIN or BEGIN TRAN. SQL-92 does not. If you don't have an active transaction and you issue a statement that calls for one, SQL-92 starts a default transaction for you. CREATE TABLE, SELECT, and UPDATE are examples of statements that require the context of a transaction. Issue one of these and SQL starts a transaction for you.

SET TRANSACTION

On occasion, you may want transaction characteristics that are different from those set by default. You can specify different characteristics with a SET TRANSACTION statement before you issue your first statement that requires a transaction. The SET TRANSACTION statement enables you to specify mode, isolation level, and diagnostics size.

You may issue the following statement:

```
SET TRANSACTION
    READ ONLY,
    ISOLATION LEVEL READ UNCOMMITTED,
    DIAGNOSTICS SIZE 4
```

With these settings you cannot issue any statements that change the database (READ ONLY), and you have the lowest and most hazardous isolation level (READ UNCOMMITTED). The diagnostics area has a size of 4. You are making minimal demands on system resources.

In contrast, you may issue:

```
SET TRANSACTION
    READ WRITE,
    ISOLATION LEVEL SERIALIZABLE,
    DIAGNOSTICS SIZE 8
```

These settings allow you to change the database, give you the highest level of isolation, and give you a larger diagnostics area. This makes larger demands on system resources. Depending on your implementation, these settings may be the same as those used by the default transaction. Naturally, you can issue SET TRANSACTION statements with other choices for isolation level and diagnostics size.

Always setting your isolation level to SERIALIZABLE just to be on the safe side may seem reasonable. Depending on your implementation and what you are doing, however, you may not need to do so, and performance can suffer significantly if you do. Set your transaction isolation level as high as you need to, but no higher. If you don't intend to change the database in your transaction, set the mode to READ ONLY. Don't tie up any system resources that you do not need.

COMMIT

Although SQL-92 does not have an explicit transaction-starting statement, it has two that terminate a transaction: COMMIT and ROLLBACK. Use COMMIT when you have come to the end of the transaction and you want to make permanent the changes that you have made to the database (if any). You may include the optional keyword WORK (COMMIT WORK) if you wish. If an error is encountered or the system crashes while a COMMIT is in progress, you may have to roll the transaction back and try it again.

ROLLBACK

When you come to the end of a transaction, you may decide that you do not want to make permanent the changes that have occurred during the transaction. In fact, you want to restore the database to the state it was in before the transaction began. To do this, issue a ROLLBACK statement. ROLLBACK is a fail-safe mechanism. Even if the system crashes while a ROLLBACK is in progress, after the system is restored, you can restart the ROLLBACK and it restores the database to its pretransaction state.

Locking

The isolation level set either by default or by a SET TRANSACTION statement tells the DBMS how zealous to be in protecting your work from interaction with the work of other users. The main protection from harmful transactions that the DBMS gives to you is its application of locks to the database objects you are using. Sometimes it locks the table row you are accessing, preventing anyone else from accessing that record while you are using it. Sometimes it locks an entire table, if you are performing an operation that could affect the whole table. Sometimes it allows reading but not writing. Other times it prevents both. Each implementation handles locking in its own way. Some implementations are more bulletproof than others, but most up-to-date systems protect you from the worst problems that could arise in a concurrent-access situation.

Backup

Backup is a protective action that your DBA should perform on a regular basis. All elements of your system should be backed up at intervals that depend on how frequently they are updated. If your database is updated daily, it should be backed up daily. Your applications, forms, and reports may change, too, although less frequently. Whenever you make changes to them, your DBA should back up the new versions.

Keep several generations of backups. Sometimes database damage does not become evident until some time has passed. To return to the last known good version, you may have to go back several backup versions.

Many different ways exist to perform backups. One way is to use SQL to create backup tables and copy data into them. A second way is to use an implementation-defined mechanism that backs up the whole database or portions of it. This mechanism is generally much more convenient and efficient than using SQL. Finally, your installation may have a mechanism in place for backing up everything, including databases, programs, documents, spreadsheets, utilities, and computer games. If so, you may not have to do anything beyond assuring yourself that the backups are performed frequently enough to protect you.

Constraints within Transactions

To ensure that the data in your database is valid, you need to do more than just make sure that it is of the right type. Some columns, for example, should never hold a null value. Others should perhaps hold values that fall within a certain range. These types of restrictions, called *constraints,* are discussed in Chapter 5.

Constraints are relevant to transactions because they can conceivably prevent you from doing what you want. For example, suppose that you want to add data to a table that contains a column with a NOT NULL constraint. One common method of adding a record is to append a blank row to your table and then insert values into it later. The NOT NULL constraint on one column, however, causes the append operation to fail. SQL does not allow you to add a row that has a null value in a column with a NOT NULL constraint, even though you plan to add data to that column before your transaction ends. To address this problem, SQL-92 allows you to designate constraints as either DEFERRABLE or NOT DEFERRABLE.

Constraints that are NOT DEFERRABLE are applied immediately. You can set deferrable constraints to be either initially DEFERRED or IMMEDIATE. If a deferrable constraint is set to IMMEDIATE, it acts like a NOT DEFERRABLE constraint. It is applied immediately. If a DEFERRABLE constraint is set to DEFERRED, it is not enforced.

To append blank records or perform other operations that may violate DEFERRABLE constraints, you can use a statement similar to the following:

```
SET CONSTRAINTS ALL DEFERRED
```

This puts all DEFERRABLE constraints in the DEFERRED condition. It does not affect the NOT DEFERRABLE constraints. After you have performed all operations that may violate constraints, and the table is now in a state that does not violate those constraints, you can reapply them as follows:

```
SET CONSTRAINTS ALL IMMEDIATE
```

If you have made a mistake and one or more of your constraints is still being violated, you will find out now.

If you do not explicitly set your DEFERRED constraints to IMMEDIATE, SQL will do it for you when you attempt to COMMIT your transaction. If a violation is still present at that time, the transaction does not COMMIT; instead, SQL gives you an error message.

SQL's handling of constraints protects you from entering invalid data (or an invalid absence of data) while giving you the flexibility to temporarily violate constraints while a transaction is still active.

Consider a payroll example to see why being able to defer the application of constraints is important.

Assume that an EMPLOYEE table has columns EMP_NO, EMP_NAME, DEPT_NO, and SALARY. DEPT_NO is a foreign key referencing the DEPT table. Assume also that the DEPT table has columns DEPT_NO and DEPT_NAME. DEPT_NO is the primary key.

Suppose that, in addition, you want to have a table like DEPT that also contains a PAYROLL column that holds the sum of the SALARY values for employees in each department.

You can create the equivalent of this table with the following view:

```
CREATE VIEW DEPT2 AS
   SELECT D.*, SUM(E.SALARY) AS PAYROLL
      FROM DEPT D, EMPLOYEE E
      WHERE D.DEPT_NO = E.DEPT_NO
      GROUP BY D.DEPT_NO ;
```

You can also define this view equivalently as follows:

```
CREATE VIEW DEPT3 AS
   SELECT D.*,
      (SELECT SUM(E.SALARY)
         FROM EMPLOYEE E
         WHERE D.DEPT_NO = E.DEPT_NO) AS PAYROLL
      FROM DEPT D ;
```

But suppose that, for efficiency, you don't want to calculate the SUM every time you reference DEPT.PAYROLL. Instead, you want to store an actual PAYROLL column in the DEPT table. You will then update that column every time you change a SALARY.

And, to make sure that the SALARY column is accurate, you can include a CONSTRAINT in the table definition:

```
CREATE TABLE DEPT
    (DEPT_NO CHAR(5),
    DEPT_NAME CHAR(20),
    PAYROLL DECIMAL(15,2),
    CHECK (PAYROLL = SELECT SUM(SALARY)
                    FROM EMPLOYEE E WHERE E.DEPT_NO=
                    DEPT.DEPT_NO));
```

Now, suppose that you want to increase the SALARY of employee 123 by 100. You can do it with the following update:

```
UPDATE EMPLOYEE
    SET SALARY = SALARY + 100
    WHERE EMP_NO = '123' ;
```

And you must remember to do the following as well:

```
UPDATE DEPT D
SET PAYROLL = PAYROLL + 100
WHERE D.DEPT_NO = SELECT E.DEPT_NO
                    FROM EMPLOYEE E
                    WHERE E.EMP_NO = '123' ;
```

(You use the subquery to reference the DEPT_NO of employee 123.)

But you have a problem. Constraints are checked at the end of each statement. In principle, all constraints are checked. In practice, an implementation checks only those constraints that reference values that are modified by the statement.

So, after the first of the preceding UPDATE statements, the implementation checks all constraints that reference values that the statement modifies. This includes the constraint defined in the DEPT table, because that constraint references the SALARY column of the EMPLOYEE table, and the UPDATE statement is modifying that column. After the first UPDATE statement, that constraint is violated. You assume that before you execute the UPDATE statement the database is correct, and each PAYROLL value in the

DEPT table is equal to the sum of the SALARY values in the corresponding columns of the EMPLOYEE table. Then the first UPDATE statement increases a SALARY value, and this equality is no longer true. The second UPDATE statement corrects this state of affairs, and once again leaves the database values in a state for which the constraint is True. But in between the two updates, the constraint is False.

The purpose of the SET CONSTRAINTS DEFERRED statement is to let you temporarily disable or "suspend" all constraints, or only specified constraints. The constraints are deferred until either (1) you execute a SET CONSTRAINTS ON statement, or (2) you execute a COMMIT or ROLLBACK statement. Thus you would surround the previous two UPDATE statements with SET CONSTRAINTS statements:

```
SET CONSTRAINTS OFF ;
UPDATE EMPLOYEE
   SET SALARY = SALARY + 100
   WHERE EMP_NO = '123' ;
UPDATE DEPT D
   SET PAYROLL = PAYROLL + 100
   WHERE D.DEPT_NO = SELECT E.DEPT_NO
                     FROM EMPLOYEE E
                     WHERE E.EMP_NO = '123' ;
SET CONSTRAINTS ON ;
```

Note that this defers all constraints, so if you insert new rows into DEPT, the primary keys won't be checked. You have removed protection that you may want to keep. Specifying the particular constraint or constraints that you want to defer is therefore preferable. To do this, you must give the constraints names when you create them:

```
CREATE TABLE DEPT
   (DEPT_NO CHAR(5),
   DEPT_NAME CHAR(20),
   PAYROLL DECIMAL(15,2),
   CONSTRAINT PAY_EQ_SUMSAL
   CHECK (PAYROLL = SELECT SUM(SALARY)
                    FROM EMPLOYEE E WHERE
                    E.DEPT_NO = DEPT.DEPT_NO)) ;
```

You can then reference the constraints individually:

```
SET CONSTRAINTS PAY_EQ_SUMSAL OFF;
UPDATE EMPLOYEE
   SET SALARY = SALARY + 100
   WHERE EMP_NO = '123' ;
UPDATE DEPT D
   SET PAYROLL = PAYROLL + 100
   WHERE D.DEPT_NO = SELECT E.DEPT_NO
                     FROM EMPLOYEE E
                     WHERE E.EMP_NO = '123' ;
SET CONSTRAINTS PAY_EQ_SUMSAL ON;
```

If you don't specify a constraint name in the CREATE statement, then SQL generates one implicitly, and that implicit name appears in the schema information tables (catalog tables). Specifying the names explicitly is more straightforward, however.

Now suppose that, in the second UPDATE statement, you mistakenly specified an increment value of 1000. This will be allowed during the UPDATE statement, because the constraint has been deferred. But when you execute the SET CONSTRAINTS ON statement, the specified constraints are checked; and if they fail, the SET CONSTRAINTS statement raises an exception. If instead of a SET CONSTRAINTS ON statement you execute a COMMIT statement and the constraints are found to be False, then the COMMIT instead performs a ROLLBACK.

Thus you can defer the constraints only within a transaction. When the transaction is terminated, either with a ROLLBACK or a COMMIT, the constraints are both enabled and checked and must be True. The ability to defer constraints is therefore only a convenience that can be used within a transaction, and not a mechanism that could in any way make data that violates a constraint available to any other transaction.

Part V

SQL in the Real World

The 5th Wave   By Rich Tennant

And finally, do you feel your client/server environment keeps you well connected to your department?

In this part . . .

Up to now, you've looked at SQL in isolation, as if you could solve all your data handling problems by using SQL alone. Alas, reality intrudes. Many things you simply can't do with SQL, at least not with SQL by itself. By combining SQL with traditional procedural languages, such as COBOL, FORTRAN, or C, however, you can achieve results that you could not get with SQL alone. In this part, I show you how to combine SQL with procedural languages.

Chapter 14

Using SQL within Applications

*I*n every previous chapter in this book, I mostly talk about SQL statements in isolation. For example, I ask questions about data and then build SQL queries that retrieve answers to the questions. This mode of operation, interactive SQL, is a fine way to learn what SQL can do, but it's not the way SQL is typically used.

Even though SQL syntax can be described as similar to English, it is not an easy language to master. The overwhelming majority of computer users today are not fluent in SQL. You can reasonably assume that the overwhelming majority of computer users will never be fluent in SQL, even if this book is wildly successful. When a database question comes up, Joe User will probably not sit down at his terminal and enter an SQL SELECT statement to find the answer. Systems analysts and application developers are the people who are likely to be comfortable with SQL, and they typically do not make a career of entering ad hoc queries into databases. They develop applications that make queries. If you plan to perform the same operation repeatedly, you shouldn't have to rebuild it every time from the console. Write an application to do the job and then run it as often as you like. SQL can be a part of an application, but when it is, it works a little differently than it does in interactive mode.

SQL in an Application

In Chapter 2, I mention that SQL is not a complete programming language, and that to use it in an application, you need to combine it with a procedural language such as Pascal, FORTRAN, Ada, C, COBOL, PL/I, or dBASE. Because of the way it is structured, SQL has some strengths and some weaknesses. Procedural languages are structured differently and have different strengths and weaknesses. Happily, the strengths of SQL tend to make up for the weaknesses of the procedural languages, and the strengths of the procedural languages are in those areas where SQL is weak. By combining the two, you can build powerful applications with a broad range of capabilities. Recently, object-oriented rapid application development (RAD) tools such as Borland's Delphi and C++ Builder have appeared, which incorporate SQL code into applications developed by manipulating objects instead of writing procedural code.

While discussing interactive SQL in previous chapters, I often use the asterisk (*) as a shorthand substitute for "all columns in the table." If the table has numerous columns, the asterisk can save a lot of typing. A danger exists in using the asterisk this way, however, whenever you use SQL in an application program.

After your application is written, you or someone else may add new columns to a table or delete old ones. Thus the meaning of "all columns" changes. Your application, when it specifies all columns with an asterisk, may retrieve different columns than it thinks it is getting.

Such a change to a table won't affect existing programs until they have to be recompiled to fix a bug or make some change. Then the * will be expanded to include all the now-current columns. This may cause the application to fail in a way totally unrelated to the bug fix or change that was made, causing a debugging nightmare.

To be safe, specify all column names explicitly in an application, rather than using the asterisk.

SQL strengths and weaknesses

SQL is strong in data retrieval. If important information is buried somewhere in a single-table or multitable database, SQL gives you the tools you need to retrieve it. You do not need to know the order of the rows or columns in a table because SQL does not deal with the rows or columns individually. The SQL transaction-processing facilities ensure that your database operations will be unaffected by any other users that may be simultaneously accessing the same tables that you are.

A major weakness of SQL is its rudimentary user interface. It has no provision for formatting screens or reports. It accepts command lines from the keyboard and sends retrieved values to the terminal, one row at a time.

Sometimes a strength in one context can be a weakness in another. One strength of SQL is its ability to operate on an entire table simultaneously. It doesn't matter whether the table has one row, a hundred rows, or a hundred thousand rows; a single SELECT statement can extract the data you want. SQL cannot operate on one row of a multirow table at a time, however, and sometimes you do want to deal with each row individually.

Procedural language strengths and weaknesses

In contrast to SQL, procedural languages are designed for one-row-at-a-time operation. This allows the application developer precise control over the way a table is processed. This high level of control is a great strength of procedural languages. A concomitant weakness exists, however. The application developer must have detailed knowledge of the way data is stored in the database tables. The order of the database's columns and rows is significant and must be taken into account.

Because of the step-by-step nature of procedural languages, they have the flexibility to produce user-friendly screens for data entry and viewing. You can also produce printed reports of great sophistication, with any desired layout.

Problems in combining SQL with a procedural language

In view of how the strengths of SQL complement the weaknesses of procedural languages and vice versa, trying to combine them in such a way that you can benefit from their strengths and not be penalized by their weaknesses makes sense. As valuable as such a combination may be, some challenges must be overcome before it can be practically achieved.

Contrasting operating modes

A big problem in combining SQL with a procedural language is that SQL operates on tables a set at a time, whereas procedural languages work on them a row at a time. Sometimes this is not a big deal. You can separate set operations from row operations, doing each with the appropriate tool. Other times, however, you may want to search a table for records meeting certain conditions and perform different operations on the records depending on whether or not they meet the conditions. This requires both the retrieval power of SQL and the branching capability of a procedural language. Embedded SQL gives you this combination of capabilities by allowing you to "embed" SQL statements at strategic locations within a program that you have written in a conventional procedural language.

Data type incompatibilities

Another hurdle to the smooth integration of SQL with any procedural language is that SQL's data types are different from those of all major procedural languages. This shouldn't be surprising, because the data types defined for any procedural language are different from the types for the other procedural languages. No standardization of data types exists across languages. In releases of SQL prior to SQL-92, data type incompatibility was a major concern. In SQL-92, however, the CAST statement addresses the problem. As I discuss in Chapter 8, you can use CAST to convert a data item from the procedural language's data type to one recognized by SQL, as long as the data item itself is compatible with the new data type.

Hooking SQL into Procedural Languages

Though many potential difficulties exist with integrating SQL into procedural languages, it can be done. In many instances, it *must* be done to produce the desired result in the allotted time — or at all. Luckily, several methods for combining SQL with procedural languages are available to you. I discuss three of them — *embedded SQL, module language,* and *RAD tools* — in the following section.

Embedded SQL

The most common method of mixing SQL with procedural languages is called *embedded* SQL. The name is descriptive: SQL statements are dropped right into the middle of a procedural program, wherever they are needed. As you may expect, an SQL statement that appears suddenly in the middle of, for instance, a C program can present a challenge for a compiler that is not expecting it. For that reason, programs containing embedded SQL are usually passed through a preprocessor before being compiled or interpreted. The preprocessor is warned of the imminent appearance of SQL code by the EXEC SQL directive.

As an example of embedded SQL, look at a program written in Oracle's Pro*C version of the C language. The program, which accesses a company employee table, prompts the user for an employee name and then displays that employee's salary and commission. It then prompts the user for new salary and commission data and updates the employee table with it.

```
EXEC SQL BEGIN DECLARE SECTION;
    VARCHAR uid[20];
    VARCHAR pwd[20];
    VARCHAR ename[10];
    FLOAT salary, comm;
    SHORT salary_ind, comm_ind;
EXEC SQL END DECLARE SECTION;
EXEC SQL INCLUDE SQLCA;
main()
{
    int sret;           /* scanf return code */
    /* Log in */
    strcpy(uid.arr,"FRED");     /* copy the user name */
    uid.len=strlen(uid.arr);
    strcpy(pwd.arr,"TOWER");    /* copy the password */
    pwd.len=strlen(pwd.arr);
    EXEC SQL WHENEVER SQLERROR STOP;
    EXEC SQL WHENEVER NOT FOUND STOP;
EXEC SQL CONNECT :uid;
printf("Connected to user: percents \n",uid.arr);
    printf("Enter employee name to update:   ");
    scanf("percents",ename.arr);
    ename.len=strlen(ename.arr);
    EXEC SQL SELECT SALARY,COMM INTO :salary,:comm
             FROM EMPLOY
             WHERE ENAME=:ename;
    printf("Employee: percents salary: percent6.2f comm:
        percent6.2f \n",
           ename.arr, salary, comm);
    printf("Enter new salary:  ");
    sret=scanf("percentf",&salary);
    salary_ind = 0;
    if (sret == EOF !! sret == 0)    /* set indicator */
        salary_ind =-1;   /* Set indicator for NULL */
    printf("Enter new commission:  ");
    sret=scanf("percentf",&comm);
    comm_ind = 0;   /* set indicator */
    if (sret == EOF !! sret == 0)
        comm_ind=-1;          /* Set indicator for NULL */
    EXEC SQL UPDATE EMPLOY
             SET SALARY=:salary:salary_ind
             SET COMM=:comm:comm_ind
             WHERE ENAME=:ename;
```

(continued)

(continued)

```
printf("Employee percents updated. \n",ename.arr);
    EXEC SQL COMMIT WORK;
    exit(0);
```

You don't have to be an expert in C to understand the essence of what this program is doing and how the program does it. First, SQL declares host variables. Next, C code controls the user login procedure, and then SQL sets up error handling and connects to the database. C code then solicits an employee name from the user and places it in a variable. An SQL SELECT statement retrieves the named employee's salary and commission data and stores them in the host variables :salary and :comm. C then takes over again and displays the employee's name, salary, and commission and then solicits new values for salary and commission. It also checks to see that an entry has been made, and if one has not, it sets an indicator. Next, SQL updates the database with the new values. C then displays an "operation complete" message. SQL commits the transaction, and C finally exits the program.

You can intermix the commands of two languages like this because of the preprocessor. The preprocessor separates the SQL statements from the host language commands, placing the SQL statements in a separate external routine. Each SQL statement is replaced with a host language CALL of the corresponding external routine. The language compiler can now do its job. The way the SQL part is passed to the database is implementation-dependent. You, as the application developer, don't have to worry about any of this. The preprocessor takes care of it. You should be concerned about a few things, however, that do not appear in interactive SQL.

Declaring host variables

Some information must be passed between the host language program and the SQL segments. You do this with host variables. In order for SQL to recognize the host variables, you must declare them before you use them. Declarations are included in a declaration segment that precedes the program segment. The declaration segment is announced by the following directive:

```
EXEC SQL BEGIN DECLARE SECTION
```

The end of the declaration segment is signaled by

```
EXEC SQL END DECLARE SECTION
```

Every SQL statement must be preceded by an EXEC SQL directive. The end of an SQL segment may or may not be signaled by a terminator directive. In COBOL, the terminator directive is "END-EXEC"; in FORTRAN, it is the end of a line; and in Ada, C, Pascal, and PL/I, it is a semicolon.

Converting data types

Depending on the compatibility of the data types supported by the host language and those supported by SQL, you may have to use CAST to convert certain types. You can use host variables that have been declared in the DECLARE SECTION. Remember to prefix host variable names with a colon (:) when you use them in SQL statements, as in the following example:

```
INSERT INTO FOODS
    (FOODNAME, CALORIES, PROTEIN, FAT, CARBOHYDRATE)
    VALUES
    (:foodname, :calories, :protein, :fat, :carbo)
```

Module language

Module language provides another method of using SQL with a procedural programming language. With module language, you explicitly put all of the SQL statements into a separate SQL module.

An SQL module is simply a list of SQL statements. Each of the SQL statements is called an SQL *procedure* and is preceded by a specification of the name of the procedure and the number and types of the parameters.

Each SQL procedure contains a single SQL statement (the next version of the SQL standard will support procedures with multiple SQL statements, with loops and conditional structures). In the host program, you explicitly call an SQL procedure at whatever point in the host program you wish to execute the SQL statement in that procedure. You call the SQL procedure as if it were a host language subprogram.

Thus, an SQL module and the associated host program are essentially a way of explicitly hand-coding the result of the SQL preprocessor for embedded syntax.

Embedded SQL is much more common than module language. Most vendors offer some form of module language, but few emphasize it in their documentation. Module language does have several advantages. First, because the SQL is completely separated from the procedural language, you can hire the best SQL programmers available to write your SQL modules, whether they have any experience with your procedural language or not. In fact, you can even defer deciding on which procedural language to use until after your SQL modules are written and debugged. Second, you can hire the best programmers in your procedural language, even if they know nothing about SQL. Third, and probably most important, no SQL is mixed in with the procedural code, so your procedural language debugger will work. This could save you considerable development time.

Once again, what can be looked at as an advantage from one perspective may be a disadvantage from another. Because the SQL modules are separated from the procedural code, when you are trying to understand how the program works, following the flow of the logic is not as easy as it is in embedded SQL.

Module declarations

The syntax for a module is as follows:

```
MODULE [module-name]
    [NAMES ARE character-set-name]
    LANGUAGE {ADA|C|COBOL|FORTRAN|MUMPS|PASCAL|PLI}
    [SCHEMA schema-name]
    [AUTHORIZATION authorization-id]
    [temporary-table-declarations...]
    [cursor-declarations...]
    [dynamic-cursor-declarations...]
    procedures...
```

As indicated by the square brackets, the module name is optional. Naming it anyway is probably a good idea, just to help keep things from getting too confusing. The optional NAMES ARE clause specifies a character set. If you do not include a NAMES ARE clause, the basic set of SQL characters is used. The LANGUAGE clause tells the module which language it is to be called from. The compiler must know what the calling language is, because it's going to make the SQL statements appear to the calling program as if they are subprograms in that program's language.

Although the SCHEMA clause and the AUTHORIZATION clause are both optional, you must specify at least one of them. You could also specify both. The SCHEMA clause specifies the default schema, and the AUTHORIZATION clause specifies the authorization identifier. The authorization identifier establishes the privileges you have. If you do not specify an authorization ID, the DBMS uses the authorization ID associated with your session to determine the privileges your module is allowed. If you don't have the privilege to perform the operation your procedure calls for, your procedure isn't executed.

If your procedure requires temporary tables, declare them with the temporary table declaration clause. Declare cursors and dynamic cursors before any procedures that use them. Declaring a cursor after a procedure is permissible as long as that procedure does not use the cursor. Doing this for cursors used by later procedures may make sense. I discuss cursors in Chapter 18.

Module procedures

Finally, after all these declarations, the functional parts of the module are the procedures. An SQL module language procedure has a name, parameter declarations, and an executable SQL statement. The procedural language program calls the procedure by its name and passes values to it through the parameters that are declared. A procedure can contain only one SQL statement, which performs the function of the procedure. Procedure syntax is as follows:

```
PROCEDURE procedure-name
    (parameter-declaration [, parameter-declaration ]... )
    SQL statement ;
```

The parameter declaration is of the form

```
parameter-name data-type
```

or

```
SQLCODE
```

or

```
SQLSTATE
```

Parameters may be either input parameters, output parameters, or both. SQLCODE and SQLSTATE are status parameters through which errors are reported. I discuss them in detail in Chapter 19.

Object-oriented RAD tools

By using state-of-the-art RAD tools, you can develop sophisticated applications without knowing how to write a single line of code in C, Pascal, COBOL, or FORTRAN. Instead, you choose objects from a library and place them in appropriate spots on the screen.

Objects of different standard types have characteristic properties, and selected events are appropriate for each object type. You can also associate a method with an object. The method is a procedure written in a procedural language. Building very useful applications without writing any methods is possible, however.

Although you can build complex applications without using a procedural language, sooner or later you will probably need SQL. SQL has a richness of expression that is difficult, if not impossible, to duplicate with the object paradigm. As a result, full-feature RAD tools offer you a mechanism for injecting SQL statements into your object-oriented applications. Borland's C++ Builder is an example of an object-oriented development environment that offers SQL capability.

In Chapter 4, I show how to create database tables with C++ Builder. That operation, of course, represents only a small fraction of C++ Builder's capabilities. The tool's primary purpose is the development of applications that process the data in database tables. The developer places objects on forms and then customizes the objects by giving them properties, events, and possibly methods as well. Out of sight of the developer, C++ Builder converts the graphic representation of the application into a C++ program, which can then be compiled and run.

Although RAD tools such as C++ Builder are able to deliver high-quality applications in short amounts of time, they are usually specific to one or a small number of platforms. C++ Builder, for instance, runs only under Microsoft Windows. Keep that in mind if you think you may want to migrate your application to a different platform.

RAD tools such as C++ Builder represent the beginning of the eventual merger of relational and object-oriented database design. The structural strengths of relational design and SQL will both survive. They will be augmented by the rapid and comparatively bug-free development that comes from object-oriented programming.

Chapter 15

ODBC

*I*n the last several years, computers have become increasingly interconnected, both within and between organizations. This connectedness has brought about the need for sharing database information across networks. The major obstacle to the free sharing of information across networks is the incompatibility of the operating software and applications running on different machines. A major step toward overcoming this incompatibility has been the creation and ongoing evolution of SQL.

Unfortunately, "standard" SQL is not all that standard. Even DBMS vendors who claim to be SQL-92-compatible have included extensions in their implementations that make them incompatible with the extensions in the implementations of other vendors. The vendors are loathe to give up their extensions, because their customers have designed them into their applications and have become dependent on them. Another way is needed to make cross-DBMS communication possible, something that does not require vendors to "dumb down" their implementations to the lowest common denominator. That other way is ODBC.

What is ODBC?

ODBC (Open DataBase Connectivity) is a standard interface between a database and an application that is trying to access the data in the database. Having such a standard allows any application front end to access any database back end by using SQL. The only requirement is that the front end and the back end both adhere to the ODBC standard. ODBC 3.0 is the current version of the standard. Access is accomplished by supplying the system with a *driver* that is specifically designed to interface with a particular back-end database. The front end of the driver, the side that goes to the application, rigidly adheres to the ODBC standard. It looks the same to the application regardless of what database engine is on the back end. The back end of the driver is customized to the specific database engine it is addressing. With this architecture, applications do not have to be customized to or even aware of what back-end database engine controls the data they are using. The driver masks the differences between back ends.

The ODBC Interface

The ODBC interface is essentially a set of definitions that is accepted as standard. The definitions cover everything needed to establish communication between an application and the database that holds its data. Defined are the following:

- ✔ **A function call library.** The ODBC function calls provide for connecting to a back-end database engine, executing SQL statements, and passing results back to the application.
- ✔ **Standard SQL syntax.**
- ✔ **Standard SQL data types.**
- ✔ **Standard protocol for connecting to a database engine.**
- ✔ **Standard error codes.**

To perform an operation on a database, include the appropriate SQL statement as an argument of an ODBC function call. As long as you use the ODBC-specified standard SQL syntax, the operation works regardless of what database engine is on the back end.

The Components of ODBC

The ODBC interface consists of four functional components. Each component plays a role in giving ODBC the flexibility that allows it to provide transparent communication from any compatible front end to any compatible back end. Between the user and the data that the user wants lie the four layers of the ODBC interface, as follows:

- ✔ **Application:** The part of the ODBC interface closest to the user is the application. Of course, even systems that don't use ODBC include an application. Nonetheless, including the application as a part of the ODBC interface makes sense. The application must be cognizant that it is communicating with its data source through ODBC. It must connect smoothly with the ODBC driver manager, in strict accordance with the ODBC standard.

✔ **Driver manager:** The driver manager is a *dynamic link library (DLL)*, generally supplied by Microsoft. It loads appropriate drivers for the system's (possibly multiple) data sources and directs function calls coming from the application to the appropriate data sources via their drivers. It also handles some ODBC function calls directly and detects and handles some types of errors.

✔ **Driver:** Because data sources can differ from each other (in some cases, they can be very different indeed), you need a way to translate standard ODBC function calls into the native language of each different data source. Translation is the job of the driver DLL. Each driver accepts function calls through the standard ODBC interface and then translates them into code understandable to its associated data source. When the data source responds with a result set, the driver reformats it in the reverse direction into a standard ODBC result set. The driver is the key element that allows any ODBC-compatible application to manipulate the structure and the contents of an ODBC-compatible data source.

✔ **Data source:** The data source could be a lot of different things. It could be a relational DBMS and associated database residing on the same computer as the application. It could be the same thing on a remote computer. It could be an *ISAM* (Indexed Sequential Access Method) file with no DBMS, either on the local or a remote computer. It may include a network, or it may not. The myriad of different forms that the data source can take requires that a custom driver be available for each one.

ODBC in a Client/Server Environment

In a client/server system, the interface between the client part and the server part is called the *application programmer's interface (API)*. An API can be either proprietary or standard. A *proprietary* API is one in which the client part of the interface has been specifically designed to work with one particular back end on the server. The actual code that forms this interface is a driver, and in a proprietary system it is called a *native driver.* I discuss native drivers in more detail in Chapter 16. A native driver is optimized for use with a specific front-end client and its associated back-end data source. Because native drivers are optimized for both the specific front-end application and the specific DBMS back end that they are working with, the drivers tend to pass commands and information back and forth quickly, with a minimum of delay.

If your client/server system always accesses the same type of data source, and you are sure that you will never need to access data on another type of data source, you may want to use the native driver supplied with your DBMS. On the other hand, if you may, at some time in the future, need to access data that is stored in a different form, using an ODBC interface now could save you from having to do a lot of rework later.

ODBC drivers are also optimized to work with specific back-end data sources, but they all have the same front-end interface to the Driver Manager. It stands to reason that any driver that has not been optimized for a particular front end is probably not as fast as a native driver specifically designed for that front end. A major complaint about the first generation of ODBC drivers was their poor performance compared to native drivers. Recent benchmarks, however, have shown that ODBC 3.0 drivers are quite competitive in performance to native drivers. The technology is now mature enough that sacrificing performance to gain the advantages of standardization is no longer necessary.

ODBC and the Internet

Database operations over the Internet are different in several important ways from database operations on a client/server system. The most visible difference from the user's point of view is the client portion of the system, which includes the user interface. In a client/server system, the user interface is part of an application that communicates with the data source on the server via ODBC-compatible SQL statements. Over the World Wide Web, the client portion of the system is a Web browser, which communicates with the data source on the server via *HTML* (HyperText Markup Language).

Because anyone with a Web browser can access data that is accessible on the Web, the act of putting a database on the Web is called *database publishing*. Databases placed on the Web are potentially accessible by many more people than can access data on a LAN server. Furthermore, on the Web, you usually don't have very strict control over who those people are. Thus, the act of putting data on the Web is more akin to publishing to the world than it is to sharing with a few coworkers. See Figure 15-1 for illustrations comparing client/server systems with Web-based systems.

Server extensions

In the Web-based system, communication between the browser on the client machine and the Web server on the server machine takes place in HTML. A system component called a *server extension* translates the HTML into ODBC-compatible SQL, which is then understood and acted upon by the database server, which in turn deals directly with the data source. In the reverse direction, the result set generated by a query is sent from the data source, through the database server, to the server extension, which translates it into a form that the Web server can handle. The results are then sent over the Web to the Web browser on the client machine, where they are displayed to the user. Figure 15-2 shows the architecture of such a system.

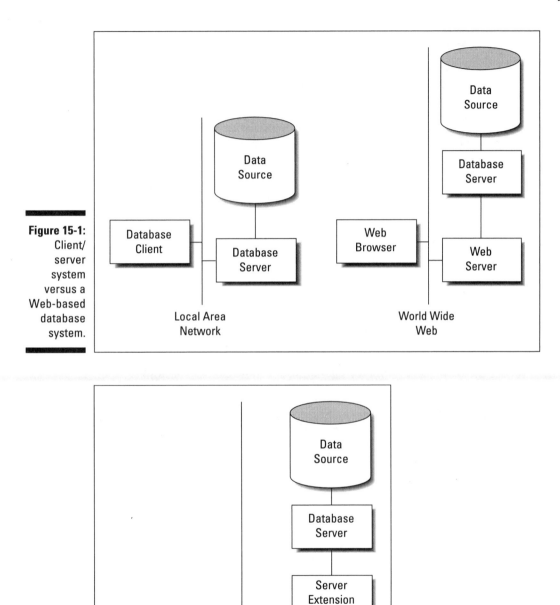

Figure 15-1:
Client/
server
system
versus a
Web-based
database
system.

Figure 15-2:
Web-based
database
system with
server
extension.

Client extensions

Web browsers were designed as, and are optimized to be, easy to understand and use interfaces to Web sites of all kinds. The most popular ones, Netscape Navigator and Microsoft Internet Explorer, were not designed as or optimized to be database front ends. In order for meaningful interaction with a database to occur over the Internet, the client side of the system needs functionality that the browser does not provide. To fill this need, several types of *client extensions* have been developed. These extensions include helper applications, Navigator plug-ins, ActiveX controls, Java applets, and scripts. The extensions communicate with the server via HTML, which is the language of the Web. Any HTML dealing with database access is translated into ODBC-compatible SQL by the server extension before being forwarded to the data source.

Helper applications

The first generation of client extensions were helper applications. A *helper application* is a standalone program that runs on the user's PC. It is not integrated with a Web page and does not display in a browser window. One major use of a helper application is as a viewer for graphics file formats not supported by the browser. To use a helper application, the user must first download it from its source site and install it on her browser. From then on, when she downloads a file in that format, the browser automatically invokes the viewer to display the file. One negative feature of this scheme is that the entire data file must be downloaded into a temporary file before the helper application is started. Thus, for large files, your wait can be quite long before you see any part of your downloaded file.

Netscape Navigator plug-ins

Netscape Navigator plug-ins are similar to helper applications in that they help process and display information that the browser cannot handle alone. They differ in that they work only with Netscape browsers and are much more closely integrated with them. The tighter integration allows a plug-in-enhanced browser to start displaying the first part of a file before the download operation has completed. The ability to display early output while later output is still being downloaded is a significant advantage. The user does not have to wait nearly as long before starting to work. A large and ever-growing number of Netscape plug-ins are available that enable enhancements such as sound, chats with similarly equipped users, animation, video, and interactive 3-D virtual reality. Aside from these uses, some plug-ins facilitate accessing remote databases over the Web.

ActiveX controls

Microsoft's ActiveX controls provide similar functionality to Netscape's plug-ins but operate by an entirely different technology. ActiveX is based on Microsoft's earlier OLE technology. Netscape has committed to support ActiveX as well as other strategic Microsoft technologies in the Netscape

environment. Of course, Microsoft's own Internet Explorer is also compatible with ActiveX. Between the two of them, Netscape and Microsoft control
an overwhelming majority of the browser market.

Java applets

Java is a C++-like language that was developed by Sun specifically for the
development of Web client extensions. After a connection is made between a
server and a client over the Web, the appropriate Java applet is downloaded
to the client, where the applet commences to run. The applet, which is
imbedded in an HTML page, provides the database-specific functionality
that the client needs to provide flexible access to server data. Figure 15-3 is
a schematic representation of a Web database application with a Java applet
running on the client machine.

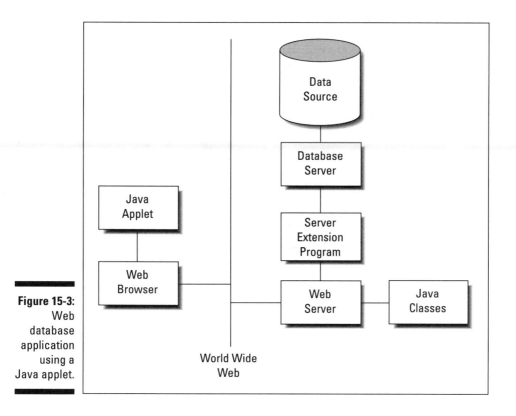

Figure 15-3:
Web
database
application
using a
Java applet.

One major advantage of Java applets is that they are always up to date. Because the applets are downloaded from the server every time they are used as opposed to being retained on the client, the client is always guaranteed to have the latest version whenever it runs one. If you are responsible for the server, you never have to worry about losing compatibility with some of your clients when you upgrade the server software. Just make sure that your downloadable Java applet is compatible with the new server configuration, and all your clients automatically become compatible, too.

Scripts

Scripts are the most flexible tools for creating client extensions. Using one of the new scripting languages, such as Netscape's JavaScript or Microsoft's VBScript, you have maximum control over what happens at the client end. You can put validation checks on data entry fields, allowing the rejection and correction of invalid entries without ever going out onto the Web. This can save a good deal of time as well as reduce traffic on the Web, thus benefiting other users as well. As with Java applets, scripts are imbedded in an HTML page and execute as the user interacts with that page.

ODBC and an Intranet

An *intranet* is a local or wide area network that operates exactly like a simpler version of the Internet. Because an intranet is entirely contained within a single organization, you don't need complex security measures such as firewalls. (I talk more about intranets in Chapter 17.) All the tools designed for application development on the World Wide Web operate equally well as development tools for intranet applications. You can use ODBC on an intranet in the same way that you use it on the Internet. If you have multiple different data sources, clients using Web browsers and the appropriate client and server extensions can communicate with them with SQL that passes through HTML and ODBC stages, until at the driver, the ODBC-compliant SQL is translated into the database's native command language and executed.

Chapter 16

SQL on the Internet

*T*he Internet, and particularly that portion of it known as the World Wide Web, has mushroomed in importance in the last couple of years. Just about every aspect of computing seems to be viewed in light of how it relates to the Web. Database is no exception. The World Wide Web lives up to its name. It provides a web of connectivity that envelops the globe. Anyone anywhere who has an Internet connection can access data residing on a Web server on the other side of town or, just as easily, on the other side of the world.

The ability to make your data available to anyone anywhere in the world opens up a whole new kind of database usage. This new usage, database publishing, is more akin to book publishing or radio broadcasting than it is to the point-to-point communication characteristic of operations on a local area network. The information you make available on the Web can be accessed and used by thousands or even millions of people that you will never meet. The most popular sites on the Web today receive more than a million visits, or *hits,* a day. You can make a substantial impact with your Web-based database, even if you are nowhere near that league.

The LAN is SQL's Ancestral Home

SQL was originally created by IBM to facilitate communication between large databases residing on mainframe computers and users on client machines that were connected to those mainframes by a local area network (LAN). SQL gradually became a *defacto* standard means, and then an official ANSI and ISO standard means, of communicating between users and databases. Companies producing relational databases designed to operate across local area networks embraced the SQL standard and made it the communications medium of choice on systems in which the user was located on a different machine from the database, with a LAN running between them.

SQL, coupled with ODBC, enabled an application running on a user's machine to simultaneously access data located on two or even more server machines. This combination proved to be a great boon to organizations whose information processing infrastructure had grown up over time without the benefit of centralized planning. Different machines, running different operating systems and different applications, could share information. Marvelous as this kind of flexibility is, it pales in comparison with what is possible over the Internet.

How the Internet Differs from a Classic LAN

A *local area network* (LAN) is a collection of computers that are all in physical proximity (that's where the *local* comes from). The computers, forming nodes on the network, are interconnected by wired or wireless communication links. Many local area networks are small, having anywhere from 10 to 50 nodes. Large organizations may be served by LANs that have more than a thousand nodes. In either case, you can exercise some centralized control over the network. This makes specifying a proprietary database interface possible, and you can expect all the users to be using access tools that are compatible with it.

The Internet is an entirely different story. It has millions of nodes, and they are not in physical proximity. No one has centralized control over what goes on. In this environment, the owner of a database server cannot make any assumptions about what kind of access tools the user has. The user has a Web browser, possibly supplemented with a plug-in that hosts the client end of a client-server database system. Because the most popular Web browsers run on all the popular client platforms, the client software does not have to be specifically tailored to run on a specific back-end database.

Note: The ordinary Web browser, such as Netscape Navigator or Microsoft Internet Explorer, comes close to being that Holy Grail of database access, the Universal Front End. If it existed, the Universal Front End would interface seamlessly with any database server that you want. It would allow the user to easily create tables, manipulate data, and operate database applications regardless of what kind of server the database is on or what kind of DBMS is controlling it. By itself, a browser cannot do this, of course. But by downloading the appropriate Netscape plug-in or ActiveX component (see Chapter 15 for more about these) before attempting to deal with the database, the browser can come very close. When a connection is established, state-of-the-art database publishers check the client machine for the appropriate plug-in. If they find it, they download the client part of their application and proceed. If they do not find the appropriate plug-in, they download the plug-in, followed by the client part of their application. This whole sequence can be relatively transparent to the user.

Two areas where operation on the Internet may differ significantly from operation on a LAN are network protocol and security. If you are considering allowing remote access to your database from over the Internet, you should carefully consider the impact of these two aspects of operation.

Network protocol

In order for the nodes on a network to communicate with each other, they must all speak the same "language." When one node sends a message, it must be formatted in such a way that the intended receiving node can understand it and take appropriate action. The people who first hooked personal computers together to form local area networks were not concerned with making their systems compatible with the Internet. At that time, the Internet was running only on large mainframe computers that ran the UNIX operating system and that were located at government organizations and research universities. The personal computer world seemed far removed from that of the mainframes used by "big science." Consequently, the "languages," or protocols, that were developed for PC LANs were different from what the Internet used.

Today, many PC LANs still operate with protocols that have evolved from those early PC protocols. The IPX/SPX protocol and the NetBEUI protocol are probably the most common of these. In contrast, the Internet uses a protocol named TCP/IP (Transmission Control Protocol/Internet Protocol). Anyone who wants to engage in database operations over the Web must do so using TCP/IP. Generally, this doesn't require any kind of a hardware change, but it can require a software reconfiguration.

Security

Security is a much bigger issue on the Internet than it is on any organizational LAN. On a LAN, you can be reasonably sure that no one is going to purposely try to sabotage your system. On the Internet, that would be a very foolish and dangerous assumption to make. All kinds of people are out there on the Internet, and some of them may want to hurt you — just for the sheer, twisted fun of it. Competitors or even enemies may have stronger reasons to give you trouble. When you are exposing your database server to the Internet, you must take significant extra precautions, beyond what would be normal for a LAN.

The principal defense against attacks by hackers or other malefactors on the Internet is to install a firewall between your organizational network and the Internet. A *firewall* is a software system, or combination of hardware and software, that insulates your network from the Internet. All traffic, both in and out, must pass through the firewall. The firewall authenticates the packets passing through it according to standards that you set up. It passes packets that meet your criteria and throws away those that don't. It also allows you to monitor traffic for suspicious activity and to trace attempts at breaching your security.

 When you make the decision to take the big step of putting your server on the Internet, be sure to provide adequate protection to sensitive information that you do not want inquisitive outsiders to know or malicious outsiders to damage.

From Client/Server to Internet-based Database

Most database systems found on LANs are structured according to client/server architecture. Data is stored on one or more servers whose specific task is providing access to that data. Smaller, client machines are spread throughout the organization. They host the user interface of the applications that access the database. Users, interacting with the client part of the application, access the data on the server by communicating over the LAN.

Compelling reasons exist to make database data available over the Internet. A commercial enterprise may want certain of its operational data to be available to vendors or customers with which it works closely. Such an enterprise may want to make detailed information about its products available to the general public, in hopes that some of them will become customers. Entities that are in the information dissemination business, such as libraries, may want to make their information available to a wider audience than those who are able to make a physical visit. For these and other reasons, many groups have decided to establish a presence on the Internet.

Beyond putting up a simple Web page, many organizations are engaging in *database publishing,* making selected internal information available to those who access their Web site. Some such information is freely available to anyone who logs in to the Web site. Using passwords, publishers can restrict access to authorized users, enabling them to access proprietary databases on the site or databases for which a fee is being charged.

The client/server architecture provides many of the key ingredients of a successful Web database publishing installation. Clients on the Web have similar equipment and operating environments to what is typical for clients on a corporate LAN. The database server of a Web-based system is no different from what serves that purpose on a LAN. Yes, you must address protocol and security issues, but good solutions exist for both. Investigating how client/server architecture may be applied to Web database publishing makes sense.

Two-tier client/server architecture

The original implementation of client/server computing on PC LANs used a two-tier architecture. This architecture had two main elements — the database client and the database server — connected by the LAN. You can implement a two-tier client/server system in several ways. One way, the so-called *fat client* architecture, places most of the computational burden on the client machine and relatively little on the server. A second major architecture is the *thin client* (also called *fat server*) model. Here, most of the computation is done by the server and the client provides little more than the user interface. Figure 16-1 is a schematic representation of a two-tier client/server system.

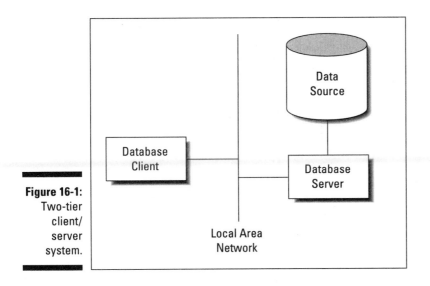

Figure 16-1:
Two-tier
client/
server
system.

Regardless of how a two-tier client/server system is implemented, all the necessary functions are performed by either the database client software on the client machine or by the database server software on the server machine.

Three-tier client/server architecture

Three-tier client/server architecture is a relatively new development that is rapidly replacing the older two-tier model. It adds another functional block or level to the server side of the system. This new functional block, often called *middleware,* assumes some of the responsibilities normally handled by both the database client and the database server, allowing both of them to be *thinner*. Thinning the client is good, because potentially so many of them exist, and the less capable the client machines need to be, the cheaper overall the system will be. Thinning the database server is also good because, when freed of computational tasks, the server can concentrate on moving data into and out of the database, speeding up operations. The higher level of modularization in a three-tier system also makes maintenance and troubleshooting easier. Figure 16-2 is a schematic representation of a three-tier client/server system.

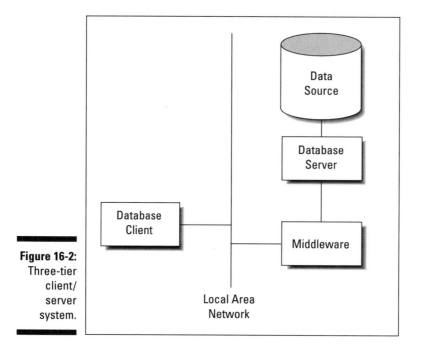

Figure 16-2:
Three-tier
client/
server
system.

Two-tier Web architecture

The traditional architecture of the World Wide Web can also be viewed as a two-tier structure. A Web server hosts HTML (HyperText Markup Language) pages, which are accessible over the Internet to Web browsers running on client machines. This architecture is similar to a two-tier client/server system in that the Web browser on an Internet client performs the same function as the user interface running on a client/server database client. The Web server performs a similar job to that of the client/server database server — dispensing information. The main differences are that a Web browser is thinner than even the thinnest database client in a thin-client client/server system, and a Web server is incapable of the database manipulation required of even a thin-server implementation of a client/server system. This state of affairs is fine as long as you are not trying to perform database operations over the Web. If all you are doing is putting HTML pages up for people to read, you don't need to do anything more. Figure 16-3 shows the structure of a two-tier Web system.

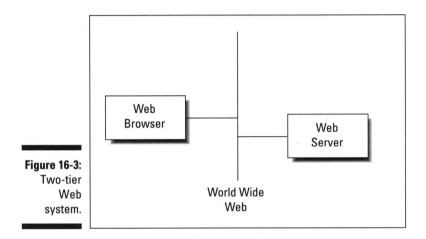

Figure 16-3: Two-tier Web system.

Three-tier Web database architecture

To effectively perform database operations over the Web, you must combine elements from a two-tier client/server system with elements from a two-tier Web system to produce a composite three-tier solution. On the client side, the Web browser, perhaps enhanced by a Netscape plug-in or ActiveX component, provides the database application user interface. On the server side, the database server interfaces directly with the data source, just as it does in a classic client/server system.

The three-tier Web database architecture differs from the three-tier client/ server database architecture in the *middleware*. The third tier (middleware) of a three-tier Web database system incorporates the Web server of a two-tier system and adds to it a *server extension program*. The signals and protocols handled by the Web server grew up in the Web environment and are accepted as standards in that realm. The signals and protocols that the database server is accustomed to seeing grew up in the client/server environment and are accepted as standards in that realm. The server extension program translates between these two incompatible standards. When requests are traveling from the client out on the Web to the data source behind the database server, the server extension program translates HTML to a form that the database server can understand, such as ODBC-compliant SQL. When result sets are traveling in the opposite direction, the server extension program translates them back into HTML for transmission over the Web. Figure 16-4 schematically shows the structure of a three-tier Web database system.

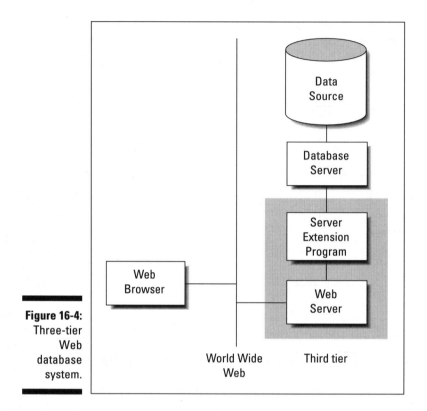

Data
Source

Database
Server

Server
Extension
Program

Web
Browser

Web
Server

World Wide
Web

Third tier

Figure 16-4:
Three-tier
Web
database
system.

The Role of SQL

SQL was originally developed as a means for a remote client to communicate
with a database. Local area networks (or wide area networks) passed the
SQL from client to server, encoding it according to a network protocol on
the source end and decoding it at the destination end. A Web-based system
adds an additional level of complication. The Web browser on the client end
transforms a user request into packets in TCP/IP format for transmission
over the Web. At the server end, the Web server passes these packets on to
the server extension program, which translates them back into SQL that the
database server can understand and respond to. So, whether you are
accessing a database over the Web or on a LAN, SQL is the means by which
communication is conducted.

Where ODBC fits in

Whereas SQL is a standard language for communicating with a database, database vendors comply with that standard (commonly called SQL-92) to a greater or lesser extent. An application using SQL for database access is by no means guaranteed to successfully communicate with a DBMS that claims to be SQL-92 compliant. You have two ways to address this problem. One is to write native drivers for all the popular database servers. A *native driver* is specifically written to communicate with a particular database server, and no other. For example, Netscape provides native drivers for Informix, Oracle, and Sybase databases and is working on a native driver for IBM's DB2 database. Microsoft provides native driver support for its own SQL Server database.

Native drivers are fast and efficient because they are specifically written for the database client and database server that they are connecting. The disadvantage is that a different native driver must be written for each database that you want to access — for each database client to which you want that access to be provided. The magnitude of the task of providing all those drivers for all those combinations of clients and servers motivated Microsoft to develop, and the industry to adopt, ODBC as a standard method of conveying SQL statements from clients to servers. If the SQL on the client end is always ODBC compliant, only one driver must be written for each type of server, and far fewer different server types exist than do clients. ODBC-compliant drivers are now available for the overwhelming majority of servers that anyone would want to connect to.

Java and SQL

Java is a language developed by Sun Microsystems specifically for use on the World Wide Web. It is similar in many respects to C++, but simpler to learn and use. People maintaining Web sites create applications written in Java, called *applets,* that reside on their Web server. When a user connects to a database server, the server downloads an applet to the user's browser, where it serves as a client-side extension to the browser. This system allows the user to access much more of the functionality available on the server than what's possible with just a "plain vanilla" browser.

SQL is a data sublanguage. It was never meant to be a complete language in itself, but was designed to be embedded in programs written in some other "host" language. Java can serve the function of being that host language just as well as can C++, Basic, or any other commonly used programming language.

Sun has published a specification for JDBC (Java DataBase Connectivity) that performs the same function that ODBC performs in making a client-generated SQL statement understandable to a wide array of possible database servers. The JDBC standard provides writers of Java applets with the ground rules they need to produce applets that will work with multiple, different database servers.

Chapter 17

Database on the Organizational Intranet

A dramatic transformation is sweeping through organizations of all types, large and small. Organizational LANs are being converted into intranets. If you work in a company, you will likely be a witness to some of the changes that are happening right under your nose! What is an intranet, and how does it compare to a LAN? How does it relate to the Internet, from which it derives its name?

LAN versus Intranet

An intranet differs from a *LAN* (local area network) in that the client user interface is always the same, a Web browser, regardless of the hardware the client runs or the operating system it uses. Platform independence is a big advantage in an organization with a heterogeneous installed base: Because you have to learn the Web browser interface only once, all applications then become easier to learn.

Physically, an intranet can be virtually identical to the LAN that it replaces. A network connects one or more servers to multiple-client machines, all located fairly close to each other. The difference is in the software, and possibly in the network protocols, as well. A database client on a LAN may run a database application, potentially requiring substantial client computing power in the process. A client on an intranet may run a browser, supplemented by a plug-in, ActiveX component, or Java applet. In general, a much less capable (and cheaper) machine can do the job.

The database server on a LAN takes ODBC-compliant SQL (or database native commands) from the network interface as input and performs appropriate operations on the database, possibly returning a result set to the client. On an intranet, a Web server and server extension program stand between the network and the database server. As is the case with the LAN, this combination delivers ODBC-compliant SQL or database native commands to the server. The interface the database server sees is the same, regardless of whether it connects to a LAN or an intranet.

One thing that may be different between the two environments (although the database server may never know it) is the network protocol. An intranet must use TCP/IP. A LAN may use TCP/IP, but it may just as well be using IPX/SPX or NetBEUI. Even if you convert an existing IPX/SPX network to an intranet, the protocol change is almost as easy as it would be if your LAN was already using TCP/IP. No big deal.

Internet-Intranet Commonality and Contrast

The organizational intranet is truly a child of the Internet. It is a "chip off the old block," a smaller version of its parent. An intranet has clients running browsers, just like the Internet. An intranet has servers hosting Web pages and database sources, just like its parent. And like the Internet, a network that runs the TCP/IP protocol connects these elements. Anything that works on the Internet also works on an intranet.

Although the Internet and intranets are similar, you find there are important differences, too. The Internet is huge and essentially uncontrollable. Neither you nor anyone else can exercise any degree of authority over it. Even the world's largest intranet is small compared to the Internet, and because a single organization completely contains that intranet, it is subject to that organization's control.

Security is another big area of difference. For all practical purposes, the Internet has no security. Anybody can get an Internet account and do what they please with it. If you connect your organizational network directly to the Internet, you multiply the threats to the integrity of your data. Get expert advice and put a robust firewall in place before you make the connection. Being so ill-protected would make Charlie Brown's pal Linus run for his security blanket — or the nearest intranet. On an intranet, you see far fewer security concerns. You have control over physical access to all the computers on the network. You can control not only who has network access, but also what they are allowed to do.

Intranets enjoy one of the biggest advantages of the Internet, while at the same time they avoid one of the Internet's biggest disadvantages. Intranets, like the Internet, give you the advantage of a single, easy-to-learn user interface — that of the browser your organization has established as a standard. Once your users learn this one interface, they are a major step closer toward fluency in any network application your organization uses. Unlike the Internet, intranets are not subject to strong attacks by outside hackers or other undesirable characters. No wonder so many organizations are converting their LANs to intranets.

A Database is Safer and Faster on the Intranet

You have an easier time writing database applications for the intranet (assuming they are never exposed to the Internet) than writing Internet database applications. The main reason is that you don't need to be paranoid about database security. On the Internet, there is plenty of reason to be paranoid about security.

To allow an Internet user to view some aspect of your database, you typically download a Web page with a data-entry form that contains invisible, embedded SQL statements. The Internet user then enters data into the form that translates "behind the scenes" into an SQL statement. It is easy for an Internet user to save an HTML page locally and make changes to it. A hostile person can change any embedded SQL statements in your form to statements that destroy data or cause some other unintended effect, then submit the modified form. Your server may then proceed to self-destruct. Even if you plug this particular security breach, there are plenty of others.

A hacker of only moderate skill and cleverness has numerous ways to attack you. You don't ever want to become a target of a highly skilled hacker. At any rate, you shouldn't worry about this problem if you're on an intranet, because (theoretically) everyone who has access to the system is a friend.

Speed is another advantage of intranets. The Internet is congested, and response time is often slow. This situation is bound to get worse before it gets better. Your own intranet should be faster. If it isn't, you can upgrade it until it is.

The added speed makes better use of your users' time and also gives you some added options. You can make more use of graphics and multimedia than you can on the Internet. A word of advice: Make very little use of graphics and multimedia effects in applets you place on your Internet Web server, because the download times for these large files are excessive. On a high-bandwidth intranet, this is not nearly so much of an issue. You can spruce up the user interface and make your applet more appealing, without worrying overmuch about download times.

Intranet Challenges

Along with the advantages of switching your LAN to an intranet, you also face some possible disadvantages. One of these is the *HTTP* (HyperText Transfer Protocol) that forms the basis for all Web traffic. HTTP operates on a higher level than the popular LAN protocols and thus does not handle large amounts of data as efficiently. For applications that heavily update database files, operating over an intranet may be noticeably slower than on a LAN running on the same hardware.

Aside from speed, another HTTP characteristic is that it is stateless. SQL allows you to encapsulate a series of statements in a transaction to protect them from harmful interactions with the statements of other users. The transaction also protects the statements from system failures that occur after only some of the statements have been executed. (Take a look at Chapter 13 for more details.) Because HTTP is stateless, there is no way to specify that a transaction is operating. Thus, you can't use transactions on an intranet (or on the Internet either). You can find ways around this problem, but they add complication to application development and slow the operation of any application that uses them.

Note: To say that HTTP is *stateless* does not mean that HTTP is a protocol without a country. It means that mechanisms do not exist for tracking how many of a sequence of operations have actually been performed and for informing the server that a series of related operations is now complete.

Don't panic! You can use cookies as one possible solution to the lack of transactions over the Web. A *cookie* is a data file that a server sends to a client that gets stored on the client's hard disk. It can contain up to 4,000 bytes of information. Each time the client connects to that server, the cookie gets sent to the server along with the request for the server's Web page. In this way, the client and server can exchange state information, allowing a partially completed transaction to pick up where it left off. Newer development tools, through state management features, offer more advanced solutions to the lack of persistent connections across the Web.

The Intranet Back End

The intranet back end is the stuff on the server side of the Web. Back-end elements consist of the data source, the database server, and the middleware that connects them to the Web. The middleware may take several different forms but always includes a Web server, which interfaces directly with the Web. In addition to the Web server, the middleware usually also includes some sort of server extension that connects the Web server to the database server.

The middleware, whatever form it takes, transforms requests coming in from the Web to the standard form the database server is accustomed to receiving. It doesn't matter what the database server is — Microsoft SQL Server, Borland InterBase, Informix, Oracle, Sybase SQL Server, or anything else. As far as the server can tell, it is dealing with an ordinary LAN client. It neither knows nor cares that an intranet is involved in its interactions with its clients.

Building Intranet Database Applications

Building database applications that are to run over an intranet requires skill in two different, and largely disjoint, areas. If you are an expert at producing client/server database applications you may be unaware of the most elementary aspects of Web programming. On the other hand, if you're a whiz at Web programming, you may not be a programming pundit with client/server database applications. Practitioners with a high level of skill in both areas are rare. Because of this situation, tool vendors produce tools specifically aimed at Web database development that require less skill than those that traditionally have been available.

Traditional application-development tools

Back in my day, I used to walk 16 miles to school, through slippery mud flats in the spring and waist-deep snow drifts in the winter. . . . Wait a minute. That's a different book. What I mean is, in the early days of Web database development, conditions were pretty primitive. The tools available for database application development were not particularly appropriate for interfacing to a Web server. For their part, Web page design tools were not designed for connecting Web pages to databases either. Web pages were created and formatted using HTML. People wrote server extension programs from scratch using PERL, C, C++, or shell scripts, according to the Common Gateway Interface (CGI) protocol. State management programming required another tool.

To do a good job, you had to understand the interfaces of the Web server and the database server on a low level, and you had to be expert in your language of choice. Development was slow and laborious. There were also significant performance issues, particularly if you were using PERL. PERL is an interpretive language, and the interpreter is over 500K in size. Every time a Web browser made a request, this 500K file would have to be loaded and a PERL script executed. This tended to make database access slow and to load down the server, slowing operation for other users too. You can still write server extensions this way today, if you want to, but now there are better alternatives.

New object-oriented tools

To make Web-based database development an endeavor that mere mortals can pursue with some hope of success, tools vendors are marketing visually oriented development tools that automate much of the job. You no longer need to know C++, PERL, or any similar procedural language. Furthermore, you don't need to be fluent in HTML. With the new generation of tools, you can develop highly functional and visually pleasing Web database applications by pointing to and clicking on icons, and by dragging and dropping objects onto a work surface. Aside from giving their tools a visual orientation, tools vendors provide you with wizards that take much of the drudgery out of application development. You can concentrate on the creative part of the job, rather than getting bogged down in low-level details.

It doesn't take a rocket scientist, or even a skateboard technician, to figure out that database on the Web, both Internet and intranet, is really important and getting more so. Consequently, it is no surprise that a number of companies offer improved development tools for this area. I won't attempt to cover the field, which is changing almost daily, but here are a couple of representative products.

Borland's IntraBuilder

Borland's IntraBuilder is one of the leading examples of the new generation of Web database development tools. Specifically designed for building intranet applications, IntraBuilder owes much of its excellent functionality and ease of use to its descent from Borland's Delphi, one of the most capable and popular development tools for client/server applications. IntraBuilder takes the best of Delphi's database access technology and marries it with complete Web support and visual tools for rapid design of Web forms and reports.

IntraBuilder helps you create "live" Web sites rather than mere static Web pages. Where a static Web page merely displays the information it contains and is difficult to update, you can change a live Web site from your client-side browser. With this capability, Web-based information need never be out of date. IntraBuilder includes a set of tools based on Netscape's JavaScript language that you can use to generate both client-side and server-side scripts.

IntraBuilder provides native driver access to PC databases such as Access, Approach, Paradox, and Visual dBASE, as well as to SQL databases such as Oracle, DB2, Sybase, Informix, InterBase, and Microsoft SQL Server. In addition, it provides ODBC access to any ODBC-compliant data source. You can use IntraBuilder to develop robust, flexible, high-performing, and easy-to-create and maintain intranet database applications.

NetDynamics' NetDynamics Studio

The visual application development tool NetDynamics Studio provides a drag-and-drop programming environment. The tool automatically generates server-side Java, HTML, and SQL code. NetDynamics Studio features an array of Wizards to help you create application features without having to do any manual coding. You can customize the provided default HTML page layouts or create your own with the HTML Editor. Security Wizards enforce security, and there is integration with third-party security mechanisms and encrypted session IDs.

Query-By-Example, as well as SQL, gives you a choice of how to communicate with your data sources. Developer-defined event triggers are available, allowing you to initiate an action when a specified event occurs. The API contains more than 200 classes and 2,500 methods that you can use as building blocks in creating custom applications.

New general purpose tools

Products in this category are general purpose development tools. They are more flexible than the products in the preceding category and consequently require a higher level of skill on your part. These tools are still a big step up from a plain-vanilla language compiler by incorporating a visual design paradigm, automatic generation of code for standard components, and an integrated development environment.

Borland's C++ Builder

As a general purpose Windows 95 and NT development tool, you can use C++ Builder to create stand-alone EXE and DLL files, drivers, action games — practically anything. Although it has broad general applicability, C++ Builder is well-endowed in the database development area. It includes an extensive array of tools and utilities that specifically target creating database applications. A key feature of the C++ Builder database application development support is the data-aware component. You can drop these easy-to-use and fast-executing components into your applications, speeding both development and execution.

Microsoft's Visual C++

Visual C++ is Microsoft's visual application development environment that uses the C++ language. Like C++ Builder, you can use Visual C++ to create any kind of stand-alone program. You can apply the Microsoft development environment to Web database application development as easily as you can apply it to any other kind of development. Visual C++ makes it easy to include ActiveX components in your programs, as well as elements from the Microsoft Foundation Classes library. You can use the templates in the Active Template Library that's included to quickly build custom components.

Borland's JBuilder

JBuilder is a visual application development tool specifically designed to develop Java applications and applets. In structure and features JBuilder has a lot in common with C++ Builder, because both are descendants of Borland's popular Delphi development environment. However, where Delphi produces Pascal code and C++ Builder produces C++ code, JBuilder produces Java code. JBuilder's drag-and-drop development structure is based on Sun's JavaBeans standard. Any applications you develop according to the JavaBeans standard can run on any platform that supports Java.

JBuilder includes what Borland is calling DataDirector architecture, which supports all JDBC- and ODBC-compliant data sources. In addition JBuilder has native drivers for Oracle, Sybase, Informix, InterBase, and other desktop and client/server database-management system.

Microsoft's Visual J++

Visual J++ is Microsoft's visual development environment for creating applications and applets in an extended version of Java that includes ActiveX controls. Visual J++ includes all the things you expect in a full-featured development environment, including a visual debugger, wizards for building applets and ActiveX controls, editor, compiler, and a class viewer to promote easy comprehension of Java objects. Microsoft promotes Visual J++ as an improved version of Java — improved because of its ActiveX support.

The Java–ActiveX battle

A battle is raging for control of the Web development tools market. Sun originally envisioned Java as a cross-platform language that would allow Web-based applications to be completely platform-independent. It wouldn't matter what hardware or operating system you developed an application on, it would run on any other hardware or operating system that supported a standard Web browser. This idea caught on like a brushfire on a dry summer day in Malibu. People started building Java applets for mainframes, mini-computers, PCs, and even Sun workstations. Java became an overnight success.

At first, Microsoft did not perceive the sudden emergence of the Web as a threat to its dominance of the personal-computer software marketplace, so Microsoft mounted only a modest effort in the Web area. Coming late to the realization that a platform-independent Web was indeed a serious problem for the Intel-Microsoft axis, Microsoft went on *red alert* and started developing a strategy to deflect any move toward platform independence back into the Microsoft Windows camp.

Microsoft's weapon of choice in the battle is the ActiveX control. You can speed development of your Java applications and applets with pre-built ActiveX controls or create your own custom ActiveX controls. Such applications can run within a browser on any platform, but you must develop the applications on either a Windows 95 or Windows NT machine. Because the overwhelming majority of computers in the world are Intel machines running Windows, Microsoft has been able to gain substantial support for its view of the future of the Web and of Java.

Meanwhile, Sun and a host of other companies who view Microsoft as intent on taking over the world, are fighting to keep Java "pure." The companies want to make sure that pure Java has no extensions that will tie it to any one development platform, such as Windows. Java would retain the idea that brought it into existence in the first place — platform independence.

After the battle is over, and the world is safe for either pure or extended Java (whichever wins), one thing will still be true: SQL will mediate any communication between the applet/application and its corresponding data source on the server.

Part VI
Advanced Topics

The 5th Wave   By Rich Tennant

"UNFORTUNATELY, THE ADMINISTRATOR'S NOT VERY FAULT-TOLERANT."

In this part . . .

You can approach SQL on many levels. In earlier parts, I cover the major topics that you are likely to encounter in most applications. This part deals with subjects that are significantly more complex. SQL deals with data a set at a time. Cursors come into play only if you want to violate that paradigm and deal with the data a row at a time. Error handling is important to every application, simple or sophisticated. However, it can be approached either simplistically or on a much deeper level. The more depth you give to your error handling, the better off your users are if problems arise. In this part, I give you a view of the depths as well as of the shallows.

Chapter 18

Cursors

As I mention in Chapter 14, a major incompatibility between SQL and the most popular application development languages is that SQL operates on data an entire set of rows at a time, while the procedural languages operate on only a single table row at a time. A cursor enables SQL to retrieve (or update, or delete) a single row at a time so that you can use SQL in combination with an application written in any of the popular languages.

A cursor acts like a pointer that locates a specific table row. When a cursor is active, you can perform a SELECT, UPDATE, or DELETE operation on the row at which the cursor is pointing.

Cursors are valuable if you want to retrieve selected rows from a table, check their contents, and perform different operations based on those contents. SQL can't perform this sequence of operations by itself. SQL can retrieve the rows, but procedural languages are better at making decisions based on field contents. Cursors enable SQL to retrieve rows from a table one at a time and then feed the result to procedural code for processing. By placing the SQL code in a loop, you can process the entire table one row at a time.

In embedded SQL, the most common flow of execution looks like this:

```
EXEC SQL DECLARE CURSOR statement
EXEC SQL OPEN statement
Procedural code
Start loop
    Procedural code
    EXEC SQL FETCH
    Procedural code
    Test for end of table
End loop
EXEC SQL CLOSE statement
Procedural code
```

The SQL statements in this listing are DECLARE, OPEN, FETCH, and CLOSE. In the following sections, I discuss each of these statements in detail.

If you can perform the operation you want with normal SQL (set-at-a-time) statements, do so. Declare a cursor, retrieve table rows one at a time, and use your system's host language only in those instances when normal SQL cannot give you the results you want.

Declaring a Cursor

To use a cursor, you first must declare its existence to the DBMS. Do this with a DECLARE CURSOR statement. The DECLARE CURSOR statement does not actually cause anything to happen. It just announces the name of the cursor to the DBMS and specifies what query the cursor is going to operate on. An SQL-92 DECLARE CURSOR statement has the following syntax:

```
DECLARE cursor-name [INSENSITIVE][SCROLL] CURSOR FOR
    query expression
    [ORDER BY order-by expression]
    [FOR updatability expression] ;
```

Note: The cursor name uniquely identifies a particular cursor, so it must be different from that of any other cursor name in the current module or compilation unit.

To make your application more readable, give the cursor a meaningful name. Relate it to the data that the query expression requests or to the operation that your procedural code performs on the data.

The query expression

The query expression can be any legal SELECT statement. The rows that the SELECT statement retrieves are the ones that the cursor steps through one at a time. These rows are the scope of the cursor.

The query is not actually performed when the DECLARE CURSOR statement is read. You cannot retrieve data until you execute the OPEN statement. The row-by-row examination of the data starts after you enter the loop that encloses the FETCH statement.

The ORDER BY clause

You may want to process your retrieved data in a particular order, depending on what your procedural code is going to do with the data. You can sort the retrieved rows before processing them, using the optional ORDER BY clause. The clause has the following syntax:

```
ORDER BY sort-specification [ , sort-specification ]...
```

You can have multiple sort specifications, each of which has the following syntax:

```
( column-name | unsigned-integer )
   [ COLLATE BY collation-name ] [ ASC | DESC ]
```

In all cases, you sort by a column, but you can specify the column either by its name or by using an integer to designate the column. If you sort by column name, the column must be one of those in the select list of the query expression. Columns that are in the table but not in the query select list do not work as sort specifications. If you sort by unsigned integer, the integer represents the position of the column in the query select list. The number 1 represents the first column specified in the query's select list, 2 specifies the second, and so on.

As an example, suppose that you want to perform an operation, not supported by SQL, on selected rows of the CUSTOMER table. You could write a DECLARE CURSOR statement similar to the following:

```
DECLARE cust1 CURSOR FOR
   SELECT CUST_ID, F_NAME, L_NAME, CITY, STATE, PHONE
      FROM CUSTOMER
   ORDER BY STATE, L_NAME, F_NAME ;
```

In this example, the SELECT statement retrieves rows sorted first by state, then by last name, and finally by first name. The statement retrieves all customers in Alaska (AK) before it retrieves the first customer from Alabama (AL). The statement then sorts customer records from Alaska by the customer's last name. For example, Aaron comes before Abbott. In cases where the last name is the same, sorting then goes by first name. George Aaron comes before Henry Aaron. You can obtain the same result with the following alternative syntax:

```
DECLARE cust1 CURSOR FOR
    SELECT CUST_ID, F_NAME, L_NAME, CITY, STATE, PHONE
        FROM CUSTOMER
    ORDER BY 5, 3, 2 ;
```

In this formulation, you order the rows first by the fifth column in the query select list (STATE), then by the third column (L_NAME), and finally by the second column (F_NAME).

Have you ever had to make 40 copies of a 20-page document on a photocopy machine that did not have a collator attached? What a drag! You must make 20 stacks on tables, desks, and any other flat surfaces in sight and then walk by the stacks 40 times, placing a sheet on each stack as you go by. This ordering process is called *collation*. A similar process plays a role in SQL.

In Chapter 5, I define a collation as a set of rules that determine how strings in a character set compare with each other. A character set has a default collation sequence that defines the order in which elements are sorted. However, you can apply a collation sequence other than the default to a column. To do so, use the optional COLLATE BY clause. Your implementation probably supports several common collations. You can pick one and then make the collation either ascending or descending by appending an ASC or DESC keyword to the clause.

In a DECLARE CURSOR statement, you can specify a calculated column that does not exist in the underlying table. In such a case, the calculated column does not have a name that you can use in the ORDER BY clause. You can give it a name in the DECLARE CURSOR query expression, which enables you to identify the column later. Consider the following example:

```
DECLARE revenue CURSOR FOR
    SELECT model, units, price,
        units * price AS extprice
        FROM TRANSDETAIL
    ORDER BY model, extprice DESC ;
```

In this example, because no COLLATE BY clause is in the ORDER BY clause, I use the default collation sequence. Notice that the fourth column in the select list results from a calculation made on the data in the second and third columns. The fourth column is an extended price and has the name extprice. In the ORDER BY clause, I first sort by model name and then by extprice. The sort on extprice is descending, as specified by the DESC keyword; the transactions with the highest dollar value are processed first. The default sort order is ascending (ASC), because sorts are in ascending order if you do not specify a sort order.

After you specify a sort order in an ORDER BY clause, that sort order is effective until you explicitly change it. Thus if you have a sort specification list that includes a DESC sort and you want the next sort to be in ascending order, you must explicitly specify ASC for that next sort. For example:

```
ORDER BY A, B DESC, C, D, E ASC, F
```

is equivalent to

```
ORDER BY A ASC, B DESC, C DESC, D DESC, E ASC, F ASC
```

The rule is to default to the first explicit ASC or DESC to the left, otherwise to ASC if no explicit ASC or DESC is to the left.

Unsigned integers as sort specifications have been deprecated

Using an unsigned integer in a sort specification is deprecated in SQL-92. When a feature is deprecated in an ANSI standard, the feature is considered either obsolete or undesirable. Using the feature is discouraged, and it will probably be dropped in the next release of the standard. Deprecating a feature in one version of a standard gives people time to eliminate the feature from their products before the next version of the standard comes out.

SQL originally included integers in the ORDER BY clause as a way to reference select list elements that were expressions (and therefore didn't have column names):

```
SELECT E_NM, SALARY+COMMISSION
    FROM EMPLOYEE ORDER BY 2 ;
```

There was originally no other way to reference that second column. SQL-92 then introduced the AS clause as a way to give names to select list elements:

```
SELECT E_NM AS EMP_NAME,
    SALARY+COMMISSION AS PAY FROM
    EMPLOYEE ORDER BY PAY ;
```

The AS clause provides more readable names, and gives identifying names to expression columns. The latter use makes integers in ORDER BY unnecessary, so the feature was deprecated.

The updatability clause

On some occasions, you may want to update or delete table rows that you access via a cursor. At other times, you may want to guarantee that you cannot make such updates or deletions. SQL-92 gives you considerable control over this issue with the updatability clause of the DECLARE CURSOR statement. If you want to prevent updates and deletions within the scope of the cursor, use the clause

```
FOR READ ONLY
```

To make updates of specified columns only, leaving all others protected from changes, use

```
FOR UPDATE OF column-name [ , column-name ]...
```

Of course, any columns listed must appear in the DECLARE CURSOR's query expression. If you don't include an updatability clause, the default assumption is that all columns listed in the query expression are updatable. In that case, an UPDATE statement can update all the columns in the row to which the cursor is pointing, and a DELETE statement can delete that row.

Sensitivity

The query expression in the DECLARE CURSOR statement determines the rows that fall within the scope of a cursor. Consider a possible problem: What if a statement in your program, located between the OPEN and the CLOSE statements, changes the contents of some of those rows so that they no longer satisfy the query? What if such a statement deletes some of those rows entirely? Does the cursor continue to process all the rows that originally qualified, or does it recognize the new situation and ignore rows that no longer qualify or that have been deleted?

Changing the data in columns that are part of a DECLARE CURSOR query expression after some but not all of the query's rows have been processed results in a big mess. Your results are likely to be inconsistent and misleading. To avoid this problem, make your cursor insensitive to any changes that statements within its scope may make. Add the INSENSITIVE keyword to your DECLARE CURSOR statement. As long as your cursor is open, it is insensitive to table changes that otherwise affect rows qualified to be included in the cursor's scope. A cursor cannot be both insensitive and updatable. An insensitive cursor must be read-only.

Think of it this way: A normal SQL statement, such as UPDATE, INSERT, or DELETE, operates on a set of rows in a database table (perhaps the entire table). While such a statement is active, SQL's transaction mechanism protects it from interference by other statements acting concurrently on the same data. If you use a cursor, however, your "window of vulnerability" to harmful interaction is wide open. You are at risk from the moment that you open a cursor until you close it. If you open one cursor and start processing through a table and then open a second cursor while the first is still active, the actions you perform with the second cursor can affect what the statement controlled by the first cursor sees. For example:

```
DECLARE C1 CURSOR FOR SELECT * FROM EMPLOYEE
    ORDER BY SALARY ;
DECLARE C2 CURSOR FOR SELECT * FROM EMPLOYEE
    FOR UPDATE OF SALARY ;
```

Now, say you open both cursors and fetch a few rows with C1 and then update a salary with C2 to increase its value. This can cause a row that you have already fetched with C1 to appear again on a later fetch of C1.

The peculiar interactions possible with multiple open cursors, or opened cursors and set operations, are the sort of concurrency problems that transaction isolation avoids. If you operate this way, you are asking for trouble. So remember: Don't operate with multiple open cursors.

Scrollability

Scrollability is a capability that cursors did not have prior to SQL-92. In implementations adhering to SQL-86 or SQL-89, the only allowed movement of the cursor was sequential, starting at the first row retrieved by the query expression and ending with the last row. SQL-92's inclusion of the SCROLL keyword in the DECLARE CURSOR statement gives you the capability to access rows in any order you want. The syntax of the FETCH statement controls the movement of the cursor. I describe the FETCH statement later in this chapter.

One limitation to SQL-92's scrollability is that a scrollable cursor must be read-only. You cannot perform updates or deletes within the scope of a scrolled cursor.

Opening a Cursor

Although the DECLARE CURSOR statement specifies which rows to include in the cursor, it doesn't actually cause anything to happen, because DECLARE is a declaration and not an executable statement. The OPEN statement actually brings the cursor into existence. It has the following form:

```
OPEN cursor-name ;
```

To open the cursor used as an example in the previous discussion of the ORDER BY clause, use the following:

```
DECLARE revenue CURSOR FOR
    SELECT model, units, price,
          units * price AS extprice
      FROM TRANSDETAIL
    ORDER BY model, extprice DESC ;
OPEN revenue ;
```

You can't fetch rows from a cursor until you open the cursor. The moment you open a cursor, the values of variables referenced in the DECLARE CURSOR statement become fixed, as do all current date-time functions. Consider the following example:

```
DECLARE CURSOR C1 FOR SELECT * FROM ORDERS
WHERE ORDERS.CUSTOMER = :NAME
AND DUE_DATE < CURRENT_DATE ;
NAME := 'Acme Co';    @hy@hyA host language statement
OPEN C1;
NAME := 'Omega Inc.';   @hy@hyAnother host statement
...
UPDATE ORDERS SET DUE_DATE = CURRENT_DATE;
```

The OPEN statement fixes the value of all variables referenced in the declare cursor, and also fixes a value for all current date-time functions. Thus the second assignment to the name variable (NAME := 'Omega Inc.') has no effect on the rows that the cursor fetches. (That value of NAME is used the next time you open C1.) And, even if the OPEN statement is executed a minute before midnight and the UPDATE statement is executed a minute after midnight, the value of CURRENT_DATE in the UPDATE statement is the value of that function at the time the OPEN statement executed. This is true even if DECLARE CURSOR doesn't reference the date-time function.

The fix is in (for date-times)

There is a similar "fixing" of date-time values in set operations. Consider:

```
UPDATE ORDERS SET RECHECK_DATE =
   CURRENT_DATE WHERE....;
```

Now suppose that you have a lot of orders. You begin executing this statement at a minute before midnight. At midnight, the statement is still running, and it doesn't finish executing until five minutes after midnight. It doesn't matter. If a statement has any reference to CURRENT_DATE (or TIME or TIMESTAMP), the value is fixed when the statement begins, so all of the ORDERS rows in the statement get the same RECHECK_DATE. Similarly, if a statement references TIMESTAMP, the whole statement uses only one time stamp value, no matter how long the statement runs.

Here's an interesting example of an implication of this rule:

```
UPDATE EMPLOYEE SET
   KEY=CURRENT_TIMESTAMP;
```

You may expect that statement to set a unique value in the key column of each EMPLOYEE. You'd be disappointed: It sets the same value in every row.

So when the OPEN statement fixes date-time values for all statements referencing the cursor, it treats all of those statements as something like an extended statement.

Fetching Data from a Single Row

While the DECLARE CURSOR statement specifies the name of the cursor and its scope and the OPEN statement collects the table rows selected by the DECLARE CURSOR query expression, the FETCH statement actually retrieves the data. The cursor always points either to one of the rows in the scope of the cursor or to the empty space between two rows. You can specify where the cursor points with the orientation clause in the FETCH statement.

Syntax

The syntax for the FETCH command is

```
FETCH [[orientation] FROM] cursor-name
   INTO target-specification [, target-specification ]...
```

There are six orientation options: NEXT, PRIOR, FIRST, LAST, ABSOLUTE, and RELATIVE. The default option is NEXT, which was the only orientation available in versions of SQL prior to SQL-92. It moves the cursor from wherever it is to the next row in the set specified by the query expression. If the cursor is located before the first record, it moves to the first. If it points to record n, it moves to record n+1. If the cursor points to the last record in the set, it moves beyond that record and notification of a no data condition is returned in the SQLCODE system variable. (Take a look at Chapter 19 for details on SQLCODE and the rest of SQL's error-handling facilities.)

The target specifications are either host variables or parameters respectively, depending on whether embedded SQL or module language is using the cursor. The number and types of the target specifications must match the number and types of the columns specified by the query expression in the DECLARE CURSOR statement. So, in the case of embedded SQL, when you fetch a list of five values from a row of a table, five host variables must be there to receive those values, and they must be the right types.

Orientation of a scrollable cursor

Because the SQL-92 cursor is scrollable, you have other choices besides NEXT. If you specify PRIOR, the pointer moves to the row immediately preceding its current location. If you specify FIRST, it points to the first record in the set, and if you specify LAST, it points to the last record.

An integer value specification must accompany ABSOLUTE and RELATIVE. For example, FETCH ABSOLUTE 7 would move the cursor to the seventh row from the beginning of the set. FETCH RELATIVE 7 would move the cursor seven rows beyond its current position. FETCH RELATIVE 0 leaves the cursor at its current location.

FETCH RELATIVE 1 has the same effect as FETCH NEXT. FETCH RELATIVE 1 has the same effect as FETCH PRIOR. FETCH ABSOLUTE 1 gives you the first record in the set, and interestingly, FETCH ABSOLUTE -1 gives you the last record in the set. Any other negative value specification returns the *no data* exception condition code (+100) in the SQLCODE variable. Specifying FETCH ABSOLUTE 0 also returns the *no data* exception condition code, as does FETCH ABSOLUTE 17 if only 16 rows are in the set.

Positioned DELETE and UPDATE statements

You can perform delete and update operations on the row that the cursor is currently pointing to. The syntax of the DELETE statement is as follows:

```
DELETE FROM table-name WHERE CURRENT OF cursor-name ;
```

If the cursor is not currently pointing to a row, this statement generates an error condition, and no deletion occurs.

The syntax of the UPDATE statement is as follows:

```
UPDATE table-name
   SET column-name = value [,column-name = value]...
   WHERE CURRENT OF cursor-name ;
```

The value you place into each specified column must be either a value expression, the keyword, or the keyword DEFAULT. If the cursor has an ORDER BY clause, you cannot update the columns used in the ordering. If an attempted positioned update operation returns any error, the update isn't performed.

Closing a Cursor

After you finish with a cursor, good practice is to close it. Leaving a cursor open as your application goes on to deal with other issues may cause no harm, but then again it may. Also, open cursors consume system resources. Make a habit of closing your cursors after they serve their purpose.

If you close a cursor that was insensitive to changes made while it was open, reopen it; the reopened cursor will now reflect any such changes.

Chapter 19

Error Handling

● ●

● ●

*W*ouldn't it be great if every application you wrote worked perfectly every time? Yeah, and it also would be really cool to win $57 million in the Oregon state lottery. Unfortunately, both possibilities are about as likely. Error conditions of one sort or another are inevitable, so it's helpful to know what caused them. SQL-92 has two mechanisms for returning error information to you — the *status parameters* (or *host variables*) SQLCODE and SQLSTATE. Based on the contents of either of these parameters, you can take different actions to remedy the error condition.

For example, the WHENEVER clause enables you to take a predetermined action whenever a specified condition (such as SQLCODE having a negative value) is met. You can also find detailed status information about the SQL statement you just executed in the diagnostics area. In this chapter, I explain these helpful error handling facilities and how to use them.

SQLCODE

Prior to SQL-92, versions of the SQL standard contained only one mechanism for returning error information: SQLCODE. SQLCODE is an integer variable that updates after the execution of every SQL statement. If the executed statement is successful, SQLCODE assumes a value of zero. If the statement does not produce an error but encounters a *no-data condition*, SQLCODE assumes a value of 100. A no-data condition occurs, for example, if you execute a SELECT on a table that has no rows or a FETCH on a table if the cursor is already located on the last record. A no-data condition may or may not be an error, depending on the situation. Any result besides successful completion (0) or no data (100) is an error of some sort and returns a negative number. Table 19-1 shows the possibilities.

Table 19-1	SQLCODE **Values**
Execution State	SQLCODE
Successful completion	0
No data	100
Error	A negative number

The SQL standard has never specified which particular error conditions produce a particular value in SQLCODE. Consequently, implementors have all come up with their own specifications. Naturally, these specifications often do not agree with each other. So, if you want to migrate an application from one DBMS to another, you may need to recode all of the error handling, which, unfortunately, can amount to rewriting a major portion of the entire application.

Because so many of the applications already written depend on the values of SQLCODE that various implementors have established, it was not practical for SQL-92 to establish standard meanings for the negative numbers that denote various error conditions. To do so would have caused a retrofit nightmare for almost everyone who had already written an SQL application. Instead SQL-92 standardized a new status parameter, SQLSTATE. With the standardization of SQLSTATE, SQLCODE has been deprecated. Of course, SQLCODE isn't cursed in the literal sense. SQLCODE still works the way it has in the past; however, its use is discouraged. I recommend using SQLSTATE for all new applications instead. Although SQL-92 still supports SQLCODE, it may be dropped from a future release of the standard, so it's a good idea to switch to SQLSTATE wherever possible.

SQLSTATE

SQLSTATE does the same thing that SQLCODE does, just in a more standard-ized way. SQLSTATE specifies a large number of conditions as opposed to two (successful completion and no data) for SQLCODE. The variety of standard conditions makes migrating applications that use SQLSTATE from one DBMS platform to another much easier.

Another difference between the two error conditions is that SQLCODE is defined as an integer but SQLSTATE is a five-character string. In SQLSTATE, only the uppercase letters A through Z and the numerals 0 through 9 are valid characters. The five-character string is divided into two groups: a two-character class code and a three-character subclass code. Figure 19-1 illustrates the SQLSTATE layout.

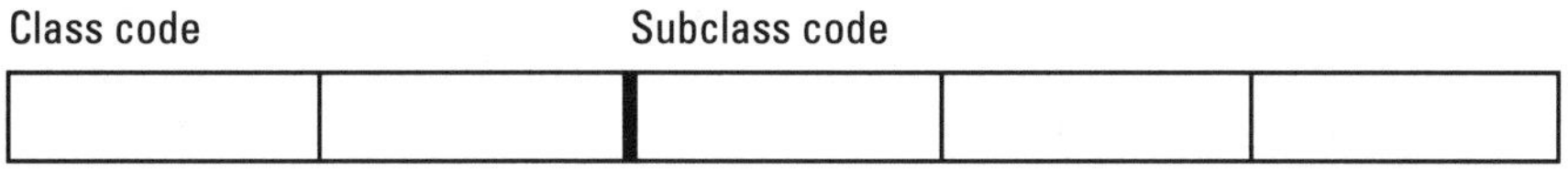

Figure 19-1:
SQLSTATE
status
parameter
layout.

Class code   Subclass code

The SQL-92 standard defines any class code starting with the letters A through H or the numerals 0 through 4, and thus these class codes mean the same thing in any implementation. Class codes starting with I through Z or 5 through 9 are left open for implementors to define. These codes are left to the implementors because the SQL specification cannot anticipate every condition that may come up in every implementation. Clearly, however, implementors should use discretionary class codes as little as possible to avoid the migration problems that can occur with SQLCODE. Ideally, implementors should use the standard codes most of the time and the nonstandard codes only under the most unusual circumstances.

In SQLSTATE, a class code of 00 indicates successful completion. Class code 01 means that statement executed successfully but produced a warning. Class code 02 indicates the no-data condition and thus is equivalent to an SQLCODE of 100. Any SQLSTATE class code other than 00, 01, or 02 indicates that the statement did not execute successfully.

Because SQLSTATE updates after every SQL operation, you can check it after every statement executes. If SQLSTATE contains 00000 (successful completion), proceed with the next operation. If it contains anything else, you may want to branch out of the main line of your code to handle the situation. The specific class code and subclass code that a SQLSTATE contains determines which of several possible actions you should take.

To use SQLSTATE in a module language program (as described in Chapter 14), include a reference to it in your procedure definitions, as shown in the following example:

```
PROCEDURE NUTRIENT
    (SQLSTATE, :foodname CHAR (20), :calories SMALLINT,
        :protein DECIMAL (5,1), :fat DECIMAL (5,1),
        :carbo DECIMAL (5,1))
INSERT INTO FOODS
    (FOODNAME, CALORIES, PROTEIN, FAT, CARBOHYDRATE)
    VALUES
    (:foodname, :calories, :protein, :fat, :carbo) ;
```

At the appropriate spot in your procedural language program, you make values available for the parameters (perhaps by soliciting them from the user) and then call up the procedure. The syntax of this varies from one language to another, but it most likely looks something like this:

```
foodname = "Okra, boiled" ;
calories = 29 ;
protein = 2.0 ;
fat = 0.3 ;
carbo = 6.0 ;
NUTRIENT(state, foodname, calories, protein, fat, carbo);
```

The status of SQLSTATE is returned in the variable state. Your program can examine this variable and then take the appropriate action based on the variable's contents.

Older implementations of SQL support only SQLCODE. Newer ones support both SQLCODE and SQLSTATE. If your implementation supports SQLSTATE, use it instead of SQLCODE. SQLSTATE provides all the information that SQLCODE does, and it is more precisely specified. Also SQLSTATE is guaranteed to be supported in future releases of the SQL specification.

The WHENEVER Clause

What's the point in knowing that an SQL operation didn't execute successfully if you can't do anything about it? If an error occurs, you don't want your application to continue executing as if everything is fine. You need to be able to acknowledge the error and do something to correct it. If you can't correct the error, at the very least you want to inform the user of the problem and bring the application to a graceful termination. The WHENEVER clause is the SQL mechanism for dealing with execution exceptions.

The WHENEVER clause is actually a declaration and as such is located in your application's SQL declaration section, ahead of the executable SQL code. The syntax is as follows:

```
WHENEVER condition action ;
```

The condition may be either SQLERROR or NOT FOUND. The action may be either CONTINUE or GOTO *address*. SQLERROR is True if SQLCODE is negative or if SQLSTATE has a class code other than 00, 01, or 02. NOT FOUND is True if SQLCODE is 100 or if SQLSTATE is 02000.

If the action is CONTINUE, nothing special takes place and the execution continues normally. If the action is GOTO *address* (or GO TO *address*), execution branches to the designated address in the program. At the branch address, you can put a conditional statement that examines SQLCODE or SQLSTATE and takes different actions based on what it finds. Following are some examples of this:

```
WHENEVER SQLERROR GO TO error_trap ;
```

or

```
WHENEVER NOT FOUND CONTINUE ;
```

The GO TO option is simply a macro: The implementation (that is, the embedded language precompiler) inserts the following test after every EXEC SQL statement:

```
IF SQLSTATE <> '00000' THEN GOTO error_trap;
```

The CONTINUE option is essentially a NO-OP that says "ignore this."

The Diagnostics Area

Although SQLSTATE can give you more information about why a particular statement failed than SQLCODE can, SQLSTATE is still pretty brief. So SQL-92 provides for the capture and retention of additional status information in a diagnostics area. The additional status information can be particularly helpful in cases where the execution of a single SQL statement generates multiple errors. SQLCODE and SQLSTATE only report the occurrence of one of them, but the diagnostics area has the capacity to report on multiple (hopefully all) errors.

The diagnostics area is a DBMS-managed data structure that has two components, a header and a detail area. The header contains general information about the last SQL statement that was executed. The detail area holds information about each code (either error, warning, or success) that the statement generated.

In Chapter 13, I cover the SET TRANSACTION statement. In this statement, you can specify DIAGNOSTICS SIZE. The SIZE you specify is the number of detail areas allocated for status information. If you do not include a DIAGNOSTICS SIZE clause in your SET TRANSACTION statement, your DBMS assigns its default number of detail areas, whatever that happens to be.

The header area contains five items, listed in Table 19-2.

Table 19-2	The Diagnostics Header Area
Item	*Data Type*
NUMBER	Exact numeric, scale 0
MORE	Character string, length 1
COMMAND_FUNCTION	Character varying, length <= 128
DYNAMIC_FUNCTION	Character varying, length <= 128
ROW_COUNT	Exact numeric, scale 0

The NUMBER field lists the number of detail areas filled with data as a result of the execution of the statement. The MORE field contains either 'Y' or 'N'; 'Y' if the diagnostics area holds all the conditions that the DBMS detects, and 'N' if more conditions are detected than the detail area can hold. COMMAND_FUNCTION contains a character string that is the SQL statement that generates the diagnostic entry. If a dynamic SQL statement generates the entry, COMMAND_FUNCTION contains either EXECUTE or EXECUTE IMMEDIATE, and DYNAMIC_FUNCTION holds the dynamic SQL statement itself. ROW_COUNT holds the number of rows the SQL statement affects.

The detail areas contain data on each individual error, warning, or success condition. Each detail area contains 17 items, as shown in Table 19-3.

Table 19-3	The Diagnostics Detail Area
Item	*Data Type*
CONDITION_NUMBER	Exact numeric, scale 0
RETURNED_SQLSTATE	Character string, length 5
CLASS_ORIGIN	Character varying, length <= maximum length of an identifier
SUBCLASS_ORIGIN	Character varying, length <= maximum length of an identifier
CONSTRAINT_CATALOG	Character varying, length <= maximum length of an identifier
CONSTRAINT_SCHEMA	Character varying, length <= maximum length of an identifier

Item	Data Type
CONSTRAINT_NAME	Character varying, length <= maximum length of an identifier
CONNECTION_NAME	Character varying, length <= maximum length of an identifier
ENVIRONMENT_NAME	Character varying, length <= maximum length of an identifier
CATALOG_NAME	Character varying, length <= maximum length of an identifier
SCHEMA_NAME	Character varying, length <= maximum length of an identifier
TABLE_NAME	Character varying, length <= maximum length of an identifier
COLUMN NAME	Character varying, length <= maximum length of an identifier
CURSOR_NAME	Character varying, length <= maximum length of an identifier
MESSAGE_TEXT	Character varying, length <= maximum length of an identifier
MESSAGE_LENGTH	Exact numeric, scale 0
MESSAGE_OCTET_LENGTH	Exact numeric, scale 0

CONDITION_NUMBER holds the sequence number of the detail area. If a statement generates five status items that fill up five detail areas, the CONDITION_NUMBER for the fifth one is five. To retrieve a specific detail area for examination, use a GET DIAGNOSTICS statement (described later in this chapter) with the desired CONDITION_NUMBER. RETURNED_SQLSTATE holds the SQLSTATE value that caused this detail area to be filled.

CLASS_ORIGIN tells you the source of the value returned in SQLSTATE. If the SQL standard defines the value, the CLASS_ORIGIN is 'ISO 9075'. If your DBMS implementation defines the value, CLASS_ORIGIN holds a string identifying the source of your DBMS. SUBCLASS_ORIGIN acts similarly to CLASS_ORIGIN.

CLASS_ORIGIN is important. If you get an SQLSTATE such as '22012', the values indicate that it is in the range of standard SQLSTATEs, so you know that it means the same thing in all SQL implementations. However, if the SQLSTATE is '22500', the first two characters are in the standard range and indicate a data exception, but the last three characters are in the implementation-defined range. And if SQLSTATE is '900001', it is completely in the implementation-defined range.

So how do you find out the detailed meaning of '22500' or the meaning of '900001'? You must look in the implementor's documentation. Which implementor? If you are using CONNECT, you may be connecting to various products. To determine which one produced the error condition, look at CLASS_ORIGIN and SUBCLASS_ORIGIN: They have values that identify each implementation. You can test the CLASS_ORIGIN and SUBCLASS_ORIGIN to see if they identify implementors for which you have the SQLSTATE listings. The actual values placed in CLASS_ORIGIN and SUBCLASS_ORIGIN are implementor-defined, but they also are expected to be self-explanatory company names.

If the error reported is a constraint violation, the CONSTRAINT_CATALOG, CONSTRAINT_SCHEMA, and CONSTRAINT_NAME identify the constraint being violated.

The constraint violation information is probably the most important information that GET DIAGNOSTICS provides. Consider an EMPLOYEE table such as the following:

```
CREATE TABLE EMPLOYEE
(ID CHAR(5) CONSTRAINT EMP_PK PRIMARY KEY,
SALARY DEC(8,2) CONSTRAINT EMP_SAL CHECK SALARY > 0,
DEPT CHAR(5) CONSTRAINT EMP_DEPT
   REFERENCES DEPARTMENT) ;
```

And possibly a DEPARTMENT table such as this:

```
CREATE TABLE DEPARTMENT
   (DEPTNO CHAR(5),
   BUDGET DEC(12,2) CONSTRAINT DEPT_BUDGET
   CHECK(BUDGET >= SELECT SUM(SALARY) FROM EMPLOYEE
       WHERE EMPLOYEE.DEPT=DEPARTMENT.DEPTNO),
   ...);
```

Now consider an INSERT as follows:

```
INSERT INTO EMP VALUES(:ID_VAR, :SAL_VAR, :DEPT_VAR);
```

Now suppose that you get an SQLSTATE of '23000'. You look it up in your SQL documentation, and it says "integrity constraint violation." Now what? That SQLSTATE value means that either

✔ The value in ID_VAR is a duplicate of an existing ID value: You have violated the PRIMARY KEY constraint.

✔ The value in SAL_VAR is negative: You have violated the CHECK constraint on SALARY.

✔ The value in DEPT_VAR isn't a valid key value for any existing row of DEPARTMENT: You have violated the REFERENCES constraint on DEPT.

✔ The value in SAL_VAR is large enough that the sum of the employees' salaries in this department exceeds the BUDGET: You have violated the CHECK constraint in the BUDGET column of DEPARTMENT. (Recall that if you change the database, all constraints that may be affected are checked, not just those defined in the immediate table.)

Under normal circumstances, you would need to do a lot of testing to figure out what is wrong with that INSERT. But you can find out what you need to know by using GET DIAGNOSTICS as follows:

```
DECLARE CONST_NAME_VAR CHAR(18) ;
GET DIAGNOSTICS EXCEPTION 1
    CONST_NAME_VAR = CONSTRAINT_NAME ;
```

Assuming that SQLSTATE is '23000', this GET DIAGNOSTICS sets CONST_NAME_VAR to either 'EMP_PK', 'EMP_SAL', 'EMP_DEPT', or 'DEPT_BUDGET'. Notice that, in practice you also want to obtain the CONSTRAINT_SCHEMA and CONSTRAINT_CATALOG, to uniquely identify the constraint given by CONSTRAINT_NAME.

This use of GET DIAGNOSTICS, determining which of several constraints has been violated, is particularly important in the case where ALTER TABLE was used to add constraints that did not exist when you wrote the program.

```
ALTER TABLE EMPLOYEE
    ADD CONSTRAINT SAL_LIMIT CHECK(SALARY < 100000) ;
```

Now if you insert into EMPLOYEE or update the SALARY column of an EMPLOYEE, you get an SQLSTATE of '23000' if SALARY exceeds 100000. You can program your INSERT statement so that, if you get an SQLSTATE of '23000', and you don't recognize the particular constraint name that GET DIAGNOSTICS returns, you can display a helpful message, such as Invalid INSERT: Violated constraint SAL_LIMIT.

CONNECTION_NAME and ENVIRONMENT_NAME identify the connection and environment to which you are connected at the time the SQL statement is executed.

If the report deals with a table operation, CATALOG_NAME, SCHEMA_NAME, and TABLE_NAME identifies the table. COLUMN_NAME identifies the column within the table that caused the report to be made. If the situation involves a cursor, CURSOR_NAME gives it its name.

Sometimes a DBMS produces a string of natural language text to explain a condition. The MESSAGE_TEXT item is for this kind of information. The contents of this item depend on the implementation; SQL-92 doesn't explicitly define them. If you do have something in MESSAGE_TEXT, its length in characters is recorded in MESSAGE_LENGTH and its length in octets is recorded in MESSAGE_OCTET_LENGTH. If the message is in normal ASCII characters, MESSAGE_LENGTH equals MESSAGE_OCTET_LENGTH. If, on the other hand, the message is in Kanji or some other language whose characters require more than an octet to express, MESSAGE_LENGTH differs from MESSAGE_OCTET_LENGTH.

To retrieve diagnostic information from a diagnostics area header, use the following:

```
GET DIAGNOSTICS status@sub1 = item@sub1 [, status@sub2 =
          item@sub2]...
```

Status@subn is a host variable or parameter; *item@subn* can be any of the keywords NUMBER, MORE, COMMAND_FUNCTION, DYNAMIC_FUNCTION, or ROW_COUNT.

To retrieve diagnostic information from a diagnostics detail area the syntax is as follows:

```
GET DIAGNOSTICS EXCEPTION condition-number
   status@sub1 = item@sub1 [, status@sub2 = item@sub2]...
```

Again *status@subn* is a host variable or parameter, and *item@subn* is any of the 17 keywords for the detail items listed in Table 19-3. The condition number is (surprise!) the detail area's CONDITION_NUMBER item.

Part VII
The Part of Tens

The 5th Wave   By Rich Tennant

Re'al Pro·gram·mers

Real Programmers code in pen.

In this part . . .

*I*f you've read this far, congratulations! You may now consider yourself an SQL weenie. To raise your status that final degree from weenie to wizard, however, you must master two sets of ten rules. But don't make the mistake of just reading the section headings. Taking some of these headings at face value could have dire consequences. All the tips in this part are short and to the point, so reading them all in their entirety shouldn't be too much trouble. Put them into practice and you can be a true SQL wizard.

Chapter 20

Ten Common Mistakes

*I*f you are reading this book, you must be interested in building relational database systems. Nobody studies SQL for the fun of it. SQL is the language you use to build database applications. A necessary prelude to building a database application is creating a database for it to work on. But many projects go awry before the first line of the application is coded. If you don't get the database definition right, your application is doomed, no matter how well it is written. Here are ten common database creation mistakes that you would be wise to avoid.

Believe that Your Clients Know What They Need

Generally, if a client calls you in to design a database system, he has a problem and the client's current methods are not working. Often clients believe that they know what the problem is and what needs to be done to solve it. They figure that all they need to do is tell *you* what to do.

Giving clients exactly what they ask for is usually a sure-fire prescription for disaster. Most users (and their managers) are not trained in the analytical methods needed to find out what the problem really is, so they have no chance of determining the best solution.

What you must do is tactfully convince the client that you are the expert in systems analysis and design and that you must do a proper analysis to uncover the real cause of the problem that has manifested itself. Usually the real cause of the problem is hidden from view.

Don't Worry about Project Scope

At the beginning of a development project, your client tells you what he wants the new application to accomplish. Unfortunately, the client always forgets to tell you something — usually several things. Somewhere along the way, these new requirements crop up and are tacked onto the project. If you are being paid on a project basis rather than an hourly basis, this kind of growth in scope can change what was once a profitable project into a loser. Make sure that everything you are obligated to deliver is specified in writing before you start the project.

Consider Only Technical Factors

Often application developers look at potential projects in terms of their technical feasibility and base their estimates of effort and time on that determination. However, issues of cost maximums, resource availability, schedule requirements, and organization politics can have a major effect on the project. In fact, these issues may turn a project that is technically feasible into a nightmare. Make sure that you understand all relevant factors before starting any development project. You may decide it makes no sense to proceed. You're better off coming to that conclusion at the beginning than to realize it after you expend considerable effort.

Don't Ask for User Feedback

Listen to the managers. The users themselves don't have any clout. Better yet, ignore the managers, too. They usually don't have a clue anyway. It may be true that data-entry clerks don't have much organizational clout, and many managers have only a dim understanding of some aspects of their areas of responsibility. But isolating yourself from one or both of these groups is almost certain to result in a system that solves a problem that nobody has. Communication with your clients is critical.

Always Use Your Favorite Development Environment

Chances are good that you have spent months or even years becoming proficient in the use of a particular DBMS or application development environment. Your favorite environment, no matter what it is, has strengths and weaknesses. Occasionally, you come across a development task that makes heavy demands in an area where your preferred development environment is weak. Rather than kludge together something that is not really the best solution, bite the bullet. You have two options: Either climb the learning curve of a more appropriate tool and then use it or candidly tell your clients that their job would best be done with a tool that you are not expert in using. Suggest that they hire someone who can become productive with that tool immediately. Professional conduct of this sort raises your clients' respect for you. (Unfortunately, if you work in an office instead of for yourself, that conduct may also get you laid off or fired.)

Always Use Your Favorite System Architecture

Nobody can be an expert at everything. Database management systems that work in a teleprocessing environment are different from those that work in client/server, resource sharing, and distributed database environments. The one or two that you are expert in may not be the best for the job at hand. Choose the best architecture anyway, even if it means passing on this job. Not getting the job is better than getting it but producing a system that does not serve the client's needs.

Design Database Tables in Isolation

Incorrect identification of data objects and their relationships to each other leads to database tables that are prone to introducing errors into the data, which can destroy the validity of any results. To design a sound database, you must consider the overall organization of the data objects and carefully determine how they relate to each other. Usually, no one *right* way exists. You must determine what is appropriate, considering the present and projected future needs of your client.

Skip Design Reviews

Nobody's perfect. Even the best designer and developer can miss important points that are evident to someone looking at the situation from another perspective. Actually, if you must present your work to a formal design review, it makes you more disciplined in your work, probably helping you avoid numerous problems that you may otherwise have experienced. Have a competent professional review your proposed design before you start development.

Skip Beta Testing

Any database application complex enough to be truly useful is also complex enough to contain bugs. Even if you test it in every way you can think of, it's sure to contain failure modes you cannot uncover. Beta testing means giving the application to people who do not understand it as well as you do. They're likely to have all kinds of problems that you never encountered because you knew too much. You need to fix such things before the product goes officially into use.

Skip Documenting

If you think your application is so perfect that it never needs to be looked at even once more, think again. The only thing you can be absolutely sure of in this world is change. Count on it. Six months from now, you aren't going to remember why you designed things the way you did, unless you carefully document what you did and why you did it that way. If, heaven forbid, you transfer to a different department or win the lottery and retire, your replacement has almost no chance of modifying your work to meet new requirements if you didn't document your design. Without documentation, your replacement may need to scrap the whole thing and start from scratch. Don't just document your work adequately — overdocument it. Put in more detail than you think is reasonable. If you come back to this project after six or eight months away from it, you'll be glad you did.

Chapter 21

Ten Retrieval Tips

A database can be a virtual treasure trove of information, but like the treasure of the Caribbean pirates of long ago, the stuff you really want is probably buried and hidden from view. The SQL SELECT statement is the tool you can use to dig up this hidden information. Even if you have a clear idea of what you want to retrieve, translating that idea into SQL can be a real challenge. If your formulation is just a little off, you may end up with wrong results that are so close to what you expect that they mislead you. To reduce the chances of being misled, follow these ten principles.

Verify that the Database Is Structured Appropriately

If you retrieve data from a database and your results don't seem reasonable, check the database design. A lot of poorly designed databases are in use, and if you are working with one, fix the design before you try any other remedy. Remember — good design is a prerequisite of data integrity.

Perform Your Query on a Test Database First

Create a test database that has exactly the same structure as your production database but with only a few representative rows in the tables. Choose the data so that you know in advance what the result of your query should be. Run the query on the test data and see if the result matches your expectations. If it doesn't, you may need to reformulate your query.

Build several sets of test data and be sure to include odd cases, such as empty tables and extreme values at the very limit of allowable ranges. Try to think of extremely unlikely scenarios, and check for proper behavior when they occur. In the course of checking for unlikely cases, you may gain insight into problems that are more likely to happen.

Triple-check Any Query that Contains a Join

Joins are notorious for being counterintuitive. If your query contains one, make sure it is doing what you expect before you add WHERE clauses or other complicating factors.

Triple-check Any Query that Contains a Subselect

Because subselects can entangle data taken from one table with data taken from another, they are frequently misapplied. You must make sure that the data the inner SELECT retrieves is the data that the outer SELECT needs to produce the desired end result. If you have two or more levels of subselects, you need to be even more careful.

Use a GROUP BY Clause with the Set Functions to Summarize Data for Groups within a Table or View

Say you have a table (NATIONAL) giving the name (PLAYER), team (TEAM), and number of home runs hit (HOMERS) by every baseball player in the National League. You can retrieve the team homer total for all teams with a query like this:

```
SELECT TEAM, SUM (HOMERS)
   FROM NATIONAL
   GROUP BY TEAM ;
```

This query lists each team, followed by the total number of home runs hit by all the players on that team.

Be Aware of Restrictions on the Use of the GROUP BY Clause

Suppose you want a list of power hitters in the National League. Consider the following query:

```
SELECT PLAYER, TEAM, HOMERS
   FROM NATIONAL
   WHERE HOMERS >= 20
   GROUP BY TEAM ;
```

In most implementations, this query returns an error. Generally, only columns used for grouping or columns used in a set function may appear in the select list. The following formulation works:

```
SELECT PLAYER, TEAM, HOMERS
   FROM NATIONAL
   WHERE HOMERS >= 20
   GROUP BY TEAM, PLAYER, HOMERS ;
```

Because all the columns you want to display appear in the GROUP BY clause, the query succeeds and delivers the results you want. This formulation has the effect of sorting the resulting list first by TEAM, then by PLAYER, and finally by HOMERS.

Use Parentheses with the Logical Connectives AND, OR, and NOT

Sometimes when you mix AND and OR, SQL does not process the expression in the order you expect. Use parentheses in complex expressions to make sure the result you get is the one you intended to get. The few extra keystrokes are a small price to pay for better-quality results.

Don't Grant Retrieval Privileges to People Who Shouldn't Have Them

Many people don't use the security features available on their DBMS. They just don't want to bother with them, and they consider misuse and misappropriation of data to be something that only happens to other people. Don't wait to get burned. Establish and maintain security for all databases that have any value.

Back Up Your Databases Regularly

Data is hard to retrieve after a power surge, fire, earthquake, or mortar attack destroys your hard disk. Make frequent backups and remove the backup media to a safe place.

Handle Error Conditions Gracefully

Whether you are making ad hoc queries from the console or embedding queries in an application, on occasion SQL returns an error message rather than the desired results. At the console, you can decide what to do next based on the message returned and then take appropriate action. In an application, the situation is different. The application user probably doesn't know what action is appropriate. Put extensive error handling into your applications to cover every conceivable error that may occur. Creating error handling takes a lot of effort, but it is better than having the user stare quizzically at a frozen screen.

Part VIII
Reference Material

"HE SAID THE ONLY HEAVY METAL HE WAS INTO WAS MAINFRAMES."

In this part . . .

For completeness, and as a potentially valuable reference, this part contains appendixes that list every one of SQL-92's 134 reserved words and that list which of the features described in this book are guaranteed to be present in Entry Level SQL, Intermediate Level SQL, and Full SQL. Part VIII also contains a glossary of important terms.

Appendix A
SQL-92 Reserved Words

ABSOLUTE	CONVERT	FULL
ACTION	CORRESPONDING	GET
ADD	CROSS	GLOBAL
ALLOCATE	CURRENT_DATE	HOUR
ALTER	CURRENT_TIME	IDENTITY
ARE	CURRENT_TIMESTAMP	IMMEDIATE
ASSERTION	CURRENT_USER	INITIALLY
AT	DATE	INNER
BETWEEN	DAY	INPUT
BIT	DEALLOCATE	INSENSITIVE
BIT_LENGTH	DEFERRABLE	INTERSECT
BOTH	DEFERRED	INTERVAL
CASCADE	DESCRIBE	ISOLATION
CASCADED	DESCRIPTOR	JOIN
CASE	DIAGNOSTICS	LAST
CAST	DISCONNECT	LEADING
CATALOG	DOMAIN	LEFT
CHAR_LENGTH	DROP	LEVEL
CHARACTER_LENGTH	ELSE	LOCAL
COALESCE	END-EXEC	LOWER
COLLATE	EXCEPT	MATCH
COLLATION	EXCEPTION	MINUTE
COLUMN	EXECUTE	MONTH
CONNECT	EXTERNAL	NAMES
CONNECTION	EXTRACT	NATIONAL
CONSTRAINT	FALSE	NATURAL
CONSTRAINTS	FIRST	NCHAR

NEXT	SQLSTATE
NO	SUBSTRING
NULLIF	SYSTEM_USER
OCTET_LENGTH	TEMPORARY
ONLY	THEN
OUTER	TIME
OUTPUT	TIMESTAMP
OVERLAPS	TIMEZONE_HOUR
PAD	TIMEZONE_MINUTE
PARTIAL	TRAILING
POSITION	TRANSACTION
PREPARE	TRANSLATE
PRESERVE	TRANSLATION
PRIOR	TRIM
READ	TRUE
RELATIVE	UNKNOWN
RESTRICT	UPPER
REVOKE	USAGE
RIGHT	USING
ROWS	VALUE
SCROLL	VARCHAR
SECOND	VARYING
SESSION	WHEN
SESSION_USER	WRITE
SIZE	YEAR
SPACE	ZONE

Appendix B

Entry, Intermediate, and Full Subsets of SQL-92

● ●

*T*here are three levels of adherence to the SQL-92 specification: entry, intermediate, and full.

Entry SQL-92

Entry SQL-92 is similar to SQL-89, with just a few differences. The main differences are:

- ✔ The addition of SQLSTATE status variable and parameter
- ✔ The addition of the AS clause to allow the naming of columns in a select list
- ✔ The addition of interfaces to the Ada, C, and MUMPS languages
- ✔ The allowance of commas and parentheses in parameter lists
- ✔ The requirement that colons precede parameter names in procedures in modules
- ✔ The allowance of delimited identifiers that are enclosed in double quotation marks. Within the quotes you can have any character, including blanks and punctuation. A delimited identifier can even be the same as a reserved word, for example:

    ```
    "Rate-of-pay"

    "New Salary after adjustment"

    "select"
    ```

- ✔ The clarification of the semantics of WITH CHECK OPTION
- ✔ The correction of various errors in the SQL-89 specification

Intermediate SQL-92

Intermediate SQL-92 includes features that several vendors have already implemented, features that are relatively easy to implement, and features of high value to users. The most significant of these various features are:

- ✔ Dynamic SQL (partial)
- ✔ Cascade DELETE
- ✔ The FULL OUTER JOIN operator
- ✔ The INTERSECT and EXCEPT set operators
- ✔ The CASE expression
- ✔ CAST data type conversion capability
- ✔ Better handling of isolation levels in transactions
- ✔ Row and table value constructors (partial)
- ✔ Schema manipulation statements
- ✔ Character string operations and functions (SUBSTRING, TRIM, concatenation, and FOLD)
- ✔ Enhancements to the LIKE predicate
- ✔ The UNIQUE predicate
- ✔ User-defined constraint names
- ✔ The GET DIAGNOSTICS statement
- ✔ Support for multiple modules in one application
- ✔ Domain support
- ✔ Support for character sets beyond the default
- ✔ Variable length character strings
- ✔ Datetime and interval data types and some of their associated operations
- ✔ Scrolled cursors
- ✔ Explicit DEFAULT VALUES allowed in INSERT statements and row value constructors
- ✔ A flag for use when writing portable applications

Full SQL-92

Full SQL-92 includes everything the standard defines. In addition to the features of entry and intermediate SQL-92, it also includes:

- ✔ Full dynamic SQL
- ✔ Deferred constraint checking and named constraints
- ✔ Full row and table value constructor support
- ✔ A fuller implementation of subqueries
- ✔ UPDATEs and DELETEs that reference the table they modify
- ✔ Additional operations on datetime and interval data
- ✔ The UNION JOIN and CROSS JOIN operators
- ✔ Cascade UPDATE
- ✔ BIT and BIT VARYING data types
- ✔ Assertions
- ✔ Temporary tables
- ✔ Internationalization features, including character translation

Glossary

● ●

ActiveX control A reusable software component that can be added to an application, reducing development time in the process. ActiveX is a Microsoft technology and ActiveX components can only be used by developers who work on Windows development systems.

Aggregate function A function that produces a single result based on the contents of an entire set of table rows. Also called a set function.

Alias A short substitute or "nickname" for a table name.

Applet A small application stored on a Web server that is downloaded to and executed on a Web client that connects to the server.

Application Programmer's Interface (API) A standard means of communicating between an application and a database or other system resource.

Assertion A constraint that is specified by a CREATE ASSERTION statement (rather than by a clause of a CREATE TABLE statement). Assertions commonly apply to more than one table.

Back end That part of a DBMS that interacts directly with the database.

Catalog A named collection of schemas.

Client That part of a DBMS that displays information on a screen and responds to user input (the front end).

Client-server system A multiuser system in which a central processor (the server) is connected to multiple intelligent user workstations (the clients).

CODASYL DBTG database model The network database model. *Note:* This use of the term "network" refers to the structuring of the data ("network" as opposed to "hierarchy"), rather than to network communications.

Collating sequence The ordering of characters in a character set. All collating sequences for character sets that have the Latin characters (a, b, c) define the obvious ordering (a,b,c,...). But, they differ in the ordering of special characters (+, -, <, ?, etc.) and in the relative ordering of the digits and the letters.

Column A component of a table that holds a single attribute of the table.

Composite key A key made up of two or more table columns.

Conceptual view The schema of a database.

Concurrent access Two or more users operating on the same rows in a database table at the same time.

Constraint A restriction you specify on the data in a database.

Constraint, deferred A constraint that is not applied until you change its status to immediate or until you COMMIT the encapsulating transaction.

Cursor An SQL feature that specifies a set of rows, an ordering of those rows, and a current row within that ordering.

Data Control Language (DCL) That part of SQL that protects the database from harm.

Data Definition Language (DDL) That part of SQL used to define, modify, and eradicate database structures.

Data Manipulation Language (DML) That part of SQL that operates on database data.

Data redundancy Having the same data stored in more than one place in a database.

Data source A source of data used by a database application. It could be a DBMS or a data file.

Data sublanguage A subset of a complete computer language that deals specifically with data handling. SQL is a data sublanguage.

Database A self-describing collection of integrated records.

Database, organizational A database containing information used by an entire organization.

Database, personal A database designed for use by a single person on a single computer.

Database, workgroup A database designed to be used by a department or workgroup within an organization.

Database administrator (DBA) The person ultimately responsible for the functionality, integrity, and safety of a database.

Database engine That part of a DBMS which directly interacts with the database (part of the back end).

Database publishing The act of making the contents of a database available on the Internet or an intranet.

Database server The server component of a client-server system.

DBMS A database management system.

Deletion anomaly An inconsistency in a multitable database that occurs when a row is deleted from one of its tables.

Descriptor An area in memory used to pass information between an application's procedural code and its dynamic SQL code.

Diagnostics area A data structure managed by the DBMS that contains detailed information about the last SQL statement executed and any errors that occurred during its execution.

Distributed data processing A system in which data is distributed across multiple servers.

Domain The set of all values that a database item can assume.

Domain integrity A property of a database table column where all data items in that column fall within the domain of the column.

Driver That part of a database management system that interfaces directly with a database.

Driver manager A component of an ODBC-compliant database interface. On Windows machines it is a dynamic link library (DLL) that coordinates the linking of data sources with appropriate drivers.

Entity integrity A property of a database table that is entirely consistent with the real-world object that it models.

File server The server component of a resource sharing system. It does not contain any database management software.

Firewall A piece of software, or a combination of hardware and software that isolates an intranet from the Internet, allowing only trusted traffic to travel between them.

Flat file A collection of data records having minimal structure.

Foreign key A column or combination of columns in a database table that references the primary key of another table in the database.

Front end That part of a DBMS that interacts directly with the user.

Functional dependency A relationship between or among attributes of a relation.

Hierarchical database model A tree-structured model of data.

Host variable A variable within an application written using embedded SQL.

HTML (HyperText Markup Language) A standard formatting language for Web documents.

Implementation A particular relational DBMS running on a specific hardware platform.

Index A table of pointers used to rapidly locate rows in a data table.

Information schema The system tables, which hold the database's meta-data.

Insertion anomaly An inconsistency introduced into a multitable database when a new row is inserted into one of its tables.

Internet A worldwide network of computers.

Intranet A network that uses World Wide Web hardware and software, but access is restricted to users within a single organization.

IPX/SPX A local area network protocol.

Java A platform-independent compiled language designed specifically for Web application development.

JavaScript A simplified, interpreted version of Java.

JDBC (Java DataBase Connectivity) A standard interface between a Java applet or application and a database. The JDBC standard is modeled after the ODBC standard.

Join A relational operator that combines data from multiple tables into a single result table.

Logical connectives Used to connect or change the truth value of predicates to produce more complex predicates.

Meta-data Data about the structure of the data in a database.

Modification anomaly A problem introduced into a database when a modification (insertion, deletion, or update) is made to one of the tables in the database.

Module language A form of SQL in which SQL statements are placed in modules, which are called by an application program written in a host language.

Nested query A statement that contains one or more subqueries.

NetBEUI A local area network protocol.

Netscape plug-in A software component that is downloaded from a Web server to a Web client, where it is integrated with the client's browser, providing additional functions.

Network database model A way of organizing a database so that redundancy of data items is minimized by allowing any data item (node) to be directly connected to any other.

Normalization A technique that reduces or eliminates the possibility that a database will be subject to modification anomalies.

ODBC (Object DataBase Connectivity) A standard interface between a database and an application that is trying to access the data in that database. ODBC is defined by an international (ISO) and a national (ANSI) standard. The most recent version is called SQL-92.

Oracle A relational database management system marketed by Oracle Corporation.

Parameter A variable within an application written in SQL module language.

Precision The maximum number of digits allowed in a numeric data item.

Predicate A statement that may be either true or false.

Primary key A column or combination of columns in a database table that uniquely identifies each row in the table.

Procedural language A computer language that solves a problem by executing a procedure in the form of a sequence of steps.

Query A question you ask about the data in a database.

Rapid Application Development tool A proprietary graphically oriented alternative to SQL. There are a number of such tools on the market.

Record A representation of some physical or conceptual object.

Referential integrity A state in which all the tables in a database are consistent with each other.

Relation A two-dimensional array of rows and columns, containing single-valued entries and no duplicate rows.

Reserved words Words that have a special significance in SQL and cannot be used as variable names or in any other way that differs from their intended use.

Row value expression A list of value expressions enclosed in parentheses and separated by commas.

Scale The number of digits in the fractional part of a numeric data item.

Schema The structure of an entire database. The database's meta-data.

Schema owner The person who created the schema.

SEQUEL A data sublanguage created by IBM that was a precursor of SQL.

Set function A function that produces a single result based on the contents of an entire set of table rows. Also called an aggregate function.

SQL An industry standard data sublanguage, specifically designed to create, manipulate, and control relational databases. SQL-92 is the latest version of the standard.

SQL, dynamic A means of building compiled applications where all data items are not identifiable at compile time.

SQL, embedded An application structure in which SQL statements are embedded within programs written in a host language.

SQL, interactive A real-time conversation with a database.

SQL/DS A relational database management system marketed by IBM Corporation.

Subquery A query within a query.

Table A relation.

TCP/IP (Transmission Control Protocol/ Internet Protocol) The network protocol used by the Internet and by intranets.

Teleprocessing system A powerful central processor connected to multiple dumb terminals.

Transaction A sequence of SQL statements whose effect is not accessible to other transactions until all of the statements are executed.

Transitive dependency One attribute of a relation depends on a second attribute, which in turn depends on a third attribute.

Translation table Tool for converting character strings from one character set to another.

Update anomaly A problem introduced into a database when a table row is updated.

Value expression An expression that combines two or more values.

Value expression, conditional A value expression that assigns different values to arguments, based on whether a condition is true.

Value expression, datetime A value expression that deals with DATE, TIME, TIMESTAMP, or INTERVAL data.

Value expression, numeric A value expression that combines numeric values using the addition, subtraction, multiplication, or division operators.

Value expression, string A value expression that combines character strings with the concatenation operator.

Value function A function that performs an operation on a single character string, number, or datetime.

View A database component that behaves exactly like a table, but has no independent existence of its own.

Virtual table A view.

World Wide Web An aspect of the Internet that has a graphical user interface. The Web is accessed by applications called Web browsers, and information is provided to the Web by installations called Web servers.

Index

Title	Author	ISBN	Price
The Internet For Macs® For Dummies® 2nd Edition	by Charles Seiter	ISBN: 1-56884-371-2	$19.99 USA/$26.99 Canada
The Internet For Macs® For Dummies® Starter Kit	by Charles Seiter	ISBN: 1-56884-244-9	$29.99 USA/$39.99 Canada
The Internet For Macs® For Dummies® Starter Kit Bestseller Edition	by Charles Seiter	ISBN: 1-56884-245-7	$39.99 USA/$54.99 Canada
The Internet For Windows® For Dummies® Starter Kit	by John R. Levine & Margaret Levine Young	ISBN: 1-56884-237-6	$34.99 USA/$44.99 Canada
The Internet For Windows® For Dummies® Starter Kit, Bestseller Edition	by John R. Levine & Margaret Levine Young	ISBN: 1-56884-246-5	$39.99 USA/$54.99 Canada

MACINTOSH

Mac® Programming For Dummies®	by Dan Parks Sydow	ISBN: 1-56884-173-6	$19.95 USA/$26.95 Canada
Macintosh® System 7.5 For Dummies®	by Bob LeVitus	ISBN: 1-56884-197-3	$19.95 USA/$26.95 Canada
MORE Macs® For Dummies®	by David Pogue	ISBN: 1-56884-087-X	$19.95 USA/$26.95 Canada
PageMaker 5 For Macs® For Dummies®	by Galen Gruman & Deke McClelland	ISBN: 1-56884-178-7	$19.95 USA/$26.95 Canada
QuarkXPress 3.3 For Dummies®	by Galen Gruman & Barbara Assadi	ISBN: 1-56884-217-1	$19.99 USA/$26.99 Canada
Upgrading and Fixing Macs® For Dummies®	by Kearney Rietmann & Frank Higgins	ISBN: 1-56884-189-2	$19.95 USA/$26.95 Canada

MULTIMEDIA

Multimedia & CD-ROMs For Dummies® 2nd Edition	by Andy Rathbone	ISBN: 1-56884-907-9	$19.99 USA/$26.99 Canada
Multimedia & CD-ROMs For Dummies® Interactive Multimedia Value Pack, 2nd Edition	by Andy Rathbone	ISBN: 1-56884-909-5	$29.99 USA/$39.99 Canada

OPERATING SYSTEMS:

DOS

MORE DOS For Dummies®	by Dan Gookin	ISBN: 1-56884-046-2	$19.95 USA/$26.95 Canada
OS/2® Warp For Dummies® 2nd Edition	by Andy Rathbone	ISBN: 1-56884-205-8	$19.99 USA/$26.99 Canada

UNIX

MORE UNIX® For Dummies®	by John R. Levine & Margaret Levine Young	ISBN: 1-56884-361-5	$19.99 USA/$26.99 Canada
UNIX® For Dummies®	by John R. Levine & Margaret Levine Young	ISBN: 1-878058-58-4	$19.95 USA/$26.95 Canada

WINDOWS

MORE Windows® For Dummies® 2nd Edition	by Andy Rathbone	ISBN: 1-56884-048-9	$19.95 USA/$26.95 Canada
Windows® 95 For Dummies®	by Andy Rathbone	ISBN: 1-56884-240-6	$19.99 USA/$26.99 Canada

PCS/HARDWARE

Illustrated Computer Dictionary For Dummies® 2nd Edition	by Dan Gookin & Wallace Wang	ISBN: 1-56884-218-X	$12.95 USA/$16.95 Canada
Upgrading and Fixing PCs For Dummies® 2nd Edition	by Andy Rathbone	ISBN: 1-56884-903-6	$19.99 USA/$26.99 Canada

PRESENTATION/AUTOCAD

AutoCAD For Dummies®	by Bud Smith	ISBN: 1-56884-191-4	$19.95 USA/$26.95 Canada
PowerPoint 4 For Windows® For Dummies®	by Doug Lowe	ISBN: 1-56884-161-2	$16.99 USA/$22.99 Canada

PROGRAMMING

Borland C++ For Dummies®	by Michael Hyman	ISBN: 1-56884-162-0	$19.95 USA/$26.95 Canada
C For Dummies® Volume 1	by Dan Gookin	ISBN: 1-878058-78-9	$19.95 USA/$26.95 Canada
C++ For Dummies®	by Stephen R. Davis	ISBN: 1-56884-163-9	$19.95 USA/$26.95 Canada
Delphi Programming For Dummies®	by Neil Rubenking	ISBN: 1-56884-200-7	$19.99 USA/$26.99 Canada
Mac® Programming For Dummies®	by Dan Parks Sydow	ISBN: 1-56884-173-6	$19.95 USA/$26.95 Canada
PowerBuilder 4 Programming For Dummies®	by Ted Coombs & Jason Coombs	ISBN: 1-56884-325-9	$19.99 USA/$26.99 Canada
QBasic Programming For Dummies®	by Douglas Hergert	ISBN: 1-56884-093-4	$19.95 USA/$26.95 Canada
Visual Basic 3 For Dummies®	by Wallace Wang	ISBN: 1-56884-076-4	$19.95 USA/$26.95 Canada
Visual Basic "X" For Dummies®	by Wallace Wang	ISBN: 1-56884-230-9	$19.99 USA/$26.99 Canada
Visual C++ 2 For Dummies®	by Michael Hyman & Bob Arnson	ISBN: 1-56884-328-3	$19.99 USA/$26.99 Canada
Windows® 95 Programming For Dummies®	by S. Randy Davis	ISBN: 1-56884-327-5	$19.99 USA/$26.99 Canada

SPREADSHEET

1-2-3 For Dummies®	by Greg Harvey	ISBN: 1-878058-60-6	$16.95 USA/$22.95 Canada
1-2-3 For Windows® 5 For Dummies® 2nd Edition	by John Walkenbach	ISBN: 1-56884-216-3	$16.95 USA/$22.95 Canada
Excel 5 For Macs® For Dummies®	by Greg Harvey	ISBN: 1-56884-186-8	$19.95 USA/$26.95 Canada
Excel For Dummies® 2nd Edition	by Greg Harvey	ISBN: 1-56884-050-0	$16.95 USA/$22.95 Canada
MORE 1-2-3 For DOS For Dummies®	by John Weingarten	ISBN: 1-56884-224-4	$19.99 USA/$26.99 Canada
MORE Excel 5 For Windows® For Dummies®	by Greg Harvey	ISBN: 1-56884-207-4	$19.95 USA/$26.95 Canada
Quattro Pro 6 For Windows® For Dummies®	by John Walkenbach	ISBN: 1-56884-174-4	$19.95 USA/$26.95 Canada
Quattro Pro For DOS For Dummies®	by John Walkenbach	ISBN: 1-56884-023-3	$16.95 USA/$22.95 Canada

UTILITIES

Title	Author	ISBN	Price
Norton Utilities 8 For Dummies®	by Beth Slick	ISBN: 1-56884-166-3	$19.95 USA/$26.95 Canada

VCRS/CAMCORDERS

Title	Author	ISBN	Price
VCRs & Camcorders For Dummies™	by Gordon McComb & Andy Rathbone	ISBN: 1-56884-229-5	$14.99 USA/$20.99 Canada

WORD PROCESSING

Ami Pro For Dummies®	by Jim Meade	ISBN: 1-56884-049-7	$19.95 USA/$26.95 Canada
MORE Word For Windows® 6 For Dummies®	by Doug Lowe	ISBN: 1-56884-165-5	$19.95 USA/$26.95 Canada
MORE WordPerfect® 6 For Windows® For Dummies®	by Margaret Levine Young & David C. Kay	ISBN: 1-56884-206-6	$19.95 USA/$26.95 Canada
MORE WordPerfect® 6 For DOS For Dummies®	by Wallace Wang, edited by Dan Gookin	ISBN: 1-56884-047-0	$19.95 USA/$26.95 Canada
Word 6 For Macs® For Dummies®	by Dan Gookin	ISBN: 1-56884-190-6	$19.95 USA/$26.95 Canada
Word For Windows® 6 For Dummies®	by Dan Gookin	ISBN: 1-56884-075-6	$16.95 USA/$22.95 Canada
Word For Windows® For Dummies®	by Dan Gookin & Ray Werner	ISBN: 1-878058-86-X	$16.95 USA/$22.95 Canada
WordPerfect® 6 For DOS For Dummies®	by Dan Gookin	ISBN: 1-878058-77-0	$16.95 USA/$22.95 Canada
WordPerfect® 6.1 For Windows® For Dummies® 2nd Edition	by Margaret Levine Young & David Kay	ISBN: 1-56884-243-0	$16.95 USA/$22.95 Canada
WordPerfect® For Dummies®	by Dan Gookin	ISBN: 1-878058-52-5	$16.95 USA/$22.95 Canada

Fun, Fast, & Cheap!™

NEW!

The Internet For Macs® For Dummies® Quick Reference

by Charles Seiter

ISBN:1-56884-967-2
$9.99 USA/$12.99 Canada

NEW!

Windows® 95 For Dummies® Quick Reference

by Greg Harvey

ISBN: 1-56884-964-8
$9.99 USA/$12.99 Canada

SUPER STAR

Photoshop 3 For Macs® For Dummies® Quick Reference

by Deke McClelland

ISBN: 1-56884-968-0
$9.99 USA/$12.99 Canada

SUPER STAR

WordPerfect® For DOS For Dummies® Quick Reference

by Greg Harvey

ISBN: 1-56884-009-8
$8.95 USA/$12.95 Canada

Title	Author	ISBN	Price
DATABASE			
Access 2 For Dummies® Quick Reference	by Stuart J. Stuple	ISBN: 1-56884-167-1	$8.95 USA/$11.95 Canada
dBASE 5 For DOS For Dummies® Quick Reference	by Barrie Sosinsky	ISBN: 1-56884-954-0	$9.99 USA/$12.99 Canada
dBASE 5 For Windows® For Dummies® Quick Reference	by Stuart J. Stuple	ISBN: 1-56884-953-2	$9.99 USA/$12.99 Canada
Paradox 5 For Windows® For Dummies® Quick Reference	by Scott Palmer	ISBN: 1-56884-960-5	$9.99 USA/$12.99 Canada
DESKTOP PUBLISHING/ILLUSTRATION/GRAPHICS			
CorelDRAW! 5 For Dummies® Quick Reference	by Raymond E. Werner	ISBN: 1-56884-952-4	$9.99 USA/$12.99 Canada
Harvard Graphics For Windows® For Dummies® Quick Reference	by Raymond E. Werner	ISBN: 1-56884-962-1	$9.99 USA/$12.99 Canada
Photoshop 3 For Macs® For Dummies® Quick Reference	by Deke McClelland	ISBN: 1-56884-968-0	$9.99 USA/$12.99 Canada
FINANCE/PERSONAL FINANCE			
Quicken 4 For Windows® For Dummies® Quick Reference	by Stephen L. Nelson	ISBN: 1-56884-950-8	$9.95 USA/$12.95 Canada
GROUPWARE/INTEGRATED			
Microsoft® Office 4 For Windows® For Dummies® Quick Reference	by Doug Lowe	ISBN: 1-56884-958-3	$9.99 USA/$12.99 Canada
Microsoft® Works 3 For Windows® For Dummies® Quick Reference	by Michael Partington	ISBN: 1-56884-959-1	$9.99 USA/$12.99 Canada
INTERNET/COMMUNICATIONS/NETWORKING			
The Internet For Dummies® Quick Reference	by John R. Levine & Margaret Levine Young	ISBN: 1-56884-168-X	$8.95 USA/$11.95 Canada
MACINTOSH			
Macintosh® System 7.5 For Dummies® Quick Reference	by Stuart J. Stuple	ISBN: 1-56884-956-7	$9.99 USA/$12.99 Canada
OPERATING SYSTEMS:			
DOS			
DOS For Dummies® Quick Reference	by Greg Harvey	ISBN: 1-56884-007-1	$8.95 USA/$11.95 Canada
UNIX			
UNIX® For Dummies® Quick Reference	by John R. Levine & Margaret Levine Young	ISBN: 1-56884-094-2	$8.95 USA/$11.95 Canada
WINDOWS			
Windows® 3.1 For Dummies® Quick Reference, 2nd Edition	by Greg Harvey	ISBN: 1-56884-951-6	$8.95 USA/$11.95 Canada
PCs/HARDWARE			
Memory Management For Dummies® Quick Reference	by Doug Lowe	ISBN: 1-56884-362-3	$9.99 USA/$12.99 Canada
PRESENTATION/AUTOCAD			
AutoCAD For Dummies® Quick Reference	by Ellen Finkelstein	ISBN: 1-56884-198-1	$9.95 USA/$12.95 Canada
SPREADSHEET			
1-2-3 For Dummies® Quick Reference	by John Walkenbach	ISBN: 1-56884-027-6	$8.95 USA/$11.95 Canada
1-2-3 For Windows® 5 For Dummies® Quick Reference	by John Walkenbach	ISBN: 1-56884-957-5	$9.95 USA/$12.95 Canada
Excel For Windows® For Dummies® Quick Reference, 2nd Edition	by John Walkenbach	ISBN: 1-56884-096-9	$8.95 USA/$11.95 Canada
Quattro Pro 6 For Windows® For Dummies® Quick Reference	by Stuart J. Stuple	ISBN: 1-56884-172-8	$9.95 USA/$12.95 Canada
WORD PROCESSING			
Word For Windows® 6 For Dummies® Quick Reference	by George Lynch	ISBN: 1-56884-095-0	$8.95 USA/$11.95 Canada
Word For Windows® For Dummies® Quick Reference	by George Lynch	ISBN: 1-56884-029-2	$8.95 USA/$11.95 Canada
WordPerfect® 6.1 For Windows® For Dummies® Quick Reference, 2nd Edition	by Greg Harvey	ISBN: 1-56884-966-4	$9.99 USA/$12.99/Canada

Windows® 3.1 SECRETS™
by Brian Livingston

ISBN: 1-878058-43-6
$39.95 USA/$52.95 Canada
Includes software.

MORE Windows® 3.1 SECRETS™
by Brian Livingston

ISBN: 1-56884-019-5
$39.95 USA/$52.95 Canada
Includes software.

Windows® GIZMOS™
by Brian Livingston & Margie Livingston

ISBN: 1-878058-66-5
$39.95 USA/$52.95 Canada
Includes software.

Windows® 3.1 Connectivity SECRETS™
by Runnoe Connally, David Rorabaugh, & Sheldon Hall

ISBN: 1-56884-030-6
$49.95 USA/$64.95 Canada
Includes software.

Windows® 3.1 Configuration SECRETS™
by Valda Hilley & James Blakely

ISBN: 1-56884-026-8
$49.95 USA/$64.95 Canada
Includes software.

Internet SECRETS™
by John Levine & Carol Baroudi

ISBN: 1-56884-452-2
$39.99 USA/$54.99 Canada
Includes software.

Internet GIZMOS™ For Windows®
by Joel Diamond, Howard Sobel, & Valda Hilley

ISBN: 1-56884-451-4
$39.99 USA/$54.99 Canada
Includes software.

Network Security SECRETS™
by David Stang & Sylvia Moon

ISBN: 1-56884-021-7
Int'l. ISBN: 1-56884-151-5
$49.95 USA/$64.95 Canada
Includes software.

PC SECRETS™
by Caroline M. Halliday

ISBN: 1-878058-49-5
$39.95 USA/$52.95 Canada
Includes software.

WordPerfect® 6 SECRETS™
by Roger C. Parker & David A. Holzgang

ISBN: 1-56884-040-3
$39.95 USA/$52.95 Canada
Includes software.

DOS 6 SECRETS™
by Robert D. Ainsbury

ISBN: 1-878058-70-3
$39.95 USA/$52.95 Canada
Includes software.

Paradox 4 Power Programming SECRETS™, 2nd Edition
by Gregory B. Salcedo & Martin W. Rudy

ISBN: 1-878058-54-1
$44.95 USA/$59.95 Canada
Includes software.

Paradox 5 For Windows® Power Programming SECRETS™
by Gregory B. Salcedo & Martin W. Rudy

ISBN: 1-56884-085-3
$44.95 USA/$59.95 Canada
Includes software.

Hard Disk SECRETS™
by John M. Goodman, Ph.D.

ISBN: 1-878058-64-9
$39.95 USA/$52.95 Canada
Includes software.

WordPerfect® 6 For Windows® Tips & Techniques Revealed
by David A. Holzgang & Roger C. Parker

ISBN: 1-56884-202-3
$39.95 USA/$52.95 Canada
Includes software.

Excel 5 For Windows® Power Programming Techniques
by John Walkenbach

ISBN: 1-56884-303-8
$39.95 USA/$52.95 Canada
Includes software.

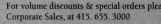

ORDER FORM

Order Center: **(800) 762-2974** *(8 a.m.–6 p.m., EST, weekdays)*

Quantity	ISBN	Title	Price	Total

Shipping & Handling Charges

	Description	First book	Each additional book	Total
Domestic	Normal	$4.50	$1.50	$
	Two Day Air	$8.50	$2.50	$
	Overnight	$18.00	$3.00	$
International	Surface	$8.00	$8.00	$
	Airmail	$16.00	$16.00	$
	DHL Air	$17.00	$17.00	$

*For large quantities call for shipping & handling charges.
**Prices are subject to change without notice.

Ship to:

Name _____

Company _____

Address _____

City/State/Zip _____

Daytime Phone _____

Payment: □ Check to IDG Books Worldwide (US Funds Only)

      □ VISA   □ MasterCard   □ American Express

Card # _____ Expires _____

Signature _____

Subtotal _____

CA residents add
applicable sales tax _____

IN, MA, and MD
residents add
5% sales tax _____

IL residents add
6.25% sales tax _____

RI residents add
7% sales tax _____

TX residents add
8.25% sales tax _____

Shipping _____

Total _____

Please send this order form to:

**IDG Books Worldwide, Inc.
Attn: Order Entry Dept.
7260 Shadeland Station, Suite 100
Indianapolis, IN 46256**

*Allow up to 3 weeks for delivery.
Thank you!*

IDG BOOKS WORLDWIDE REGISTRATION CARD

RETURN THIS REGISTRATION CARD FOR FREE CATALOG

Title of this book: **SQL For Dummies®, 2nd Edition**

My overall rating of this book: ❏ Very good [1] ❏ Good [2] ❏ Satisfactory [3] ❏ Fair [4] ❏ Poor [5]

How I first heard about this book:

❏ Found in bookstore; name: [6]

❏ Book review: [7]

❏ Advertisement: [8]

❏ Catalog: [9]

❏ Word of mouth; heard about book from friend, co-worker, etc.: [10]

❏ Other: [11]

What I liked most about this book:

What I would change, add, delete, etc., in future editions of this book:

Other comments:

Number of computer books I purchase in a year: ❏ 1 [12] ❏ 2-5 [13] ❏ 6-10 [14] ❏ More than 10 [15]

I would characterize my computer skills as: ❏ Beginner [16] ❏ Intermediate [17] ❏ Advanced [18] ❏ Professional [19]

I use ❏ DOS [20] ❏ Windows [21] ❏ OS/2 [22] ❏ Unix [23] ❏ Macintosh [24] ❏ Other: [25] _____
(please specify)

I would be interested in new books on the following subjects:
(please check all that apply, and use the spaces provided to identify specific software)

❏ Word processing: [26]

❏ Spreadsheets: [27]

❏ Data bases: [28]

❏ Desktop publishing: [29]

❏ File Utilities: [30]

❏ Money management: [31]

❏ Networking: [32]

❏ Programming languages: [33]

❏ Other: [34]

I use a PC at (please check all that apply): ❏ home [35] ❏ work [36] ❏ school [37] ❏ other: [38] _____

The disks I prefer to use are ❏ 5.25 [39] ❏ 3.5 [40] ❏ other: [41]_____

I have a CD ROM: ❏ yes [42] ❏ no [43]

I plan to buy or upgrade computer hardware this year: ❏ yes [44] ❏ no [45]

I plan to buy or upgrade computer software this year: ❏ yes [46] ❏ no [47]

Name: _____ Business title: [48] _____ Type of Business: [49] _____

Address (❏ home [50] ❏ work [51] /Company name: _____)

Street/Suite#

City [52]/State [53]/Zipcode [54]: _____ Country [55] _____

❏ **I liked this book!** You may quote me by name in future
IDG Books Worldwide promotional materials.

My daytime phone number is _____

IDG BOOKS

THE WORLD OF
COMPUTER
KNOWLEDGE

❑ YES!

Please keep me informed about IDG's World of Computer Knowledge.
Send me the latest IDG Books catalog.

BUSINESS REPLY MAIL
FIRST CLASS MAIL   PERMIT NO. 2605   FOSTER CITY, CALIFORNIA

IDG Books Worldwide
919 E Hillsdale Blvd, STE 400
Foster City, CA 94404-9691

NO POSTAGE
NECESSARY
IF MAILED
IN THE
UNITED STATES